PROVERB LORE

Being a Historical Study of the
Similarities, Contrasts, Topics, Meanings, and
Other Facets of Proverbs, Truisms, and Pithy Sayings,
As Expressed by the Peoples of Many Lands
And Times

F. Edward Hulme

Edited by

Wolfgang Mieder

"Proverbium"
in cooperation with the
Department of German and Russian

The University of Vermont
Burlington, Vermont
2007

Supplement Series

of

Proverbium
Yearbook of International Proverb Scholarship

Edited by Wolfgang Mieder

Volume 23

Cover illustration:
"Strike while the iron is hot"
John W. Barber,
*The Hand Book of Illustrated Proverbs
with Numerous Engravings and Descriptions.*
New York: George F. Tuttle, 1856, p. 151.

ISBN 0-9770731-5-7

Manufactured in the United States of America
by Queen City Printers Inc.
Burlington, Vermont

INTRODUCTION

For many languages and cultures of the world scholars have provided comprehensive books on their proverbs and proverbial phrases. Such studies trace the history, nature, and significance of the many types of proverb collections (paremiography) and they also deal with the origin and dissemination of proverbs, discuss definitions of various proverbial genres, analyze structural and stylistic aspects, comment on the use and function in different contexts, and present an idea of the meaning and significance of proverbs as communicative strategies (paremiology). For the English language there are four such inclusive accounts that were published during the past one hundred and fifty years. In the middle of the nineteenth century the theologian and philologist Richard Chenevix Trench (1807-1886) wrote his small volume *On the Lessons in Proverbs* (1853) that saw seven editions during his lifetime and several more reissues afterwards, with the last edition having appeared in 1905 with the slightly altered title of *Proverbs and Their Lessons*. The book includes a still useful survey of the origin, nature, content, distribution, meaning, and significance of proverbs in the English-speaking world. Realizing that this slim account is certainly of historical value, I prepared a reprint of it in 2003 as the thirteenth volume of the "Supplement Series" of *Proverbium: Yearbook of International Proverb Scholarship*.

There is, of course, also Archer Taylor's (1890-1973) classical study on *The Proverb* (1931) with *An Index to "The Proverb"* (1934) that this eminent scholar added to his magisterial study. The book and its 105-page index were reprinted in 1962, and some twenty years later I had the honor of reissuing *The Proverb and An Index to "The*

Proverb" (1985) once again. Taylor's volume confronts definition issues, metaphorical proverbs, proverbial types, variants, proverbs in folk narratives and literary works, loan translations, and the classical or biblical origin of many proverbs and proverbial phrases. It also treats customs and superstitions expressed in proverbs, legal, medical, and weather proverbs, and the content and style of these expressions of folk wisdom. Proverbial stereotypes, proverbial phrases and comparisons, and wellerisms are also discussed in this all-encompassing volume by the world's leading paremiologist of the twentieth century.

It fell upon me to undertake the daunting task of writing an updated treatise on proverbs with the title of *Proverbs: A Handbook* (2004). The time had come to take a new look at proverbs that was informed by the vast scholarship of the past seven decades. While my first chapter deals with the traditional problems of the definition and classification of proverbial texts, the second chapter presents six case studies on the proverbs "Big fish eat little fish," "First come, first served," "The apple doesn't fall far from the tree," "The only good Indian is a dead Indian," "Good fences make good neighbors," and "A picture is worth a thousand words." The third chapter looks at the different approaches of paremiological scholarship, with the fourth chapter including contextualized analyses of proverbs and proverbial phrases used by Lord Chesterfield, Benjamin Franklin, Abraham Lincoln, Charles Dickens, Winston S. Churchill, and Bertolt Brecht. The volume also includes various bibliographies of proverb collections and studies, reflecting the scholarship by anthropologists, cultural and literary historians, folklorists, linguists, philologists, psychologists, sociologists, theologians, and others.

There exists, however, yet another general study in English on proverbs that preceded my handbook by one hundred years, namely Frederick Edward Hulme's (1841-1909) volume on *Proverb Lore* (1902). It has long been my dream to make this significant study available again as a reprint to international proverb scholars and libraries, and it is with much pleasure that I reissue it now with my short introduction as volume 23 of the "Supplement Series" of *Proverbium*. As has been the case with other volumes of this series, the publication costs of this book have once again been underwritten in part by the pecuniary help of my former student Keir Kleinknecht and his family foundation, Gertraud and Jerry Jacobson, and Hank Schaefer. International paremiology owes a great debt to these friends, whose philanthropy has enabled me to serve proverb scholars and students worldwide by editing the *Proverbium* yearbook and the "Supplement Series" volumes.

Turning now to the exciting project at hand, let me present at least a cursory biography of Frederick Edward Hulme together with a list of the most significant publications of this incredibly prolific and versatile Englishman. He was born at Hanley, Staffordshire, England, either on March 29 (by his own claim) or March 30 (according to his birth certificate) 1841, as the only son of the landscape painter Frederick William Hulme (1816-1884) and his wife Caroline Jackson. As of 1844 the family lived at London, with Frederick Edward attending the Western Grammar School in Brompton and at the age of seventeen beginning his art studies in South Kensington. In 1866 he married Emily Napper of Henfield, Sussex, and together they raised two sons and two daughters. From 1870 to 1883 Hulme was art and drawing master at Marlborough College, where as an artist and naturalist he began publishing his eight volumes of *Familiar Wild Flowers* (1878-1905) that as his best known work included his own drawings. He also provided splendid drawings for Shirley Hibberd's five volumes of *Familiar Garden Flowers* (1879-1897) and Francis George Heath's *Sylvan Spring* (1880). Before leaving Marlborough College in 1883, he put his historical and cultural interests to work by writing *The Town, College and Neighbourhood of Marlborough* (1881).

In 1885 he became lecturer at the Architectural Association in London, and in 1886 he joined the faculty of King's College as professor of geometrical drawing (from 1896 on also of freehand drawing), serving for many years as examiner to the Department of Science and Art and the London chamber of commerce. Hulme was elected a fellow of the Linnean Society in 1869 and of the Society of Antiquaries in 1872, but despite of all of these activities and his relatively large family he found the time to write numerous quite successful books on art, botany, folklore, and history. He died on April 11, 1909 at his home in Kew and was buried at Brookwood, Surrey, after a full life of teaching, scholarship, and service as an artist, antiquarian, and naturalist.

What follows is a list of Frederick Edward Hulme's diverse publications as I have been able to verify them:

A Series of Sketches from Nature of Plant Form. London: Day, 1868.

A Series of Sixty Outline Examples of Freehand Ornaments Adapted for Class or Individual Teaching. London: Marcus Ward, 1870.

Art-Studies from Nature, as Applied to Design, for the Use of Architects, Designers and Manufacturers. London: Virtue, 1872. (with James Glaisher, Samuel Joseph Mackie, and Robert Hunt)

Catalogue of the Archaeological Collection. Marlborough: Marlborough College Natural History Society, 1873.

The Garland of the Year, or the Months. Their Poetry and Flowers. London: Marcus Ward, 1873.

Plants, Their Natural Growth and Ornamental Treatment. London: Marcus Ward, 1874.

Principles of Ornamental Art. London: Cassell, Petter, and Galpin, 1875.

Examples for Fret-Cutting and Wood-Carving. London: Marcus Ward, 1877; rpt. as *Victorian Fret-Work and Wood-Carving. Patterns and Instructions.* Mineola, New York: Dover Publications, 2005.

Bards and Blossoms; or, The Poetry, History, and Association of Flowers. London: Marcus Ward, 1877.

Familiar Wild Flowers. 8 vols. London: Cassell, Petter, and Galpin, 1878-1905.

Suggestions in Floral Design. London: Cassell, Petter, and Galpin, 1878-1879; rpt. partially as *Victorian Floral Designs in Full Color.* New York: Dover Publications, 1994.

Mathematical Drawing Instruments and How to Use Them. London: Kegan Paul, 1879.

The Town, College, and Neighbourhood of Marlborough. London: E. Stanford, 1881.

Art Instruction in England. London: Longmans, Green, and Company, 1882.

Worked Examination Questions in Plane Geometrical Drawing. London: Longmans, Green, and Company, 1882.

Myth-Land. London: Sampson Low, Marston, Searle, and Rivington, 1886.

Wayside Sketches. London: Society for Promoting Christian Knowledge, 1889.

The History, Principles and Practice of Symbolism in Christian Art. London: S. Sonnenschein, 1891; rpt. Detroit: Gale Research Company, 1969; rpt. again Poole, England: Blandford Press, 1976; rpt. once again Whitefish, Minnesota: Kessinger Publishing, 2003.

The History, Principles and Practice of Heraldry. London: S. Sonnenschein, 1892; rpt. New York: Haskell House, 1969; rpt. again Honolulu, Hawaii: University Press of the Pacific, 2004.

The Birth and Development of Ornament. London: S. Sonnenschein, 1893; rpt. Detroit: Gale Research Company, 1974.

Natural History, Lore and Legend. London: Bernard Quaritch, 1895; rpt. Landisville, Pennsylvania: Arment Biological Press, 2000.

The Flags of the World, Their History, Blazonry, and Associations. London: F. Warne, 1897; rpt. ed. by E.M.C. Carraclough and W.G. Crampton. London: F. Warne, 1978.

Cryptography; or, The History, Principles, and Practice of Cipher-Writing. London: Ward, Lock and Company, 1898.

Proverb Lore, Being a Historical Study of the Similarities, Contrasts, Topics, Meanings, and Other Facets of Proverbs, Truisms, and Pithy Sayings, as Expressed by the Peoples of Many Lands and Times. London: Elliot Stock, 1902; reissued London: Elliot Stock 1906; rpt. Detroit:

Gale Research Company, 1969; rpt. again Whitefish, Minnesota: Kessinger Publishing, 2003.

Butterflies and Moths of the Country-Side. London: Hutchinson, 1903.

Wild Fruits of the Country-Side. London: Hutchinson, 1907.

Familiar Swiss Flowers, Figured and Described. London: Cassell, 1908.

That Rock-Garden of Ours. London: T.F. Unwin, 1909.

Wild Flowers in Their Seasons. London: Cassell, 1909.

These titles show that F. Edward Hulme, as his name appears on his publications, had at least some interest in folklore, but he appears not to have had any particular fascination with proverbs as such. Little wonder then that his book on *Proverb Lore* (1902) is somewhat of an oddity which is not even mentioned by G.S.B. in the supplement of *The Dictionary of National Biography* (Oxford: Oxford University Press, 1912), vol. 1, pp. 321-322, or by Peter Osborne in the *Oxford Dictionary of National Biography* (Oxford: Oxford University Press, 2004), vol. 28, p. 716. Merely the anonymous entry in *Who Was Who, 1897-1915* (London: Adam & Charles Black, 1920), pp. 259-360, includes the shortened title *Proverb Lore* with its 1902 publication date. And yet, Hulme's unique treatise clearly carried on the previous work *On the Lessons in Proverbs* (1853) by Richard Chenevix Trench and together with it informed Archer Taylor's *The Proverb* (1931) and my own *The Proverb: A Handbook* (2004). As such, it is a major accomplishment in the history of paremiology and deserves to be made available again at this time.

As Frederick Edward Hulme did in many of his other books, he provides detailed descriptions of his seven chapters in the table of contents, illustrating in the bullets of these paragraphs the rich account of his informed and readable book. He too begins with a discussion of the definition, form, content, and meaning of proverbs, followed by a survey of major proverb collections. Then he moves on to the use and function of proverbs in English literature, citing many examples in their literary contexts together with explanatory comments. The book moves on to national idiosyncracies expressed in the proverbs from different languages and cultures. Next Hulme offers a discussion and explanation of numerous English proverbs relating to all walks of life. This is followed by a similar treatment of animal proverbs, with the remainder of the book looking at proverbs and their meaning as they comment on human behavior and worldview.

All of this rich proverbial material is presented in an informed and readable style, making Frederick Edward Hulme's *Proverb Lore* a fascinating treasure trove for anybody interested in proverbial matters. As such, this book deserves to be read and cited in the studies of modern proverb scholars who should ever be mindful that there is much to be learned from those who tilled the proverbial fields during earlier times.

Burlington, Vermont
Spring 2007

Wolfgang Mieder

PROVERB LORE

PROVERB LORE

*MANY SAYINGS, WISE OR OTHERWISE,
ON MANY SUBJECTS, GLEANED
FROM MANY SOURCES*

BY

F. EDWARD HULME, F.S.A.

AUTHOR OF
"WAYSIDE SKETCHES," "MYTHLAND," "NATURAL HISTORY
LORE AND LEGEND," "SYMBOLISM IN ART,"
"WILD FRUITS OF THE COUNTRYSIDE,"
'FAMILIAR WILD FLOWERS," ETC.

LONDON
ELLIOT STOCK, 62 PATERNOSTER ROW, E.C.
1902

CONTENTS

CHAPTER I

CHAPTER II

CHAPTER III

CHAPTER IV

CHAPTER V

CHAPTER VI

CHAPTER VII

PROVERB LORE

THE study of proverbs is one of exceeding interest and value. By means of it our thoughts travel back through the ages to the childhood of the world, and we see at once how amidst the surroundings that vary so greatly in every age and in every clime the common inherent oneness of humanity asserts itself: how, while fashions change, motives of action remain ; how, beneath the burning sun of Bengal or Ashanti, in the tents of the Crees, or amidst the snows of Lapland, the thoughts of men on the great problems that confront the race are strikingly at one. Hence, while the outward garb and phraseology of these proverbial utterances must neces- sarily greatly vary, we find, when we pierce below the

A

surface, a remarkable similarity of idea. When we desire to point out the foolishness of providing any place or person with anything that they are really better able to procure for themselves, the absurdity of "carrying coals to Newcastle" is pointed out, and we might at first sight very naturally say that surely here we have a popular saying that we can specially claim as a piece of English proverbial wisdom. We find, however, in the Middle Ages the popular saying, "Send Indulgences to Rome"; while even before the Christian era the Greeks were teaching the same lesson in the formula, "Owls to Athens," the woods of Attica yielding these birds in abundance, while the city itself, under the special guardianship of Pallas Athene, had, as its device and symbol, on its coinage and elsewhere, the owl, the bird associated with that goddess—coals, owls, indulgences, so different in outward seeming, teaching the self-same truth. Any attempt at classification of proverbs by nationality is exceedingly difficult, and in many cases impossible, since the more one looks into the matter the more one realises what a cosmopolitan thing a proverb is. Gratifying as it would be to patriotic feeling to gather together all the best pro- verbs in circulation in England and claim them as the product of English wit and wisdom, we should at once on investigation find that in great degree they were, perhaps in actual wording, and certainly in significance, the property of humanity at large.

The necessity of curbing the hasty tongue, the dis- praise of folly, the value of true friendship, the watch- fulness that enmity entails, the influence of womankind, the fabrication of excuses, the vainglory of boasting and pretension, the exposure of hypocrisy, the evil of ingratitude, the golden irradiation of the pathway of life by hope, the buoyant strength and confidence of youth, the sad decrepitude of old age, the retribution that awaits wrongdoers, were as keenly understood three thousand years ago as to-day, and the trite expression of these verities, crystallised into warning, encouragement, or reproof, is as much a part of the equipment of life to the date-seller of Damascus as to the ploughman in an English shire.

Proverbs have been handed down from generation to generation from the remotest ages, and were in circulation from mouth to mouth long before any written records, since in the earliest writings extant we find them given as obvious quotations. By means of them, primitive peoples entered upon a heritage of sound wisdom and good working common-sense, and had ready to hand counsels of prudence, hints for the conduct of life, warnings of its pitfalls. Much that is interesting in history, in manners and customs, is also preserved in them, and though times change it is scarcely safe to say that any proverb is obsolete. A local allusion may be understood by some old countryman that to the philosopher and savant is nought.

Time after time as we travel onwards through life we find our knowledge somewhat nebulous, our ideas in need of precision and sharpness of definition. We accept so many things, almost unconsciously, on trust, and should find it almost impossible in many cases to give an exact reason for the belief that is in us. The nature and construction of a proverb appears a thing too self-evident for any question to arise, the definition of it one of the simplest of tasks, and we do not at all realise its difficulty until we are fairly brought face to face with the problem, pen in hand, and a sheet of blank paper before us. Waiving a personal definition, we will endeavour by means of the statements of others, men whom we may more or less recognise as authorities and specialists, to arrive at a satisfactory conclusion.

Dr Johnson, in his noble dictionary, a splendid mass

of erudition,* defines a proverb as "a short sentence frequently repeated by the people ; a saw ; an adage," but this definition, as it stands, is scarcely sufficient. Having already a fair though nebulous notion of what a proverb is we may perhaps accept it, since we automatically fill in what is wanting, but if we could imagine the case of one who had no previous notion of the nature of a proverb the definition of Dr Johnson would not fill the void, since there are many colloquial phrases in constant use that are not proverbial in their nature at all.† The Doctor points out, under a second clause in his definition, that a proverb may also be a byeword of reproach, but it would appear needless to dwell specially on this. A proverb may exert its influence on us in many ways, by encouragement, by derision, by warning, and so forth, and there seems no occasion to make a special section of those that yield their lesson to us by way of reproach. As an example of the use of this class we may instance the passage of Milton, from his "Samson Agonistes"—

> " Am I not strong and proverb'd for a fool
> In ev'ry street : do they not say, how well
> Are come upon him his deserts ? "

Our readers will doubtless recall, too, how in Holy Writ it is declared that " Israel shall be a proverb and a byeword among all people."

---

* " A dictionary of the English language, in which the words are deduced from their originals, and illustrated in their different significations by examples from the best authors." This early edition is in two massive quarto volumes, and the later abridgments that are now alone seen give no conception of the value of the original work.

† The two illustrative quotations appended are from the writings of Bacon and Addison respectively. The first runs as follows:—" The proverb is true that light gains make heavy purses; for light gains come thick, whereas great come but now and then "; while the second, from Addison, declares that "the proverb says of the Genoese that they have a sea without fish, land without trees, and men without faith." This latter would appear to be rather an epigram than a proverb.

The word saw is Saxon in its origin, and is defined by our great lexicographer as "a saying, a maxim, a sentence, an axiom, a proverb." Shakespeare writes—

> "From the table of my memory
> I'll wipe away all saws of books,"

and elsewhere of another of his characters he says that "his weapons" were "holy saws of sacred writ." Perhaps, however, the best and best-known Shakespearian instance is in his graphic description of the seven ages of man in "As You Like It," where we are presently introduced to the portly Justice with eyes severe and beard of formal cut, "full of wise saws and modern instances," a well-bound encyclopædia of legal axiom, precedent, and practice.

Milton writes, somewhat more forbiddingly, of

> "Strict age and sour severity
> With their grave saws."

The word proverb is Greek in its inception, and means, literally, a wayside saying. Adage, a fairly equivalent word, is also of Greek birth. The reference in "Macbeth" will at once be recalled—

> "Letting I dare not wait upon I would,
> Like the poor cat i' the adage." *

Synesius, a Christian writer of the early part of the fifth century, affirms, in quoting from a work of Aristotle that is now lost, that "A proverb is a remnant of the ancient philosophy preserved amid many destruc-

---

* We shall later on, when we deal with proverbial philosophy suggested by the various traits of animal life, find that the cat furnishes material for several popular sayings. The particular facts here brought out are the two antagonistic points in the feline economy—a great liking for fish, and a great disliking to getting wet, so that "I dare not" becomes the insurmountable obstacle to "I would." In a sixteenth century manuscript this adage is given as "a cat doth love the fishe, but she will not wett her foote," and, with various slight modifications of diction, the proverb is an oft-quoted one.

tions on account of its brevity and fitness for use," and in like strain Agricola declares proverbs to be "short sentences into which, as in rules, the ancients have compressed life." Cervantes puts this yet more pithily in his definition, "Short sentences drawn from long experience." Howell, too, is happy in his declaration, "Sayings which combine sense, shortness, and salt." Russell declares a proverb to be "the wisdom of many and the wit of one"—the one being the man who puts into happy form a truth that many had already felt, and thereby crystallised it for the use of all future time. Bacon, less happily, declares proverbs to be "the genius, wit, and spirit of a nation"; but this definition manifestly covers a far wider area than can be justly claimed for them. We need scarcely here point out that the word spirit does not mean the courage and resolution that summon a nation to the defence of its rights. It is but the Anglicised form of the French *esprit*, a word that has no entirely satisfactory English equivalent.

Chambers hath it that "proverbs are pithy, practical, popular sayings, expressive of certain more or less general convictions," and this is a definition that really seems to cover very satisfactorily the whole ground. That of Annandale is like unto it, "A proverb is a short and pithy sentence forming a popular saying, and expressing some result of the experience of life in a keen, quaint, and lively fashion." Popularity is an essential feature, an absolute necessity. A saying of some wise man may strike us at once as one of the happiest of utterances, but if from any cause it does not find acceptance and adoption into the common speech, the absence of this popular recognition of its work debars it. It may richly deserve a place amongst the proverbs, being as pithy, as wise as any of them, and possess every essential of a proverb save the one. This one essential of general acceptance being wanting, we have left to us a golden sentence, a striking aphorism, a soul-stirring utterance. This is a point that some of the compilers of lists of proverbs have overlooked, and they have been tempted to insert in their pages brilliant wisdom-chips from the writings of divers clever men, or to coin them for themselves.

Worcester, in his dictionary, defines a proverb as "a common or pithy expression which embodies some moral precept or admitted truth," but we find in practice that some few of these popular sayings are not altogether moral in their teaching. Hazlitt affirms that this popular diction is "an expression or combination of words conveying a truth to the mind by a figure, periphrasis, antithesis, or hyperbole." Here, again, the soundness of the teaching is taken for granted.

Cooper, in his Thesaurus, A.D. 1584, translates *proverbium* as "an old sayed sawe," and this really, in spite of its great brevity, very nearly touches the root of the matter. Being "old," the popular utterance has the stamp and dignity of antiquity: it is no new-fangled thing that may or may not find a lasting resting-place in the minds and consciences of men; while, being "sayed," it is not merely a golden maxim buried deeply in the pages of some venerable tome, it has passed into the daily life and struggle for existence, and become incorporated in the popular speech. It has borne the test of time; generation after generation of the sons of men have recognised its value and accepted it.

In the "Encyclopædia Metropolitana" a proverb is defined as "a common saying, sentiment, or sentence in which all agree"; but while so common a saying, a sentence that all can agree upon, as "twice two make four," comes entirely within this definition, it is in no sense a proverb. Slavery we all feel to be an evil, and we deplore its existence, but while the sentiment does credit to our hearts, and unanimous as we may all be on the point, it is in no degree proverbial. The definition, moreover, requires from us a unanimity of acceptance, but this is by no means always forthcoming, as regards the moral teaching, for example, of some of our ancient adages. If we take, for instance, so well recognised a proverb as " Honesty is the best policy," some persons will see in it a mine of shrewd wisdom, while others will decide that the man who is honest because he thinks that it will pay best is at heart a rogue. Our acceptance or rejection of its teaching does not alter the fact that for good or ill the utterance ranks as a proverb.

The Rev. John Ward, the vicar of Stratford-on-Avon in the reign of Charles the Second, was a great collector of these items of proverbial wisdom, and his stipulations as to the correct structure of a proverb were very definite, though perhaps a little too severe. He declared that in each such utterance six things were essential. It should be short, plain in its language and teaching, in common use, figurative in its expression, ancient, true. When all these requirements are met we have, doubtless, an ideal proverb, but many excellent adages are current that cannot be thus bound in.

Horace declares, wisely enough, in his " Art of Poetry," in favour of brevity :

> " Short be the precept which with care is gained
> By docile minds, and faithfully retained,"

and it is a very valuable feature. How happy in expression, for instance, are such proverbs as " Fast bind, fast find," " Forewarned, forearmed," " Haste is waste."

That a proverb should be plain in language and teaching is, we take it, by no means an essential. It rather owes often somewhat of its value to the fact that there is something in it that compels analysis, possibly awakens doubt or resistance, startles us by an apparent contradiction, and compels us to delve at some trouble to ourselves before we grasp its significance. Ray, one of the best known students of proverb-lore, realises this when he stipulates for "an instructive sentence in which more is generally designed than expressed" as his ideal.

Quaint exaggeration of statement, the use of hyperbole, is often employed, and very happily, to compel attention. Some men seem to be so specially the children of fortune that they from the most untoward events gain increased advantage, and after a submergence that would drown most men emerge buoyantly from this sea of trouble and go cheerily on their way. Such are very happily described in the Arab proverb, "If you throw him into the sea he will come up with a fish in his mouth." To those who would attempt great tasks with inadequate means how truly may we say, "It is hard to sail across the sea in an eggshell." Of those who labour hard for results that bear no proportion to the effort made we may equally truly say, "He dives deep and brings up a potsherd." In France, if a man attempts a prodigious, or possibly impossible, task, it is said of him, "Il a la mer à boire," while the thoughtless or reckless man, who to avoid a slight and passing inconvenience will run imminent risk of grave misfortune, is said to jump into the river that he may escape the rain, "Il se jette à l'eau, peur de la pluie." The hyperbole employed startles and arouses the attention and drives the lesson home. It is especially characteristic of the Eastern mind, and the Bible, a book of the East, is full of examples of its use.

Proverbial wisdom, it must be borne in mind, deals sometimes with only one aspect of a truth. The necessary brevity often makes the teaching one-sided, as the various limitations and exceptions that may be necessary to a complete statement of a truth are perforce left

unsaid.   One proverb therefore is often in direct contradiction to another, and yet each may be equally true.
Solomon, for example, tells us to "answer a fool according to his folly, lest he be wise in his own conceit," and
he also tells us to "answer not a fool according to his
folly, lest thou also be like unto him."* These two
directions are placed one immediately after the other
of deliberate forethought that the sharp contrast may
force itself on the attention.   The two modes of action
are in direct contradiction, yet each is equally valuable
in its place, and according to circumstances one or other
of them would be the right course to pursue.   To the
restless, unstable man we may well quote the well-known
adage, "A rolling stone gathers no moss";† but, on the
other hand, it is equally true that "A tethered sheep
soon starves."   While one villager is content to remain
in the little hamlet where he was born, living hardly
throughout his life, the recipient of a scanty wage, of
soup and blankets from the vicarage or the hall, and,
finally, of a pauper grave, his schoolmate, the rolling
stone, goes out into the big world and fights his way
into a position of independence.

The fourth stipulation of Ward—figurativeness of
expression—while it may appear to somewhat clash
with his second, the demand for plainness of utterance,
is undoubtedly of great value ; but it is not an essential.
Such proverbs as "Plough, or not plough, you must pay
your rent," "The receiver is as bad as the thief," "The
child says what father says," "Misfortunes never come
singly," "Extremes meet," "Ill doers are ill deemers,"

---

* A great use is made in the Bible of this thought-compelling antithesis.
One illustration will suffice : "There is a shame that bringeth sin, and
there is a shame that is glory and grace."

　　† " The stone that is rouling can gather no mosse,
　　　　Who often remooueth is sure of losse,
　　　　The riche it compelleth to paie for his pride ;
　　　　The poore it vndooeth on euerie side."

are direct statements to be literally accepted, and to these scores more could be added. The figurative treatment is, nevertheless, still more in evidence, and very justly so. By its employment the attention is at once arrested and the memory helped. This love of picture language is specially characteristic of early days and of primitive peoples, and those who would turn away from an abstract discourse in praise of virtue, temperance, or strenuous endeavour will gladly accept the teaching if presented in more concrete form—the fairy tale, the fable, or the parable.

This figurativeness of language was a marked characteristic of the teaching of our Lord, and the common people, who would have been repulsed by dogma or exhortation, thronged gladly to the Teacher who reached their hearts through the beautiful and simple stories that fascinated them and awoke their interest. The sharp experiences of the wayward son in the far-off land, the story of the anxious housewife seeking at midnight for the lost piece of silver, the lonely traveller sore beset by thieves, the withering grain that fell amidst the roadside stones, the goodman of the house so stoutly guarding his belongings, the sheep that had strayed afar into the perils of the wilderness, the useless tares amidst the fruitful grain, the house upon the shifting sand, the widely-gathering net, the pearl of great price, have been a delight to countless generations, and will ever continue to be so.*

A proverb that is figurative in its construction may be considered as really a condensed parable. Hence Chaucer, in the prologue of " The Wife of Bathe," refers to " eke the paraboles of Salomon."

Numerous examples of these word-pictures will at

* " In manye suche parablis he spak to hem the word, as thei myghten here, and he spak not to hem withoute parable."—*Wiclif's translation of the Bible.*

" The holye scripture hath her figure and historye, her mysterye and veritie, her parable and playne doctryne."—*Bale.*

once occur to us. How expressive of the reproductive power of evil is the well-known proverb, "Ill weeds grow apace." In one of the Harleian MSS. of about the year 1490 we find it given as "Ewyl weed ys sone y-growe"; or, as another writer hath it,—

> "Ill weede groweth fast, ales, whereby the corne is lorne,
> For surely the weed overgroweth the corn."

In France it is "Mauvaise herbe croit toujours," and in Italy "Erba mala preste cresce," and in some kindred form it appears in the proverb lore of almost all people. How telling, again, the picture and the lesson in "Still waters run deep."

> "Small griefs find tongues : full casks are ever found
> To give, if any, yet but little sound ;
> Deep waters noiseless are, and this we know,
> That chiding streams betray small depth below."—*Herrick.*

In Germany it is "Stille Wasser sind tief"—"Still waters are deep"—or "gründen tief," "are grounded deep." In its English and German dress we learn that the silent man is a thoughtful man, but in France it is rendered as "Il n'y a pire eau que l'eau qui dort"—"There is no worse water than that which sleeps"—making the considerably stronger assertion that a thoughtful man becomes thereby a distinctly dangerous member of society !

While we are reminded of the restless turmoil of the babbling brook, and gain in its contemplation a hint of the fussy activity that in shallow minds ends in little but outward show, we must nevertheless learn that the day of small things must not be despised, for "Little brooks make great rivers." Recalling the fable of the ensnared lion and the kindly and industrious mouse that came to his rescue, we learn afresh that the weak may often help the great, for "When large ships run aground, little boats may pull them off." How true, too, to experience is it that "To a crazy ship all winds are contrary," when in many lives there seem times when everything goes wrong, and the unfortunate victim of circumstances is buffeted from all directions. Another of these aqueous proverbs reminds us how in such case the most desperate remedies may be tried, for "A drowning man will catch at a straw." To profit, too, by seasons of good fortune is no less needful, for "Every tide will have an ebb," and we may not assume that the opportunities we neglect to-day will be always open to our embrace.

> "There is a tide in the affairs of men,"

we are told by Shakespeare, who doubtless knew this proverb, and transmuted it by his genius into fine gold—

> "Which, taken at the flood, leads on to fortune ;
> Omitted, all the voyage of their life
> Is bound in shallows and in miseries."

In the day of prosperity friends appear to be numerous, but adversity tries their worth, and it is too true for the credit of human nature, that "Men shut their doors against the setting sun." "Strike," then, "while the iron is hot"—"Batti il ferro quando è caldo," say in like manner the Italians. This is a proverb, however, that is met with almost universally, seeing that the necessity for prompt decision is also almost equally universal. Chaucer tells us how

> "Pandarus, whiche that stode her faste by,
> Felt iron hotte, and he began to smite."

Yet, remember, would one prosper, "Have not too many irons in the fire." These proverbs suggested by the smithy recall yet one other, and a very ancient one, "Inter malleum et incudem "—" Between the hammer and the anvil "—a position so hemmed in with danger that no way of escape seems possible.

When a continuous use of any advantage blinds us

to the need of caution, we must remember that "The pitcher goes oft to the well, but is broken at last," and what we have grown careless in the use of we may presently find that we have lost.* When this day comes another proverb—as to the folly of "shutting the stable door after the horse is stolen "—may be too late recalled. How picturesque and how true to life the well-worn adages, "A new broom sweeps clean," "A creaking door hangs long on its hinges," "One nail drives out another," as portrayed in the new-born diligence that, mayhap, will not last ; in the career that drags along despite all probabilities of its survival ; in the fickle heart and mind that lightly supplant old friends with new, or drop some hobby that a week ago seemed all-absorbing in favour of some other thing of no greater value, but possessing the attraction of novelty.

To those who live in constant nervous dread of im-pending misfortune it should be some little comfort to remember that "Every mote doth not blind a man." Things often work out better than the anticipation of them suggested. No action is unimportant, and all have their consequences, seeing "There is no hair so small but hath its shadow." If the action be wrong the results will accord, for "A crooked stick throws a crooked shadow." As one sows, so must they reap ; thistles will never yield figs, nor thorns grapes.

As the pains so the gains ; and "He that will eat the kernel must crack the nut." For everything the price must be paid, and "One cannot make pancakes without breaking eggs."† We cannot all be of high position, whatever our zeal and industry, and in every army the rank and file are far in excess of the leaders, and are yet

---

* "Or the golden bowl be broken, or the pitcher broken at the cistern."
—*Ecclesiastes* xii. 6.

† "Ou ne fait point d'omelettes sans casser les œufs," says the French-man, and the Spaniard agrees, "No se hacen tortillas sin romper huevos."

as indispensable as they. The French saying, "Toute chair n'est pas venaison"—"All meat is not venison"—comes in very happily here. When we recall how one revolts against "toujours perdrix," and how the London apprentices rebelled against being expected to eat salmon four days a week, we see that there is abundant welcome in the world for the steady workman, the diligent official, the succulent sirloin, the fragrant bloater.

That merit shall not go unrewarded, that fitness for duty may fairly hope to meet full and fair recognition is suggested in the proverb, "A stone that is fit for the wall is not left in the way," and men, sooner or later, receive the recognition of their worth that they deserve, for "The turtle, though brought in at the back door, takes the head of the table." A little influence, a friend at court, and a bribe to blind his eyes therewith have ere now been tried as an aid to fortune, for "A silver key can open an iron lock" in this fallen world it has been found. While this prescription is working the expectant suitor may amuse himself by "building castles in the air."

The commonest objects yield their lesson and are worked into the great mass of proverbial philosophy at the service of those who were daily using them, and could thus most fully realise the point of the utterance. The cooper soon found out that "Empty vessels make the most sound," and that every tub may well be expected to stand on its own bottom; and the miller early grasped the truth that "A little barrel gives but a little meal." He saw, too, that "A torn sack will hold no corn," and that "An empty sack cannot stand upright." The soldier was warned, "Draw not thy bow before thine arrow be fixed," and did not shoot before he had some definite aim. He knew, too, how prudent it was to have "two strings to one's bow," and that "A bow long bent at last waxeth weak." The woodman's ex-

perience added to the store of proverbial wisdom, " A
blunt wedge will sometimes do what a sharp axe
cannot"; that "Willows are weak, but yet they bind
other wood"; that "Oaks may fall while reeds remain";
and that "Great trees keep down little ones"; while the
gardener saw that "Ripe fruit may grow on rough wall";
and even the nursery yields the declaration that "A
burnt child dreads the fire"; and the tailor grasps the
wisdom of the advice, "Measure thy cloth thrice ere
thou cut it once." Other homely adages are—"At open
doors dogs come in," "A spur in the head is worth two
in the heels," "The rotten apple injures its neighbour,"
"Darns are bad, but better than debts."

Proverbs are of immense value, as they furnish an
inexhaustible store of epigrammatic utterances, and
many of them are of considerable archæological and
folk-lore value as keys to usages, beliefs, and so forth,
that have now passed away. The many proverbs, for
illustration, that deal with bows and arrows are sur-
vivals from remote antiquity or mediæval experience.

All proverbs, we need scarcely point out, are not of
equal value or popularity. Some, from their going
down to the solid bed-rock of human nature and common experience, have lasted for centuries, and will
continue, doubtless, while time shall last, their appeal to
humanity, while others are transient, local, restricted.
While some collections of proverbs run into thousands
of examples, it is astonishing how few in these latter
days are really in use. If our readers, to test this
matter, will turn their thoughts inwards, or consult any
of their friends, they will probably find that half a sheet
of note-paper will very comfortably suffice to put down
their stores, and if a hundred people did this their lists
would be curiously alike, showing that only a very
limited number have really nowadays found popular
acceptance. One hundred per cent. of these lists would

include "All is not gold that glitters," "There is a silver
lining to every cloud," and "Those who live in glass
houses should not throw stones," all, it will be noted,
being word-pictures. "A rolling stone gathers no
moss," and "A bird in the hand is worth two in the
bush," are also very popular proverbs, and greatly for
the same reason.

Proverbs may have more than one significance, and
smite as two-edged swords. Like the old-fashioned
flail, that has now so largely been superseded by the
thrashing-machine, they may very smartly return on
the head of the careless user of them. If, for example,
we quote the adage, "Set the saddle on the right horse,"
it may signify our intention to see that those whose
action in some matter is blameworthy shall be duly
held up to execration, or it may with the utmost kindliness desire that the "willing horse," human or equine,
shall not be imposed on, and that those shall bear the
burden that are most fit to do so.

Some proverbs are merely palpable truisms, and have
little or no claim on our consideration. They have
largely arisen from the mistaken zeal of some of the old
writers in endeavouring to force into their lists anything
that could be got together with any semblance of pro-
priety, and in such a case the sharp dividing line that
should be in evidence between proverb and platitude
was often overstepped. Should A publish a select list
of one hundred proverbs, the book of B, which contains
two hundred examples—the hundred of A, plus axioms,
platitudes to make up the double amount—is not twice
as good ; it is only half as good, because one has to
spend time and energy in separating the gold from the
dross. The following may be taken as illustrations of
the sort of thing we are protesting against :—"He that
does no good does evil," "The act proves the intention,"
"Defer not charities till death," "Diligence is the mother

B

of good luck," " Books should inspire thought, not super-
sede it," " Learn first to obey before proceeding to
govern," " Great designs require great consideration,"
" Self is a poor centre," " Affected simplicity is but
imposture," " Yield graciously or oppose firmly," " Good
cause gives stout heart and strong arm," " It is good to
begin well, better to end well," " Procrastination often
brings repentance." These, all culled from various collections, are perfectly harmless, and, indeed, praiseworthy.
As copy-book headings they might render good service,
but they want the " salt " to make them popular or
acceptable. As truisms they are superb.

The antiquity of many of our proverbs is very great,
and their parentage is enveloped in mystery. Howell,
an old writer on the subject, likens them to " natural
children legitimated by prescription and long tract of
ancestriall time," and these foundlings have certainly
been made very welcome. While the name of the
coiner is not transmitted with it, the gift he bestows on
posterity enjoys an unending popular appreciation that
the authors of soul-stirring appeals, of learned treatises,
of exquisite poems, sometimes fail to reach. It is a
piece of proverbial wisdom that " liars should have good
memories," and there is a very modern ring about it,
but St Jerome, writing in the fourth century, introduces it to clinch an argument, and refers to it as an
old proverb. Quintilian, a contemporary of Martial,
Juvenal, Tacitus, during the reigns of Titus and
Domitian, some three hundred years before the days
of Jerome, also introduced it. How many centuries
before this the proverb was in use, who can say? The
rule it lays down would be a valuable one any time this
three thousand years or more, and as political economists
tell us that supply and demand act and react upon each
other, we may reasonably assume that in the earliest
ages the demand for such an axiom would give it birth.

There is a homely ring in the saying that " He who lies
down with dogs will rise up with fleas," and we could
well imagine it starting into circulation somewhere
about the time of our great-grandfathers, when manners
were a little coarser, or at all events, a little more
coarsely expressed, and when, without circumlocution,
a spade was a spade ; but over eighteen centuries ago
Seneca quoted this proverb, and we find it in his
writings in all its homely directness—" Qui cum canibus
concumbunt cum pulicibus surgent."

Hesiod introduces many proverbs in his writings, and
we find them again referred to by Plutarch, Cicero, and
others. When St Paul warned his hearers that " Evil
communications corrupt good manners," he was quoting
a saying doubtless well known to them. It may be
found again in the writings of the poet Menander. In
the Edda we meet with many striking Scandinavian
proverbs, and one of the books of the Bible, compiled
about a thousand years before the Christian era, is
wholly devoted to proverbial teaching.

Proverbs form a branch of that great mass of folk-
lore that is more especially the possession of the
humbler denizens of our towns and rural districts, and
seem to have comparatively little sympathy with the
great ones of the earth. In " Eastward Hoe," written in
1605, we have a quaint illustration of their use—where
Touchstone declares, " I hired me a small shop, fought
low, tooke small game, kept no debt-booke, and gar-
nished my shop, for want of plate, with good wholesome thriftie sentences, as 'Touchstone, keepe thy
shoppe and thy shoppe will keepe thee,' 'Light
gaines make heavie purses,' ''Tis good to be merrie
and wise.'" A great use was made of proverbs and
mottoes during the middle ages on jewellery, pottery,
furniture, and in fact wherever they could be applied.

" Proverbs," Whateley very happily says, " are somewhat analogous to those medical formulas which, being in frequent use, are kept ready made up in the chemists' shops, and which often save the framing of a distinct prescription." The uneducated are quite willing to be supplied with happy arguments ready made,* and having tested their efficacy, are well content to abide by them. Motherwell very aptly observes that "A man whose mind has been enlarged by education, and who has a complete mastery over the riches of his own language, expresses his ideas in his own words, while a vulgar man, on the other hand, uses these proverbial forms which daily use and tradition have made familiar to him, and when he makes a remark which needs confirmation, he clinches it by a proverb." It is of course obvious here that the word vulgar is not used in the offensive sense that has in these latter days been associated with it.

With the uneducated and poorer folk an axiom never becomes hackneyed. In all such matters they are very conservative, and do not readily forsake the old paths. Rustic humour, rustic customs, rustic remedies, all conform to this well-nigh immutable law. Years ago, when we lived in a little Wiltshire village, the leading farmer had a black horse with a broad blaize of white running from between its ears to the nostrils, and anyone meeting the carter leading this animal to plough or stable would accost him as follows: "That harse of yourn looks pretty baad!" to which the carter would reply, "Yees, he looks pretty white about the faace, doant he?" Should this horse, or such a horse, be still to the fore, we do not for a moment doubt—it is only eighteen years since we left—that this formula is still flourishing in perennial youth. Everyone knew just

---

* "My reasoning your reason setteth nought by,
  But reason for reason yee so stiffly lay,
  By proverbe for proverbe that with you doe way."—*Heywood.*

what to say and when to slowly chuckle, and so everybody was entirely satisfied, and the sally was a guaranteed success. It had ripened with age, and had long passed the troublesome experimental stage.

Lord Chesterfield declared that "a man of fashion never had recourse to proverbs," but after all his opinion is not final. The utterance is often quoted, but proverbs still survive his anathema, and the ban under which he would place them has had no binding force. It is, moreover, a matter quite immaterial what the man of fashion thinks of them at all. They yet remain interesting objects of study for the philosopher, and are for the man of the busy world a storehouse of practical wisdom.

The Divine Teacher did not scruple to employ this form of speech. In the synagogue of Nazareth He reminds them of the popular proverb, "Physician, heal thyself," and at the Well of Sychar He declares that saying true, "One soweth, another reapeth."

There is reason in all things, and the "happy medium" is one of the most valuable objects one can strive after in almost every direction. A man who was continuously firing off adages and axioms would be as terrible an infliction as the inveterate anecdotist or the everlasting pun-producer. Shakespeare freely introduces this proverb-lore, and the titles of two of his plays, "Measure for Measure," and "All's Well that Ends Well," owe their titles to popular proverbs of the day. Fuller uses it very largely and effectively in his writings. Butler's "Hudibras" is overflowing with proverbial allusions, and so, too, are the writings of Rabelais, Montaigne, Cervantes, and many another who might be instanced. We shall have occasion, however, later on to dwell at length on their introduction into literature.

"Apt alliteration's artful aid" is sometimes invoked.

Such precepts as "Live and let live," "No silver, no servant," "Like likes like," "Out of debt, out of danger," "Time tryeth troth,"* and "No cross, no crown," and the Latin, "In vino veritas,"† are the more easily retained in the memory in consequence.

Another valuable aid to remembrance is found in rhyme, and many of our most widely current proverbs owe, no doubt, some at least of their popular acceptance to the catching jingle that fixes them on the ear. The following are examples :—"Who goes a borrowing goes a sorrowing," "Store is no sore," "The counsels that are given in wine will do no good to thee or thine," "Little strokes fell great oaks," "One drop of ink may make a million think." Very familiar examples are these— "Little pot, soon hot," "A stitch in time saves nine," "Many a little makes a mickle," "No gains without pains," and "Man proposes, God disposes." How true to life is it in a censorious world that "When I did well I heard it never, when I did ill I heard it ever." There is a touch of sarcasm in the following :—"As a man is friended so the law is ended," and the old saying, "In vino veritas," reappears in this, "What soberness conceals, drunkenness reveals." The equally well-known "Bis dat qui cito dat" is seen in the adage, "He giveth twice who gives in a trice," "He that by the plough would thrive, himself must either hold or drive," for "Well begun is half done," and "By hawk and by hound small profit is found." There are "No gains without pains," and it is "Better small fish than empty dish," "He that leaves certainty and sticks to chance, when fools pipe he may dance." He will find it true enough that "Great spenders are bad lenders," and so it

---

* Nearly equivalent to the delightful saying of classic times, "Veritas temporis filia."

† To some extent preserved in the modern equivalents, "La verdad está en el vino," "Dans le vin on dit la vérité."

is a case of " Help, hands, for I have no lands," and " Be the day never so long, at last it cometh to evensong." " Easy fool is knave's tool," but " He that mischief hatcheth mischief catcheth." " He has wit at will that with an angry heart can hold him still," but far better yet, " A little house well filled, a little land well tilled, a little wife well willed," for " A good wife and health is a man's best wealth."

Naturally, as rhyming proverbs are found to be valuable as aids to memory in England, they are equally esteemed elsewhere ; thus in France we have " L'homme propose et le Dieu dispose,"* and " Ami de table est variable "—" The friend of one's table is of very little value,"—while the Spaniard says, " A malas hadas, malas bragas"—" Ill fortune is shabbily attired." "Asi es el marido sin hecho, como casa sin techo"—"A husband without ability is like a house without a roof." " El que lleva la renta que adobe la venta"—"Let him who receives the rent repair the inn." Those who take the profits should also bear the expense. In Latin we have " Durum et durum not faciunt murum,"† that is to say, two hard materials do not come well together in building a wall, we must have some soft yielding substance to soften their asperities, and to bind them together. In other words, two headstrong, domineering people will never get on well alone : there must be the intervention of some gentler spirit to palliate, to excuse, to be a peacemaker, and avert friction. " Nocumentum, documentum " is another illustration. Its significance is that trouble teaches a man and opens his eyes, the wise course being to profit by our misfortunes. " Via crucis, via lucis," and " Qualis vita, finis ita " are other examples of the rhyming proverb. Portuguese examples are, " De ora em hora Deus mellora," " Agua molle em

---

* In modern Portuguese, " O homem impoem, Deus dispoem."
† In modern Portuguese, " Duro com duro nao faz bom muro."

pedra dura tanto dà até que fura," "Quem do alheio veste na praça o despe." Greek, German, Italian and other proverbs equally conform to this custom of aiding the memory by a rhyming treatment ; but enough has been brought forward to indicate the point.

Sometimes actual rhyme is absent, but there is nevertheless a certain catch or jingle in the wording that attracts the attention ; as, for example, " The law of love is better than the love of law," " Look rather on the good of evil men than on the evil of good men," " It is better to suffer without cause than to have cause for suffering," and " Take heed when thou seest no need of taking heed." A Latin example is, " Præmonitus, præmunitus," being forewarned one is forearmed, and prepared to defend oneself from a threatened mischief.

Such rhymes, alliterations, and quaint turns of diction have at all times had a great attraction to children and to primitive people, and to the great mass of mankind. That " Peter Piper picked a peck of pepper " is of overwhelmingly more interest, for instance, in the nursery than that George Piper should have ground a pound of coffee. When Cæsar reported his success to Rome in the words "Veni, vidi, vici," there can be little doubt that by both sender and recipients it was considered that he had put the matter very neatly, and the kindly Gregory and his hearers no doubt equally felt that a decidedly happy remark had been made when he hailed the fair-haired Saxon children as "Non angli sed Angeli."

A very interesting Greek inscription that reads the same either backwards or forwards is found in many English and foreign churches—" Nipson anonemata me monan opsin." In the Greek lettering the reversal is complete, but in English characters the " ps " is two letters instead of one, and when read backwards becomes " sp." The significance is, " Cleanse thy sins and not thy face only." It appears ordinarily on the font, and, less usually, on the sacred vessels, and may be taken as a fair equivalent of the scriptural precept, " Rend your heart and not your garments." Examples will be found in England in Hadleigh Church, Suffolk ; West Shefford, Berks ; Clipston Church, Northampton ; Worlingworth Church, Suffolk ; Harlow, in Essex ; Melton Mowbray, in Leicestershire, and other places. One notable and interesting example of its introduction was on the font of the Basilica of the Heavenly Wisdom at Constantinople, but on the conversion of this building into a mosque this font was destroyed.

CHAPTER II

THE collecting of proverbs appears at almost all periods
to have exercised a great fascination, and even in classic
times we find writers either amassing stores of them or
introducing them freely into their writings. Many of
these sayings arose, there is no doubt, in the leisurely
and sententious East, and from thence found their
way to the widely-spreading colonies of Greece and
Phœnicia, and in due course to Rome, where a still
greater area of diffusion was thrown open for their
dispersal. The Jewish proverbs used by our Saviour, or
by St Paul and the other apostles, can be traced back
to India, where they were in use centuries before they
found their way through Babylonia and Persia to the
shores of the Mediterranean Sea. Hesiod, Homer,
Pindar, Æsop, Solon, Aristotle, Phædrus, and many
other ancient writers introduced them. Menander
made a fine collection of them under the title of
Sententiæ Monostichæ. Pythagoras drew up a collection

of adages for his disciples, and Plato, Theophrastus, and Chrysippus accumulated stores of them. During the Roman Empire collectors of antiquarian tastes carried on the work, Zenobius and Diogenianus, during the reign of Hadrian, being perhaps the most notable and enthusiastic in this pursuit, and to these, though of much later date, we may add the names of Gregorius, Cyprius, and Macarius.

Zenobius made an epitome of the proverbs collected by two older writers, Tarraeus and Didymus, in number five hundred and fifty-two, and Diogenianus, living about the same time, the beginning of the second century, accumulated seven hundred and seventy-five. Andrew Schott edited these two lists, plus fourteen hundred from Suidas and some few others from various sources at Antwerp in the year 1612.

The Biblical book known as the Proverbs of Solomon must certainly not be overlooked, as it is a collection of quite inestimable worth, having a counsel for every emergency in the troublous life of man, an encouragement for the weak, a reproof for the froward. To the conceited man it cries " Be not wise in thine own eyes," " Cease from thine own wisdom," while man swollen up with pride is warned that " Pride goeth before destruction and an haughty spirit before a fall," so that " When pride cometh there cometh shame." The value of friendship is very fully enforced : we are warned that " A man who hath friends must show himself friendly " in turn, that we must not resent the honest counsel proffered, for " Faithful are the wounds of a friend," and we must not too hastily assume that all who profess to be our friends are really so, for " Every man is a friend to him that giveth gifts," and only adversity could prove their real value. The mischief done by the hasty tongue is repeatedly dwelt upon—" A fool's mouth is his destruction," " The words of a tale-bearer are as wounds," and "Death and life are in the power of the tongue." The man of business is warned that "Divers weights are an abomination to the Lord," while the man who honestly endeavours is encouraged to believe that his labours shall not be lost to him, for "Whoso keepeth the fig-tree shall eat the fruit thereof, while the slothful man" excuses his idleness and apathy, and "saith there is a lion without." The vindictive man is admonished that "Whoso diggeth a pit shall fall therein," while the value of forethought and common-sense is enforced in the hint, "Surely in vain is the net spread in the sight of any bird." That we should read those counsels aright, and not draw false conclusions, we are reminded that "The legs of the lame are not equal: so is a parable in the mouth of fools." *

The priceless gift of wisdom, far in value above rubies, is dwelt upon and enforced, and its saving strength referred to time after time. The wisdom enshrined in this book, if incorporated in the heart and illuminating the life, would suffice as a complete *vade mecum.*

The writings of the son of Sirach are worthy of attentive study: they will be found in the apocryphal book of Ecclesiasticus, and are of very similar character to the proverbs of Solomon.† That the one writer should appreciate the work of the other was most natural, and the wisdom of Solomon is thus eulogised:—"How wise

---

* "A wise sentence shall be rejected when it cometh out of a fool's mouth; for he will not speak it in due season."—*Ecclesiasticus* xx. 20.

† The following illustrate the nature of these precepts: "Gold is tried in the fire, and acceptable men in the furnace of adversity." "Change not a friend for any good." "Of a spark of fire a heap of coals is kindled." "How agree the kettle and the earthen pot together?" "He that can rule his tongue shall live without strife." "As the climbing up a sandy way is to the aged so is a wife full of words." "The furnace trieth the potter's vessels." "Better is the life of a poor man in a mean cottage than delicate fare in another man's house." "He that taketh away his neighbour's living slayeth him." "Every counsellor extolleth counsel." "Bountifulness is as a most fruitful garden."

wast thou in thy youth, and as a flood filled with understanding. Thy soul covered the whole earth, and thou
filledst with dark parables. Thy name went far into the
islands, and for thy peace thou wast beloved. The
countries marvelled at thee for thy songs, and proverbs,
and parables, and interpretations."

> " O Salomon, richest of all richesse,
> Fulfilled of sapience and worldly glorie,
> Ful worthy ben thy wordes to memorie
> To every wight that wit and reason can."
> CHAUCER, *The Marchantes Tale.*

This book, though spoken of as one and as the work
of Solomon, is really divided into several sections, and
was doubtless the work of different authors and the
product of different times. All was finally collected
into a single book, but there is absolutely no clue as to
how much is the fruit of the wisdom of Solomon and
how much sprang from the experience of others. Two
other contributors are mentioned in the book, Lemuel
and Agur, writers of whom nothing is elsewhere known.
The first nine chapters are chiefly a description and
commendation of wisdom, and these are followed by
others that are largely made up of sentences very loosely
strung together. The proverbs of Agur are much more
artificial in style than the others, while the proverbs of
King Lemuel are in commendation of chastity, temperance and justice, and the praise of the ideal wife.*

In the year 1676 one Henry D'Anvers collated these
proverbs, and arranged them in alphabetical sequence
as an aid to the memory. He entitled it " A Presentation of the Proverbs of Solomon in English
Dress." At the opening of the book the writer, as in

* Amongst the various commentators on this book the works of Ewald
Berthean, Hitzig, Elster, Rosenmuller, Hirzel, Stuart, Umbreit, and Noyes
may be commended to the reader who would desire detail and analysis.

the Biblical original, seeks wisdom. His search is at
first fruitless :—

> " Fare wel (said I), for yet it don't appear,
> That Wisdom (whom I seek for) dwelleth here.
> So I departed thence with speedy feet,
> When as I found that was not Wisdom's seat."

At last, however, he seeks it in the Bible, and his perseverance is here rewarded :—

> " She's glorious within, enlightened eyes
> Do see such beauty which they can't but prize.
> She hath one room all hung with Pearls (you'll see),
> King Solomon's Proverbs, full of dignity."

This simile of the pearls is to the compiler a very
attractive one, and we find it repeated more than once
in the book, as, for instance :—

> " Who searches oft in small things worth descries.
> A Pearl is small and yet of a great price :
> A Proverb is a Pearl then, rich though small,
> But Scriptural most precious is of all.
> King Solomon hath left Posterity
> A rich and everlasting Legacy :
> A cabinet of Pearls, which all may take
> Nor shall they yet their fellows poorer make ;
> You may perhaps be owner of 't, and yet
> I also may enjoy the Cabinet.
> Who will not then this Cab'net prize and keep ?
> They're precious Pearls, although they're in a heap.
> You'l say, perhap, they're mixt together ; well,
> Loke here, each Jewell hath its proper Cell ;
> And as your use requires, you may repair
> To such a Cell, and have a Jewell there."

This latter part refers to the alphabetical arrangement
under such headings as honour, diligent, slothful. On
the right-hand page all through his book he gives the
same proverbs in Latin.

The definition of proverbs by D'Anvers is a happy
one, " Short, wise sentences, containing much in a
little." He goes on to say that " they are in the Scrip-

tures sometimes called the Sayings of the Antients
(1 Sam. xxiv. 13), because delivered by the wise antient
Fathers or Elders, and therefore called the words of the
wise (Prov. i. 6); and sometimes the sayings of old
(2 Sam. xx. 18, Ps. lxxviii. 2), because the approbation
and consent of Ages went to make them the usage of
a Nation, being brought by Custom and Tradition to
every mouth."

D'Anvers carefully calls attention to a point that is
sometimes overlooked, that such figurative language is
sometimes of intent employed to veil rather than to
reveal. Hence sometimes "an obscure and enigmatical
way of speaking," and therefore called "the word of the
wise and their dark sayings," and "dark sayings of
old." And therefore it is said to our Saviour upon His
explanation of some teaching that had not been grasped
by His hearers, "Now speakest thou plainly and speakest no proverb," opposing plain speaking to proverbial
and parabolical.

The comprehensiveness of the book of Proverbs is
very happily brought out by D'Anvers when he speaks
of it as " containing not only the true Wisdom (in teaching the fear of the Lord) but all other necessary
learning as well—Ethicks, viz., matters pertaining to
moral virtues, as Prudence, Temperance, Justice. As
Oeconomicks, viz., matters of Domestick and Family-
concerns, relating to the duties of Husbands, Wives,
Parents, Children, Masters and Servants, and Politicks,
also, relating to Government and matters of State."
We may therefore, on recognition of this, find no
difficulty in assenting to his declaration that " Plato,
Aristotle, Cicero and other Heathenish School-Authors
are not to be named with Solomon who so instructs to
every good word and work."

A manuscript preserved in the Library of Trinity
College, Cambridge, is of considerable interest in the

bibliography of proverbs. It was written in the beginning of the thirteenth century and is a translation into
Latin of some of the more popular sayings of the time.
Thus, for example, the well-known adage, "A bird in
the hand is worth two in the bush," appears as "Plus
valet in manibus avis unica quam dupla silvis." "When
the dog eats his bone he loves not company," is given
as "Dum canis os rodit, sociari pluribus odit." In an old
French collection we find the equivalent of this, "Chen
en cosyn compagnie ne desire"—"The dog while in the
kitchen desires no fellow."

Another is the interesting collection got together by
Wynkyn de Worde and Peter Trevisis early in the
sixteenth century. The wording is very quaint, but we
are able to recognise many proverbs that are still in use,
the difference of their wording often making them still
more attention-compelling. How delightful, for example,
is the variation on the well-worn theme as to the
impropriety and want of delicacy in looking in a gift-
horse's mouth, "A gyuen hors may not be loked in the
tethe." The fate that may attend unasked-for offers
of assistance is graphically brought before us in the
rendering, "Profred seruyce stynketh." The difference
in result between the idle aimless wish and the strenuous
endeavour is excellently brought home to us in
"Wysshers and wolders ben smal housholders." "Be ye
dayes neuer so long at ye last cometh euensonge," when
"the ploughman homeward plods his weary way." It is
very refreshing, too, to meet another old friend, "Thou
hyttest the nayle on the heed," though in these latter
days we make a point of its being "the right nail." The
collection is entitled "Vulgaria Stambrigi."

The "Prourbes of Lydgate," a black letter-treatise of
about the same date as the book just referred to, may
also be consulted. Many of the proverbs, though some
are good, appear to have now passed out of use. We

have for instance a somewhat selfish motto, " Payne thee
not eche croked to redresse," a counsel not to worry over
other people's troubles. " Galle under suger hathe
double bytternesse," is expressive and suggestive. It
tells of lost friendship, of confidence treacherously be-
trayed, of bright hopes dashed. The advice to look at
home and to mind primarily one's own business is
brought out in the line, " Loke in thy mirrour and
deme none other wyghts." There is, as will be noted in
the examples we have given, a certain tone of cynicism
and selfishness that is not a pleasant feature and which
we would fain hope is at least one reason for many of
them having gone out of service.

Michael Apostolius of Byzantium in the middle of the
fifteenth century compiled a book of ancient proverbs,
on which he made comments and gave explanations
where he deemed it needful. The collection contained
2027 examples. The man, however, who in these
earlier days did most in this direction was Erasmus, and
his labours supplied for subsequent writers a mass of
very valuable material, for the work was one of gigantic
toil. Erasmus largely contributed in many ways to
the advancement of learning in Europe. The first
edition of his book, the " Adagia," was published in
Paris in the year 1500. The work was at once greeted
with acclamation, and fresh editions were repeatedly
called for. On each occasion Erasmus made additions,
until at length the book contained over 4000 examples.
These were mostly the proverbs to be found in the early
Greek and Roman writers. The book is a monument of
perseverance and erudition ; it still remains unrivalled,
and it became on its issue the medium through which
the knowledge of many proverbs was disseminated
throughout Europe : the similarity of many of the
proverbs of England, Holland, Germany, Italy, Spain,
was at least in some measure owing to the fact that the

C

Latin treatise of Erasmus supplied an abundant store for general appropriation.

Erasmus was one of the many who sought to reform the Church. The dissolute were denounced whatever their rank, and abuses were fulminated against with unsparing zeal, so that the people were prepared for some great change either of mending or ending. Hence it has been said that Erasmus laid the egg of the Reformation and Luther hatched it. Great enmity was aroused, and the divines who had had cause to wince, endeavoured to persuade the Pope, Leo X., to have the " Adagia " condemned. The morals and comments added to some of the proverbs told very heavily against the clergy, and they very naturally did not take kindly to the issue of such a book. The ecclesiastics, however, in session at the Council of Trent, before whom the matter was brought, liberally decided that the book was of too great value to be wholly suppressed, so they contented themselves with ordering its strict revision, everything which they deemed offensive to the papal sway and the influence of the priesthood being under their ban. This garbled version was published in Florence in the year 1575, the name of the author being suppressed, but the book had ere this passed through so many editions and had been scattered so far and wide over Europe that any action of this kind came altogether too late to be of any efficacy.

Taverner, an Englishman, issued a book of proverbs, axioms, and epigrams in the year 1539. It is in blackletter, and has avowedly been largely constructed " with newe addicions" out of the monumental work of Erasmus. It is "the Garden of Wysdome, conteyning pleasant floures, that is to saye, propre and quycke sayinges of Princes, Phylosphers, and other sortes of men, Drawen forth of good Authours by Rycharde Tauerner." His comments on the various adages are often very shrewd. " Lawes,"

he says, " be lyke spyders webbes, wherein the weakest
and most feble beastes be catched and stycke faste,
but the strongest breake out. So lawes do bynde the
poore and meane persons but the rich cobbes escape
vnpunyshed "; and again, " An angrye bodye dothe nothynge dyffer from a mad man, but in the tariannce
of tyme, sygnifyeng that wrathe is a short frensye."
Many of his "quycke sayinges " * are very happy, thus,
" Demanded what is a frend, Zeno answered an other I,
sygnifyeng that an entyer and hartye frende no lesse
loveth his frende then hymselfe." We read, too, with
interest, of "a certayne person which rose erly in the
mornynge and found his hose knawen and eaten of the
rattes, and being troubled wyth this syght, thynkyng
it a prognosticatiō (a tokē of some misfortune) he
cometh to Cato to aske his coūsaile and to know of
hym what euyl thys thyng portended. Cato maketh
hym thys answere, Certes my frend it is no mōstrouse
syght to se rattes eat mens hose, but yf thy hose had
eaten the rattes that had been a monstrouse syght."
This answer was so entirely to the point that one
would fain hope that the man of the knawen hose
went on his way rejoicing that he knew the worst.

Books of like nature with that of Taverner will be
found in the works of Florio—one of these is entitled
" Merie proverbes, Wittie Sentences and golden
Sayings," and another is the " Garden of Recreation."
This latter contains some six thousand Italian
proverbs. They doubtless passed through divers
editions ; the copies that came under our own notice
were dated 1578 and 1591 respectively.

A valuable sixteenth century collection of proverbs

---

* Quick is here used in its original sense of having life. These therefore
were lively sayings. In the Apostle's creed the quick and the dead are
referred to, and a quick set hedge is one of growing plants as contrasted
with a mere fencing or line of palings.

may be found in a rhyming treatise written by John Heywood. The first edition that we have seen is a black-letter quarto of the year 1547. It is entitled " A Dialogue, contayning in effect the number of al the Proverbs in the English tongue, compact in a matter concerning two Marriages." In an issue in 1598 that has come under our notice the title is, " A dialogue wherein are pleasantlie contrived the number of all the effectuall proverbs in our English tongue, compact in a matter concerning two marriages. Together with three hundred epigrams upon three hundred proverbs." Heywood always refers to the proverbs as already old sayings and praises them, though he at times dressed up as proverbs some of his own ideas, and altered others, depriving them of somewhat of their rugged directness.   He says of them :

> " Our common, plaine, pithie proverbes olde
> Some sense of some of whiche beying bare and rude,
> Yet to fine and fruitfull effect they allude,
> And their sentences include so large a reache
> That almost in all thinges good lessons they teache.
> This write I not to teach but to touch : for why?
> Men know this as well or better than I.
> But this and that rest : I write for this,
> Remembering and considering what the pith is,
> That by remembering of these, Proverbs may grow."

This poem on marriage may make an excellent vehicle for the introduction of these old English sayings, but as a poem it is in itself most cheerless and disagreeable, the view taken being a most unfavourable one.   One gets no notion of anything like conjugal felicity being possible, the rhymes being a snarl and a wrangle all through.

John Heywood was a friend of Sir Thomas More. His book at once sprang into popularity, and was ten times reprinted during the sixteenth century.   He also wrote the " Mery playe betwene the Pardoner and the

Frere, the Curate and Neybour Pratte." The whole tone of this is as hostile to the clergy as the other to Hymen. Another of his productions was the "Play of the Wether," where a "gentylman, wynde-miller, marchaunt, launder," and others all fall foul of the weather, and at last appeal to Jupiter. The gentleman, for instance, "wants no wynde to blow for hurt in hys huntynge," while "she that lyveth by laundry must have wether hot and clere her clothys to dry." He wrote several other plays and other things.

The following extracts from Heywood give an illustration of his rhyming treatment :—

> " The cat would eat fish and would not wet her feete.
> They must hunger in frost that will not worke in heate.
> And he that will thrive must aske leave of his wife,
> But your wife will give none, by you and her life."

> " Haste must provoke
> When the pigge is proffered to hold up the poke.
> When the sun shineth make hay : which is to say
> Take time when time com'th, lest time steale away.
> And one good lesson to this purpose I pike
> From the smith's forge, when th' iron is hot, strike."

The reasons may be sound enough, but the rhymes are deplorable. Thus "pike" is no doubt an example of "poetic license," as pick, the word he really wants, would not rhyme with strike !

> " From suspicion to knowledge of yll, for sothe,
> Coulde make ye dooe but as the flounder dothe—
> Leape out of the frying-pan into the fyre,
> And chaunge from yl peyn to wurs is smal hyre."

For badness of rhyme it would be hard to surpass this—

> " But pryde she sheweth none, her looke reason alloweth,
> She lookth as butter would not melt in her mouth."

That "newe broom swepth cleene" is the text for
another atrociously bad rhyme. It limps as follows :—

> " But since all thing is the worse of the wearing
> Decay of cleene sweeping folke had in fearing."

In the year 1586 appeared the first edition of
Camden's Britannia. The book was a very popular
one, and repeatedly issued. The author accumulated a
vast store of information, more than he found himself
able to utilise in his book, the result being yet another
book, the " Remaines." This, like the first, was received
with much favour. The title was " Remaines concerning Britaine ; but especially England and the Inhabitants thereof, their Languages, Names, Surnames,
Allusions, Anagrams, Armories, Monies, Impresses,
Apparell, Artillarie, Wise Speeches, Prouerbs, Posies,
Epitaphs." William Camden was Clarenceaux, King
of Armes, surnamed "the Learned" by some of his
contemporaries, and his heraldic and archæological
tastes are clearly seen in his choice of subjects when
dealing with so vast a theme as the thousand and one
interests that divers Englishmen would look for in such
a book ; the sportsman, the botanist, the merchant, for
example, each having their special interests quite
outside those that seemed to Camden so specially
characteristic and essential to a right comprehension
of England.

The book is a very interesting one, and full of
valuable matter, but it is with one section alone, that
on proverbs, that we now deal. His reason for their
insertion is as follows :—" Where as proverbs are concise, witty, and wise Speeches grounded upon long
experience, containing for the most part good caveats,
and therefore profitable and delightfull : I thought it
not unfit to set down here, alphabetically, some of the
selectest and most usuall amongst us, as being worthy

to have place amongst the wise Speeches." In the book
they immediately succeed these wise speeches.

We give a selection from these proverbs, held to be
worthy of such commendation. " An ynche in a miss
is as good as an ell." " Looke not to hie least a chip
fall in thine eie." " It is euill waking of a sleeping
dogge." " Many stumble at a strawe and leape over
a blocke." " Of little medling commeth great ease."
" Poore and proud, fy, fy." " Saue a thiefe fro the
gallowes and heele cut your throat." " So long goes
the pot to the water that at length it comes home
broken." " Tread a worme on the taile and it must
turne againe." " Where be no receauers there be no
theeues." * " When the skye falleth we shall have
larkes."

Though the exigencies of space prevent anything like
individual comment, we trust that our readers will not
hurry through these as a mere list to be got through.
Each is excellent, and well worthy of quiet thinking
over ; while a second theme of interest may, we think,
often be discovered in the recognition of proverbs well
known to us in a somewhat different wording, as, for
instance, Camden's version—" A man may well bring
a horse to the water, but he cannot make him drinke
without he will," and " An inche in a misse is as good
as an ell,"—proverbs in common use still, but given
here with a certain quaintness of variation that has a
charm.

Other happy utterances in the Camden collection
are : " A friend is not so soon gotten as lost." † " A
leg of a lark is better than the body of a kyte." " A
man far from good is near to harm." " A man may

* " It is a comon sayinge, ware there is no ryceyver there shoulde be no
thefe." " A Christian exhortation unto customable swearers," 1575.

† A more modern utterance shrewdly says, " There is a scarcity of friendship, but none of friends."

buy golde too deare." "One piece of a kid is worth
two of a cat." "It is a proud horse that will not bear
his own provender." "As good sit still as rise up and
fall." "Blind men should judge no colours." "He
that will have a hare for breakfast must hunt over-
night." "It is hard to teach an old dog tricks." "It
is not good to have an oare in every man's boat."
"One ill weede marreth a whole pot of pottage."
This latter is in an especial degree, in its literal
wording, a proverb of the past, though its inner significance will hold good till the end of time. It
clearly refers to a time when the herbs of the field
were utilised, and vegetable gardens did not supply
the needful requisites for the table. In these present
days well-ordered ranks of beans, onions, lettuce, and
other crops are to hand, and a mistake is scarcely
possible, but in these earlier days, when the wild
growths of the hedgerow were utilised, one can
readily see that a little ignorance in the gathering
might contribute an ingredient that would mar all—a
touch of hemlock, for instance, in lieu of parsley.

It is strikingly true, too, that as on the one hand a
soft answer turneth away wrath, so, on the contrary,
" one ill worde asketh another," and probably does not
ask in vain. It is equally true in one's experience of
life that not uncommonly " One beateth the bush and
another catcheth the birds." The necessity of caution
in permitting innovations is well brought out in, " Once
a use then ever a custom "; and the fact that there is
more skill in even the simplest art than the onlooker
quite realises is very effectively brought out in, " There
is craft in daubing." The motto of the Order of the
Garter has prepared us for " Shame take him that
shame thinketh." Other happy renderings in the
collection under consideration are, " Such an one hath
a good wit if a wise man had the keeping of it." " No

penny, no paternoster." " The beggar may sing before the thiefe," for, having no property to lose, the highwayman or the burglar have no terrors for him. " Three may keepe counsell if two be away." "Who medleth in all things may go shoe the gostlings." We have by no means exhausted the list. The only one amongst the whole collection that appears unworthy of a place is " Struggle not against the streame." This appears to point to a cowardly surrender, a floating easily down when a stout resistance should be made. A policy of " Do as the others do ; ask no questions ; raise no difficulties; make no protest; keep quiet, or shout with the majority; we are no worse than other people." We cannot recall the name of any man or woman whose life shines bright in history whose principles were built up exactly on these lines.

John Davies, a native of Hereford, in the year 1611 or thereabouts wrote a book which he called the " Scourge of Folly." The work is now a scarce one, and the world is no great loser in consequence. He was a versifier at once prolific and drearily dull. The first edition we have not seen, but that of 1620 is entitled, " The Scourge of Folly, consisting of satyricall Epigrams and others in honour of many noble Persons and worthy Friends, together with a pleasant (though discordant) Descant upon most English Proverbs and others." The epigrams are, most of them, of a most offensive character. The references to the names of the persons satirised carry now no meaning, but at the time they were written they must have been of the most grossly personal character. " Against Formias brauery and unceessant prating," "against Cleophus, the Time observer," "against faint-hearted bragging Bomelio," " against wordy Classus," are examples of the headings, and the lines that in each case are appended are grossly insolent. There are two hundred and ninety-two of

these scoundrelisms.   His proverbs are four hundred
and nineteen in number, and he adds to each a rhyming
comment of his own.   They are mostly very feeble, and
many of them much too gross for quotation.

> " Fast binde, fast finde, but Rufus, bound as fast
>   As bonds could do, to pay a debt he ought,
> Stole quite away, ere quite the day was past,
>   And nowhere can be found, though he be sought."

He lengthens and shortens the proverbs as rhythmical
exigencies call for, and his great idea throughout seems
to be to show that these old proverbs were quite absurd
and valueless, and that John Davies was the real fount
of wisdom.

We append a few of these couplets, the first line
being a proverb and the second the comment of Davies
upon it.   Anything more feeble and pointless than
the latter could scarcely be imagined.

> " A Mouse may in time bite in two a cable—
>   That may she at once if she be able."

> " No more can we have of the fox but his skin ;
>   Yes, Bones to make dice, which now is no sin."

> " Three may keep counsell if two be away,
>   And so may all three if nothing they say."

> " A dead Bee will make no Hony,
>   But from dead Bees it's had for money."

> " Ill newes are commonly true,
>   Not if a lyer made them new."

> " The Cat would eat fish but for wetting her feete,
>   To eat ere she wash is fowle and unsweete."

> " Throw no Guift at the Giver againe ;
>   Yes : if he give me a blow Ile thanke him with twaine."

> " A scabb'd Sheepe will marre a whole flocke,
>   Faith, then the Shepherd's a Knave or a Block."

> " Who is worse Shood than the Shoomaker's wife ?
>   Faith, Geese, that never wore Shoes in their life."

About this time also was published a book called
" The Crossing of Proverbs." The copy before us as
we write is, we see, dated 1616. It is on the same lines
as the preceding book, except that it is not in rhymes.
" It is far to the bottom of the sea," says the old proverb,
" Not so," says the author, " 'tis but a stone's cast." We
will spare our readers any further extracts. To give
several extracts from the " Scourge of Folly " and then
to merely add that "The Crossing of Proverbs " is just
such another book, will give a quite sufficient measure
of justice to both.

In the year 1625 the " Apothegms new and old " of
Lord Bacon made their appearance. The study was a
favourite one with him, and he often in his writings and
discourses made a very judicious use of the material he
had collected. He affirms that " Apothegms are not
only for delight and ornament but for business also and
civil use," for " they are, according to Cicero, mucrones
verborum, pointed speeches." He also calls them
Salinas, salt pits from whence one can draw the salt of
discourse. " By their sharp edge they penetrate the knots
of business, and serve to be interlaced in continued speech
or recited upon occasion by themselves." He regrets
greatly that Cæsar's book was lost. " I imagine these
apothegms were collected with judgment and care ;
for as his history, and those few letters of his which
we have and those apothegms which were his own
excel all others so I suppose would his collection of
them have done. As for those which are collected by
other writers either I have no taste in such matters, or
else their choice has not been happy." Elsewhere he
declares that the modern writers on the subject
" draw much of the dregs."

With all possible respect to the erudition of Bacon
we find his book a somewhat heavy one, the subject
appearing to call for a lightness and delicacy of touch

that he would very possibly have considered beneath the dignity of literature. If we turn, for instance, to his comments on friendship, we are referred to verse 14 of Psalm xxvii. We read, " He that blesseth his friend with a loud voice, rising early in the morning, it shall be counted a curse to him," and this calls forth the following comment : " Moderate and seasonable praises uttered upon occasion, conduce much to men's fame and fortune ; but praises immoderate, noisy, and importunately poured out, profit nothing : nay rather, do a good deal of hurt. First, they manifestly betray themselves to proceed either from excess of love and kindness, or that they are designed and affected, so that they may rather ingratiate themselves with the person commended by false encomiums rather than set him off by just and deserved eulogisms. Secondly, sparing and modest praises commonly invite such as are present to add something of their own to the commendation ; on the contrary, profuse and immoderate ones detract and take away something. Thirdly, which is the principal point, too much magnifying a man stirs up envy ; since all immoderate praises seem to tend to the reproach of others, who are no less deserving." This is quite Baconian, almost Johnsonian, in its weighty precision and formal enunciation, but a thousand proverbs thus handed over to the commentator would be a ponderous tome that few would dare to open, and the *esprit* and quaintness of these familiar utterances would be utterly lost, buried, in such a flow of exposition.

In the year 1640 was published a volume entitled, " Outlandish Proverbs." The name of the author was not given, " selected by Mr G. H." being all the information vouchsafed. As these proverbs were those in common use, the title strikes one as being particularly inappropriate. The collection was a somewhat meagre one. All gross sayings were omitted, or softened down.

That anything objectionable should be left out seems to our present ideas so entirely a matter of course that the mention of the fact appears uncalled for, nevertheless this omission differentiated the labours of Mr G. H. from much that had gone before. The softening down process is perhaps not quite so justifiable. A proverb, like a hymn, should not be edited. All that seems fair and justifiable is to accept it as it stands or else refuse it admission.

Some considerable time after the appearance of this book on "Outlandish Proverbs" a second edition appeared, but this time the title was "Jacula Prudentum, or outlandish proverbs, sentences, etc.," and the authorship was no longer veiled by mere letters but stands revealed—"selected by Mr George Herbert, Late Orator of the University of Cambridge." This second issue contains a great many more proverbs than the first, and the title, Jacula Prudentum, "javelins of the wise," indicates the value placed by Herbert upon these popular sayings.

The mystery of the anonymous publication, like that of the Waverley novels, and other cognate cases, excited some little public interest, one writer of the day advances we see the somewhat startling thesis, "It is not a thing that, hastily regarded, one would have expected from Herbert, hence the genuineness is the more probable!" This is a very sweeping and far-reaching argument, that because a thing appears well-nigh impossible there is much to be said in favour of its probability. It seems so unlikely that Bala lake will ever flood out Westminster that all prudent persons resident there will at once provide themselves with life-belts.

A well-known proverb warns us against letting the cat out of the bag, and this seems to have been just what Herbert very nearly did, another book of his, of more devotional type, "A priest to the Temple," supplying to critical eyes a clue. In it he says that "the Country Parson doth bear in mind in the morning the outlandish proverb that prayers and provender never hinder a journey." Also in one of his letters that he wrote to his brother he added, "Take this rule, and it is an outlandish one, which I commend to you now as being a father, 'The best bred child hath the best portion.'" The introduction of the title of the book and the liking for the use of proverbs were held strong proofs in favour of his being the Mr G. H. who was being sought for. As we are told that nothing succeeds like success, we are invited to admire the sapience of the mystery-hunter, but there really seems no reason why, the title of the book being in men's minds, some other person might not have thus referred to it and introduced into his book or letters proverbs that this book had brought before him and that had attracted his notice.

Most of the proverbs in the Jacula Prudentum are admirably chosen, and as many of them are now passing away from the minds of men we make no apology for quoting freely from the book.

The re-appearance of old proverbs in a slightly altered setting than that we are now familiar with, is a point of interest in these old collections that we have already referred to, but each author we consult gives us anew this pleasure. How refreshing, for instance, is Herbert's version, "Whose house is of glasse must not throw stones at another," or this, "You may bring a horse to the river, but he will drinke when and what he pleaseth," or this, yet again, "A feather in hand is better than a bird in the ayre." A proverb that is often used at the present time amongst us in its French dress is found here as "It is a poore sport that's not worth the candle."

How true and how pithily put are these, "He that studies his content wants it." "Not a long day but a good heart rids worke." "Hearken to Reason and shee will bee heard." " He that staies does the businesse." " Prosperity lets go the bridle." " Still fisheth he that catches one." "Give a clowne your finger and he will take your hand." * And this one like unto it, " Let an ill man lie in the strawe, and he looks to bee thy heire." " The back-dore robs the house." " One sword keeps another in the sheath." An excellent motto this last. The Peace Society may have its uses, but there is no doubt that this side the millennium efficient army corps and magnificent navies supply yet more cogent arguments. " Si vis pacem pare bellum."

How sound again the teaching, " He is not poor that hath little, but he that desireth much." " God provides for him that trusteth." " A cheerful look makes a dish a feast." " Sometimes the best gain is to lose." " He that sows trusts in God." " Divine ashes are better than earthlie meale."

How excellent the prudence that gives value to the following : " Send a wise man on an errand and say nothing unto him." "Although it rain cast not away thy watering-pot." " Who hath no more breade than nede must not keepe a dog." " The best remedy against an ill man is much ground between." " Love your neighbour, yet pull not down your hedge." " Send not a catt for lard." It is well, too, to remember that " Courtesie on one side only lasts not long," that a commensurate price has to be paid for everything, and so " a lion's skin is never cheape," that one's position must be frankly accepted and its duties adequately met, for " he that serves must serve," that gentle measures will often succeed better than rough ones, for " he that will take the bird must not skare it." It is at once a comfort and a warning that " none is a foole alwaies, everyone sometimes," and that the crafty at last over-

---

* Somewhat similar proverbs to this are, " If you play with boys you must take boy's play," and if you " play with a fool at home he will play with you abroad."

reach themselves and in the end Nemesis awaits them. " At length the fox is brought to the furrier," and the farmyard knows him no more.

What an excellent lesson against jumping to conclusions is seen in this, " Stay till the lame messenger come, if you will know the truth of the thing," against concluding too hastily that the work we are engaged upon is finished, for "One flower does not make a garland."

The evil wrought by the tongue is a constant and perennial theme of the moralist, and the makers of proverbs are in complete accord, " The tongue talks at the head's cost." "More have repented speech than silence." Those who suffer at the hands, or rather the tongues, of others may learn how effectually to avenge themselves, for " Pardon and pleasantnesse are great revengers of slanders," and the experiment is one that is well worth trial. In any case, " Neither prayse nor disprayse thyself : thy actions serve the turne." " The effect speakes, the tongue need not." How full of wisdom is this final cluster of pearls, this sheaf of javelins : " A gift much expected is paid, not given." "Pleasing ware is half sould." " The hole calls the thief "—a warning against putting temptation in the way and thereby causing a brother to offend. The man who has gone far on the path of reformation is not safe so long as any relic of the past yet clings round his heart, for " The horse that draws after him his halter has not altogether escaped." " Whither shall the oxe goe where he shall not labour ? " How can one hope to evade the responsibilities of his position ? The proverb is an interesting reminder of the custom once common enough, and which we ourselves have seen in Sussex and Wiltshire, on the heavy down-lands, of ploughing with a yoke of oxen. There is quaint humour in this, " The chicken is the countrey's, but the citie eateth it." " If the old dog barke he gives counsell." " A married man turns his staffe into a stake," his wandering days are over.

A not unpleasant cynicism gives point to the assertion that " Nothing dries sooner than a teare," while it is
equally one's experience of life that " When the tree is
fallen all goe with their hatchet," and that " Men speak
of the fair as things went with them there." It is a
rather touching assertion that " The reasons of the poor
weigh not," and it is too true. Their poverty makes the
poor despised and their words unheeded by many who,
richer in this world's goods, treat with contempt the
struggling and the unsuccessful. Poverty is not a crime:
it may be a badge of shame if the result of vice, or it
may be a badge of honour where a man has scorned to
stoop to shuffling dishonesties that may have enriched
some who presume to despise him.

In 1659 James Howell issued a series of proverbs,
and some of these were incorporated in Randle Cotgrave's dictionary in the following year. This latter
has been deemed " that most amusing of all dictionary
makers." He quotes many French proverbs, and then
gives English adages that more or less match them.
Thus under faim he gives " A la faim il n'y a point de
mauvais pain," which, he explains, means that " To him
who is hungry any bread seems good "—not quite a sufficiently literal translation, we should have thought, for a
dictionary-maker—and adds, "We say hungrie dogs love
durtie pudding." * Howell's proverbs were, as a whole,
not very judiciously selected, and he had the presumption and bad taste to spin out of his own imagination a
series of what he called " New Sayings which may serve
for Proverbs for posterity." These were very poor, and
posterity has declined to have anything to do with them.

In this same year, 1659, a small volume of adages,
compiled by N. R. (Nathaniel Richards), appeared.

* "The messenger (one of those dogs who are not too scornful to eat
dirty puddings) caught in his hand the guinea which Hector chucked at
his face."—"The Antiquary."

D

They are all in English, but are mostly of foreign origin, and are of no great interest or value.

A much more notable book is the "Gnomologia: Adagies and proverbs; wise sentences and witty sayings, ancient and modern, foreign and British, collected by Thomas Fuller, M.D." As the compiler gives over six thousand proverbs, we may regard the book as a fairly adequate one. He gives in it no indication of the sources from whence the adages are derived, adds no explanatory notes, and works on no system. This is equivalent to writing a natural history and leading off with panther and earwig. It is, as a matter of fact, very difficult to classify a collection of such disconnected units as proverbs. If we attempt to do it by countries we may soon find that it is in most cases quite impossible to guess where the adage originated, and the general borrowing that has been going on for centuries makes anything like a local claim to exclusive possession impossible. It would be quite easy to write out a list of fifty proverbs, illustrating them exclusively by passages from Cervantes and other Spanish writers, and, on the strength of this, claiming them as Spanish, but it would be equally easy afterwards for Dane, Russian, and German, Englishman, Italian, and Greek to come and each claim so many of these items that the speedy outcome would be an almost absolute disappearance from our list of anything purely Iberian.

There is a good deal to be said in favour of the alphabetical arrangement, but only on condition that the leading word of the adage be taken. It is a mere absurdity to take the first word. How can we reasonably put under letter A, "A rolling stone gathers no moss"? It may be objected that we are putting an extreme case, but extreme cases have to be considered as much as any others. In one book before us we find that the old author in scores of instances produces

results as grotesquely inadequate. Under the letter D,
for instance, we find, "Do not spur a willing horse,"
though surely everyone, with the exception of the compiler of the list, would at once realise that the pith of
the adage does not in any way rest in "do." We may
at once see this if we take the proverb in another of its
popular forms, "Spur not a willing horse."

The classification of these old saws according to their
subject, such as friendship, pride, industry, and the like,
is sometimes adopted, and it has many advantages ; but
we very soon find that we come to something that declines to be thus pigeon-holed. If we take the Russian
proverb, for instance, "The burden is light on the
shoulders of another," how shall we classify it? It
will clearly not come under "friendship," and it is
equally not at home in the section on "industry."
While some adages decline to fit into any section,
others we find might with almost equal appropriateness find a home under three or four headings.

Fuller defines a proverb as "much matter decocted
into a few words," and a very good definition it is. He
declares that "six essentials are necessary for the com-
pleating of a perfect Proverb. Namely that it be—

1. Short		1. Oration
2. Playne	Otherwise it is not	2. Riddle
3. Common	a proverb at all	3. Secret
4. Figurative	but a	4. Sentence
5. Antient		5. Upstart
6. True		6. Libel."

As he was evidently a little nervous that some persons
might think the subject a little beneath the dignity of
Dr Fuller, he allows an imaginary objector to have
his fling, and then proceeds to demolish him. The
"objection" raised by this anonymous disciple of Mrs
Grundy is that "it is more proper for a person of your
profession to imploy himself in reading of, and com-

menting on, the Proverbs of Solomon, to know wisdome and instruction, to perceive words of understanding. Whereas you are now busied in what may be pleasant, not profitable, yet what may inform the fleshlie not edifie the inward man." As many proverbs do undoubtedly build up the inner man this judgment is wanting in charity, and as a student ourselves in the subject we are gratified to find that the doctor declines to accept this vote of censure, and is able to make out a good case for himself. His reply is somewhat longer than a quotation permits, and one must give all or none.

In his preface, also, he alludes to "snarling persons" who have deprecated his labours. This preface of his is distinctly interesting.

"All of us," he writes therein, "forget more than we remember, and therefore it hath been my constant Custom to note down and record whatever I thought of myself, or received from Men or Books worth preserving. Amongst other things I wrote out Apothegms, Maxims, Proverbs, acute Expressions, vulgar Sayings, etc., and having at length collected more than ever any Englishman has before me I have ventur'd to send them forth to try their Fortune among the People. In ancient Times, before methodical Learning had got Footing in the Nations and instructive Treatises were written, the Observations that were from Experience were us'd to be gather'd and sum'd up into brief and comprehensive Sentences, which being so contriv'd as to have something remarkable in their Expressions might be easily remember'd and brought into Use on Occasions. They are call'd Adagies or Maxims.

"Also the Men of Business and the common People, that they might in their Affairs and Conversation signify and communicate this Sense and Meaning in short, with Smartness and with Pleasantness fell into customary little Forms of Words and trite Speeches, which

are call'd Proverbs and common Sayings. The former
of these are from Judgment, and are us'd by Men of
Understanding and Seriousness; the other are from
Wit, and are accommodate to the Vulgar and Men of
Mirth. I conceive it is not needful for me accurately
to determine which are to be call'd Adagies and Proverbs; nor nicely to distinguish the one from the other.
All that I here take upon me to do is only to throw
together a vast confus'd heap of unsorted Things, old
and new, which you may pick over and make use of,
According to your Judgment and Pleasure. Many of
these are only plain bare Expressions, to be taken
literally in their proper Meaning: others have something of the Obscure and Surprize, which, as soon as
understood, renders them pretty and notable.

"It is a matter of no small Pains and Diligence
(whatever lazy, snarling Persons may think) to pick up
so many independent Particulars as I have done, And
it is no trifling or useless thing neither: it being what
many of the most learned and wisest Men of the World
have in all Ages employ'd themselves upon. The Son
of Syrac will be held in everlasting Remembrance for
his Ecclesiasticus, but, above all, that most glorious
of Kings and wisest of Men, Solomon, wrote by Divine
Appointment and Inspiration, Proverbs, Precepts and
Counsels.

"No man ought to despise, ridicule, or any ways dis-
courage the Diligence and Kindness of those that take
Pains to bring home to others without Price those
things of Profit and Pleasure. I picked up these Sentences and Sayings at several times, according as they
casually occurr'd, and most of them so long ago that
I cannot remember the Particulars: and am now (by
reason of great Age and ill Sight) utterly unable to
review them; otherwise I would have struck out all
such as are not fit for the Company, or are indecent

to be spoke in the Presence of wise, grave, virtuous, modest, well-bred people." These closing words one can hardly accept. Years before age and failing sight had come these various items had been growing bit by bit, and the striking-out process might well have been going on at the same time as the collecting.

"Our excellent Mr Ray," as a contemporary writer terms him, was another great collector of proverbs, and he, too, made a book of them. The first edition of this work appeared in 1670, and a second in 1678. The first was altogether too gross, so that the second edition gave an opportunity, which was embraced, for some little amendment. This is beyond all doubt the coarsest set of proverbs that has come under our notice.

Ray was a Master of Arts and a Fellow of the Royal Society. The title of his book is as follows:—" A Collection of English Proverbs Digested into a convenient Method for the speedy finding any one upon occasion: with short Annotations. Wherunto are added Local Proverbs with their Explications, old Proverbial Rhythemes, Less known or Exotick Proverbial Sentences and Scottish Proverbs." The second edition was enlarged by the addition of several hundred more English Proverbs, and by an appendix of Hebrew sayings. The annotations of Ray on various proverbs are often very feeble. Thus to the adage, or saw, or whatever it may be, " I would not trust him though he were my brother," he adds to a thing sufficiently tame in itself the comment, " This is only a physiognomical observation." The truth is, our learned author, or compiler, seems to have heaped together all the old " saws," whether wise or not, and all the " modern instances " that came in his way, and to have strung at random the precious gems in company with the worthless beads.

His "convenient method" was the alphabetical one, based on the leading word of the saying. Thus, under A, for example, we get "Adversity makes a man wise, not rich," "There is no Alchemy like saving," "He that is Angry is seldom at ease," "For that thou canst do thyself rely not on Another," "Make a slow Answer to a hasty question," "The best Armour is to keep out of gun-shot."

Robert Codrington added yet another to the pile of proverb lore in his "Collection of many Select and Excellent Proverbs out of Several Languages." These he declared to be "most useful in all Discourses and for the Government of Life." He gives no preface or any kind of introductory matter, but begins at once with number one, and goes straight on till he gets to fourteen hundred and sixty-five. His adage, "You may not lose your friend to keep your jest," is a curious variant on the familiar present-day assertion that some men would rather lose a friend than a joke. His selection is on the whole a very good one. Such sayings as, "A young man old maketh an old man young," "A drunkard is not master either of his soul or his body," and "Curses prove choke-pears to those that plant them," are thought-compelling, and many such may be encountered.

A book of somewhat different character is the "Parœmiologia Anglo-Latina" of William Walker, B.D. The sub-title was "English and Latin proverbs and proverbial sentences and sayings matched together in a collection of them made out of Plautus, Petronius, Terentius, Horatius, and other authors." The particular copy that came under our notice bore the date of 1676. He concludes his short preface by the following deprecatory passage: "What will be the advantage and benefit hereof to the Commonwealth of learning I leave to others to judge and try, as not willing to show the Sun by the light of a Candle. And so, that I may not set up a great Gate before a little House I commit the Work to You, and You to God, and rest your humble Drudge, W. W."

As the author has himself raised the question as to the benefit of his book to others, one can only reply that the advantage to the Commonwealth would probably not be very great, since the translation of the old classic authors is so exceedingly free that it is practically no translation at all. It gives those who do not know the original writings no adequate idea of them, while the English is of so very colloquial a character that all the dignity of the original is lost, the result being that both the Latin and the English languages suffer in the process.

If we take, for example, "Versutior es quam rota figularis," we find that he cites three so-called equivalents, and none of them at all giving the beautiful image of the original; the first of these being, "You are as inconstant as the wind," the next, "As wavering as the weathercock," and, thirdly, "One knows not where to have you." The "Non habet plus sapientiæ quam lapis" of Plautus he renders fairly enough as "He hath no more wit than a stone," but he adds to this, "No more brains than a burbout. He is a very cod's head"; while "As wise as Solomon" cannot at all be accepted as a rendering of "Plus sapit quam Thales." The striking "Verba fiunt mortuo" has lost all its dignity when we are invited to accept as a translation, "It is of no purpose to talk to him : he'll not hear you speak : you may as well talk to the wall."

The well-known "Parturient montes, nascetur ridiculus mus" is thus Anglicised by Walker, "Great boast, little roast ; Great cry and little wool, as the fellow said when he shore his hogs "; and the equally familiar "Ad Græcas calendas" is given as, "At Nevermass, when two Sundays come together." The striking "Leporis vitam vivit"

loses much when we are invited to accept as an equivalent, "He is afraid of the wagging of a straw." The
absurdity of teaching a fish to swim, "Piscem natare
doces," is scarcely adequately rendered by, "Tell me it
snows." How pleasant a glimpse of ancient customs we
get in the "Stylum invertere." The waxen tablet—the
stile at one end sharpened for writing, at the other flat-
tened for erasing—rise before us. But all this is entirely
lost when we are invited to accept, in place of the classic
allusion, "To turn the cat in the pan," "To sing another
tune"; and certainly the pith and rhythm of "A minimo
ad maximum" suffers woful deterioration in such renderings of it as "Every mother's son of them, tag and
rag, all that can lick a dish."

The refining influences that are associated with a
study of good classic writers seem to have rather failed
when this ancient schoolmaster came beneath their
sway. Such expressions as, "Your brains are addle,"
"As subtle as a dead pig," "Chip of the old block,"
"Lean as a rake," "A cankered fellow," "A scurvy
crack," scarcely rise to the dignity of his subject. We
cannot help wondering how the school prospered in his
hands, and what sort of boys he turned out after a year
or two under his tuition.

The "Moral Essays on some of the most Curious and
Significant English, Scotch, and Foreign Proverbs," of
Samuel Palmer,* "Presbyter of the Church of England,"
deserves some little notice. The edition before us, we
note, is dated 1710. His definition of a proverb strikes
one as being an entirely satisfactory one. He tells us
that it is "an Instructive Sentence, in which more is
generally Design'd than is Express'd, and which has

---

* Our author must not be confused with a namesake, Charles Palmer,
who was Deputy Serjeant of the House of Commons, and who published
"A Collection of Select Aphorisms and Maxims extracted from the most
Eminent Authors." He gives eighteen hundred and thirteen of these: the
copy that came into our hands was dated 1748.

pass'd into Common Use and Esteem either among the
Learned or Vulgar. I take this to be its Genuine
Definition, for though the Incomparable Erasmus takes
Elegance and Novelty into the Character of a Proverb
it seems to be an Error: for a Proverb has not only
more Honour and Authority from Antiquity, but a
Sentence never comes up to that Title till it has pass'd
for Sterling some Competent time, and receiv'd its
Dignity from the Consent of an Age at least. 'Tisn't
in a Single Author's Power to convey this Reputation
to any Saying, but the Dignity grows up in the Use of
it." This appears excellent common-sense, and the dis-
tinction that he draws between the use of a saying by
the learned or the vulgar is a very happy one, and one
that no other writer appears to regard. A proverb need
not, to establish its position, be in use by all classes.
There are certain sayings from the classics or elsewhere
that find general acceptance amongst the educated, such
as the " Ad calendas Græcas," " A la Tartuffe," " Aut
Cæsar aut nullus," " Facilis est descensus Averni." These,
either in the original tongue or Anglicised, are current,
and have a full claim to recognition as proverbial sayings,
though four-fifths of the population never heard them ;
while many homely sayings that come freely to the lips
of the carter or the village blacksmith find no welcome
or recognition from the professor, the bishop, or the
banker, and yet are as truly of proverbial rank.

Our old author goes on to say : " 'Tis the Use, not
the Critical History or Notion of Proverbs I am concern'd in. To see People throw 'em at each other by
way of Jest or Repartee, without feeling their Weight,
tasting their Wit, or being better'd by the Reflection,
wou'd vex a man of any Spirit, and the Indignation
forces him to write somewhat that might Redeem these
Fragments of Wisdom from the Contempt and Ill
Treatment of the Ignorant. For as they are now us'd

very Rarely Forc'd, but will Struggle after all the
Discipline either of Power or Principles. This made
Solomon say that Oppression makes a Wise Man
Mad. Now this shou'd be consider'd, and a Wise
Man ought to foresee how far 'tis fit to press the
most contemptible Enemy: for though his Opposition
be Wicked or Ridiculous yet it may hit the Pursuer
and do him a Mischief. To drive a Coward to the
Wall recovers his Spirits, and fear of being shot thro'
the Back makes him turn his Face. The certainty
of being quite lost by Flight gives a new Turn to the
Spirits, and Naturally prompts to a Sudden and
Desperate Defence: and tho' this be not true Courage,
nor don't act up to the Regularity that Valour is distinguished by: yet it may exceed in Face, and give a
Home Thrust. He that is eager in the Pursuit may
be struck through by that Hand which trembled till it
was reinforced by Necessity. In Armies this is a
known Rule. He that Beats a Brave Enemy ought
to be glad to be Rid of him. Let him Retreat as
quick as He can, provided the Main Victory be
secure. In Private Quarrels, Just and Vnjust, this
must be heeded: in the One Case to be Implacable
is Infamous, and in the other Wicked and Dangerous.
In Both, Rashness: and if Pity don't move us to forbear and abate in our Revenge, Caution and Regard
to our own Safety Shou'd." A rat, if driven into a
corner, will fly at a man.* And it appears that even

---

*   " For a flying foe
Discreet and provident conquerors build up
A bridge of gold."—MASSINGER, *The Guardian.*

"Ouuerez tousiours a voz ennemys toutes les portes et chemins et
plustost leur faictes ung pont d'argent, affin des les renvoyer."—RABELAIS,
Gargantua.

See also the Italian proverb—"A nemico che fugge un ponte d'oro."
" Le Comte de Pitillan en parlant de la guerre soulouit dire quand ton
ennemy voudra fuir, fais luy un port d'or."—Extract from *Les divers propos*

in baiting a cat there is a right and a wrong way of going to work. It is said by old sportsmen that the fox enjoys the sport as much as anybody, but there comes a time with baited rats and cats and most other creatures when they tire of that sort of thing, and have a very definite way of indicating the fact to all whom it may concern.

The proverbial utterances of " poor Richard " were once in great vogue. They were written by Benjamin Franklin under the *nom de plume* of Richard Saunders. " Poor Richard's Almanack " was issued for twenty-six years, from 1733 to 1758, and with constantly increased acceptance. These calendars excellently combined entertainment with useful knowledge and terse concentrated wisdom. All available spaces that occurred between notable days in the months were filled in with wisdom-chips, some of them of true proverbial rank, and others the offspring of the brains of Dr Franklin.

Franklin was born on January 6th, 1706, at Boston, and there is no doubt that his sterling common-sense and quaint philosophy must have had a considerable influence in moulding the character of the early inhabitants of the United States. These almanacks were largely reprinted in Great Britain and France, and very freely quoted from, so that the area of their influence was very extensive. In the preface to the first of this long series he quaintly gives the reasons that influenced him, poor Richard, to issue it. " I might, in this place," he writes, " attempt to gain thy favour by declaring that I write Almanacks with no other view than that of the publick good, but in this I should not be sincere ; and men are now-a-days too wise to be deceived by pretences. The plain truth of

memorables des Nobles et Illustres Hommes."—Gilles Corrizot. Paris, 1571.
" Press not a falling man too far."—SHAKESPEARE, *King Henry VIII.*

the matter is, I am extremely poor, and my wife, good woman is, I tell her, excessive proud ; she cannot bear, she says, to sit spinning in her shift of tow while I do nothing but gaze at the stars, and has threatened more than once to burn all my books if I do not make some profitable use of them for the good of my family."

Next year he writes, " Your kind and charitable assistance last year in purchasing so large an impression of my almanack has made my circumstances much more easy in the world, and requires my most grateful acknowledgment. My wife has been enabled to get a pot of her own, and is no longer obliged to borrow one from a neighbour ; nor have we ever since been without something to put in it. She has also got a pair of shoes and a nice new petticoat, and for my part I have bought a second-hand coat, that I am not now ashamed to go to town or be seen there. These things have rendered her temper so much more pacifick than it used to be, that I may say I have slept more and more quietly within this last year than in the three foregoing years put together."

There is much excellent wisdom in the sayings that he got together. How full of wise warning the utterance, " There is no little enemy," or this, " There's small revenge in words, but words may be greatly avenged." Or these warnings against covetousness, " If you desire many things many things will seem but a few." " Avarice and happiness never saw each other, how then should they become acquainted ? " How quaintly sarcastic are these, " Lawyers, preachers, and tomtits' eggs, there are more of them hatched than come to perfection." " None preaches better than the ant, and she says nothing." How true again that " Poverty wants some things and luxury many things," and that " No man was glorious who was not first laborious." How valuable the counsel, " Deny self for self's sake," and that "It is less discredit to abridge petty charges than to stoop to petty gettings"; and as a hint as to the value of concentration, "Don't think to hunt two hares with one dog." Others that we marked for quotation are, "Ever since follies have pleased, fools have been able to divert"; "He that can have patience can have what he will"; "Strange that he who lives by shifts can seldom shift himself," and to these many more of equal shrewdness could be added.

We make no claim that this list of ours is complete as a bibliography of proverb-writers. All references to the works of more recent men, Trench and others, are entirely omitted, as they are so easily accessible, that all who care to do so will have no difficulty in consulting them. Amongst the earlier men's works some are good, and some are good for nothing, but we trust that our readers will feel that this excursus is not without interest, while somewhat may be added to the dignity of our subject when it is seen to how many minds it has been a fascinating study.

CHAPTER III

THROUGHOUT the Middle Ages a great use was made,
as we have seen, of these popular adages on tapestries,
rings, and in fact wherever they could be employed.
Shakespeare, it will be recalled, writes of a but mode-
rately good poetaster as one "whose poetry was

> For all the world like cutler's poetry
> Upon a knive, 'Love me, and leave me not,'" *

and we shall therefore naturally expect to find
numerous allusions to this wealth of proverb-lore in
the writings of the day. The works of the Elizabethan
dramatists are brimming over with them. Such a fund
of material as the " Book of Merry Riddles " must have
been often drawn upon. The first edition was printed
in 1600, and contained, amongst other entertaining
material, a collection of " choice and witty proverbs."
It was often re-issued, and our last chapter has revealed

* " Love me little, love me long " is found in the writings of Christopher
Marlowe : " Pray, love me little, so you love me long," in Herrick.

to us how many other collections of like nature were issued and immediately became available.

We propose to devote now some little space to exploring in search of proverbial allusions a little of the literary wealth of our country, and we may say at once that proverbs, like everything else, require discreet use, and it is not difficult to overdo the thing.   A person who would be always dragging in these adages would be a terrible nuisance in conversation, and no less so in literature. In such a case " Enough is as good as a feast."   One would quickly weary of a page or two of this sort of thing—a brochure during the days of a suggested invasion of England by " Boney "—

> " Our foes on the ocean sent plenty of ships,
>   But ' It's not the best carpenter makes the most chips ' ;
>   They promise to give Britain's sailors a beating,
>   Though ' the proof of the pudding is found in the eating.'
>   The French have big armies, but their threats are but froth,
>   For ' too many cooks do but spoil good broth ' ;
>   They are welcome Britannia to catch when they get her,
>   But though ' Brag is a good dog yet Holdfast's a better.'
>   For their threats of invasion we ne'er care a rush—
>   ' A bird in the hand is worth two in the bush ' ;
>   They may think, open-mouthed, to devour us like sharks,
>   But ' Till the sky falls we must wait to catch larks.' "

" The pleasant historie of the two angrie women of Abington " * is, despite its self-assertion of its pleasantness, rendered very tedious by this abuse and superabundance of proverbs—one of the characters in the play, one Nicholas Prouerbes, introducing them *ad nauseam*. To give any notion of the drift of the play is beside our present need. We will content ourselves,

* " The Pleasant Historie of the two Angrie Women of Abington, with the humerous mirthe of Dick Coomes and Nicholas Prouerbes, two seruingmen.   As it was lately played by the Right Honourable the Earl of Nottingham, Lord High Admirall, his Servants.   By Henry Porter, gent.   Imprinted at London for Joseph Hunt and William Farbrand, and are to be solde at the corner of Colman Street, neere Loathburie.   1599."

therefore, with some few extracts that will suffice to indicate the point before us, the excessive use of these popular adages :

"*Nicholas.* O maister Philip forbeare. You must not leape ower the stile before you come to it ; haste makes waste ; softe fire makes sweet malte ; not too fast for falling ; there's no hast to hang true men.

"*Philip.* Now will I see if my memorie will serue for some prouerbes too. O, a painted cloath were as well worth a shilling as a theefe worth a halter ; wel, after my heartie commendations, as I was at the making therof. He that trots easilie will indure. You have most learnedly proverbde it, commending the virtue of patience and forbearance, but yet you know forbearance is no quittance.

"*Nich.* I promise ye, maister Philip, you have spoken as true as steele.

"*Phil.* Father, there's a prouerbe well applied.

"*Nich.* And it seemeth vnto me that you mocke me ; do you not kno mocke age and see how it will prosper ?

"*Phil.* Why ye prouerbe booke bound up in follio, have ye no other sense to answere me but euery word a prouerbe, no other English ?"

Presently a dispute arises outside, and Nicholas is asked, " Wilt thou not go see the fraye ? " to which this inveterate proverb-monger replies :

"No indeed, even as they brew so let them bake—I will not thrust my hand into a flame and neede not—'Tis not good to have an oare in another man's boat—Little said is soone amended, and in a little medling commeth great rest. 'Tis good sleeping in a whole skin—so a man might come home by weeping-crosse. No, by Lady, a friend is not so soone gotten as lost—blessed are the peace-makers—they that strike with the sword shall be beaten with the zcabberd."

To this flow of wisdom Philip replies :

"Well said, Prouerbes, is ne're another to that purpose ?"

The too ready Nicholas makes reply:

"Yes, I could have said to you, Syr, take heede is a good reede."

His fellow serving-man at one portion of the play sees
well to call Nicholas " tripe-cheeke, fat asse," and other
epithets of like nature ; upon which he replies:

" Good words cost nought, ill words corrupt good manners,
Richard, for a hasty man never wants woe, and I had thought you
had been my friende, but I see alle is not golde that glisters, time
and truth tryeth all, and 'tis an old prouerbe and not so olde as true,
bought wit is the best.   I can see day at a little hole.   I knowe
your minde as well as though I were within you: goe to, you seeke
to quarrell, but beware of lead I wist ; so long goes the potte
to the water at length it comes home broken.   I knowe you are
as goode a man as ever drew sword, as ere lookt man in the face,
as ere broke bred or drunke drinke ; but he is propper that hath
propper conditions, be not you like the Cowe that gives a good sope
of milke and casts it downe with his heeles.   I speak, plainely, for
plaine dealing is a Iewell, yet Ile take no wrong, if hee had
a head as big as Brasse and lookt as high as Poules steple."

Coomes, not quite liking the tone of these remarks,
replies :

" Sirra, thou grashoper, thou shal skip from my sword as from
a sithe.   Ile cut thee out in collops and steakes and frye thee
with the fier I shall strike from the pike of thy Bucklet."

To this appalling threat, not best adapted to soothe
matters over, or pour oil on the troubled waters, Nicholas
replies :

" Brag's a good dog : threatened folkes liue long."

Further quotation is quite needless ; enough, amply
enough, has been brought forward to convince us how
terrible a bore the inveterate quoter of proverbs can
readily become.   We are prepared after this to
sympathise entirely with the sentiments of old Fuller :
" Adages and prouerbs are to be accounted only as Sauce
to relish Meat with, but not as substantial Dishes to
make a Meal on; and therefore were never good but upon
proper Subjects and Occasions, where they may serve
to give a lively Force and pleasant Turn to what is said:

but to apply them wrong and crack them off too thick, like Sancho in 'Don Quixote,' is abominably foppish, ridiculous and nauseous." We had our eye on Sancho Panza, but any comments that we might have made on his conduct in cracking off proverbs so thick become needless, since Fuller has already said all that need be hurled against so hardened an offender.

A very curious early manuscript has come under our notice, in which the common proverbs of the time are quoted by one of the villains. It is arranged in stanzas of six lines, each being then followed by a proverb. This latter is sometimes in two lines and sometimes in one, but is in every case attributed to the villains, " Ce dit li vilains." It deals with the proverbs current in Bretaigne, and commences :

> " Qui les proverbes fist
> Premierement bien dist
> Au tans qu'alors estoit
> Or est tout en respit.
> En ne chante ne lit
> D'annor en nul endroit
> ' Que a la bone denrée
> A mauvaise oubliée '
> Ce dit li vilains."

This quaint old French may be thus Anglicised : " He who first made proverbs spoke well to the people of his time ; now all is forgotten, people neither sing nor read of honour in any place. He who has the good ware has forgotten the bad—so says the villain." The moral does not seem somehow to quite fit, unless indeed we read it to mean that when people had abundant supply of this proverb-law they had the good, and were so enamoured of it that it had supplanted in their hearts all desire for what they once preferred— the evil that was now quite driven from their hearts and forgotten.

Another verse terminates thus :

> " Qui n'aime son mestier
> Ne son mestier lui
> Ce dit li vilains " —

" Who likes not his business his business likes not him."
Another proverb that remains a very familiar one, as to
the folly of not taking full precautions, and only shutting
the stable door when the horse has already been taken,
appears as

> " Quant le cheval est emble
> Dounke ferme fols l'estable
> Ce dit li vilains."

The date of this poem is about the year 1300. How
long the proverbs given therein date before its appearance—centuries possibly—we cannot say ; but even if
we took this poem as a point to start from, it is very
interesting to reflect that this stolen horse and his
unlocked stable have been for hundreds of years a
warning to the heedless, and as well known to the
men of Cressy and Agincourt as to those of this present
day. However men, as Cavaliers or Roundheads, Lan-
castrians or Yorkists, priests or presbyters, differed from
each other in much else, all agreed in this recognition
of the folly of not taking better care of the steed they
all knew so well.

We have an imitation of this old French poem in an
English one that was almost contemporaneous, and, as
in the preceding poem, each stanza is an amplification
of the idea in the proverb that immediately follows,
though in either case this gloss or development is not
always very much to the point.

The first verse is dedicatory, invoking the Divine
blessing :

> " Mon that wol of wysdom heren
> At wyse Hendyng he may lernen

> That wes Marcolmes sone :
> Gode thonkes out monie thewes
> For te teche fele shrewes
> For that wes ever is wone
> Jhesu Crist al folke red
> That for us all tholede ded
> Upon the rode tre
> Lene us all to ben wys
> Ant to ende in his servys.
> Amen, par charite.
> God biginning maketh god endyng
> Quoth Hendyng."

"Of fleysh lust cometh shame," and "if thou will fleysh overcome" the wisest course is flight from the temptation :

> "Wel fytht that wel flyth
> Quoth Hendyng."

If you would avoid the evils that follow hasty speech keep the tongue with all diligence in subjection, for though one's tongue has no bone in it itself it has been the cause of many a broken bone in the quarrels that it has fostered :

> "Tonge breketh bon
> Ant nad hire selve non
> Quoth Hendyng."

"Al too dere," he warns us, "is botht that ware that we may wythoute care," gather at a terrible risk to ourselves. It is the grossest folly to find a momentary pleasure in any act that will bring misery in its train, for

> "Dere is boht the hony that is licked of the thorne
> Quoth Hendyng."

Where counsel fails, experience may step in and exact a higher price for the lesson taught :

> "So that child withdraweth is hond
> From the fur ant the brond

That hath byfore ben brend
Brend child fur dredeth
Quoth Hendyng." *

The Italians still more powerfully say that "A scalded
dog dreads cold water," the meaning of this clearly
being that those who have suffered in any direction have
an exaggerated fear in consequence, and are afraid,
even when there is no cause, really, for terror. This idea
is even more strongly brought out in the old Rabbinical
adage, " He who has been bitten by a serpent fears
a piece of rope," a quite imaginable state of mind to
arrive at.†

Up till now we have shown how one writer may use
many proverbs ; we will turn to the other alternative
and seek to show how one proverb is used by many
writers. In doing so we are at once struck by the
variety of garb in which it may appear. The inner
spirit and meaning, the core, remains inviolate naturally,
but its presentation to us is by no means in one set
formula. We are warned not to judge alone by outward appearance, nor to assume too hastily precious
metal in what may prove to be but dross or a poor
counterfeit of the real thing. Hence Chaucer warns
us, " All thing which that shineth as the gold He
is no gold, as I have heard it told." Lydgate,
writing on " the Mutability of human affairs," declares
truly enough that " all is not golde that outward
showeth bright " ; while Spenser, in his " Faerie
Queene," hath it that " Gold all is not that doth golden
seem " ; and Shakespeare, in the " Merchant of Venice,"

* " Why urge yee me ? My hart doth boyle with heate
   And will not stoope to any of your lures:
   A burnt child dreads the ffyre."—Timon, c. 1590.
   † Ovid writes : " Tranquillas etiam naufragus horret aquas "—the man
who has been wrecked dreads still water. The Portuguese make the cat
the subject of their proverb—" Gato escaldado d'agua fria tem medo."

writes, " All that glisters is not gold."* Dryden's
version, in the " Hind and Panther," is very similar, " All,
as they say, that glitters is not gold "; and Herbert, in the
" Jacula Prudentum," reverses the wording into " All is
not gold that glisters." In " Ralph Roister Doister " we
find the reading, " All things that shineth is not by and
by pure gold "; while the Italians have the equivalent,
" Non é oro tutto quel che luce."

In Greene's " Perimedes," published in the year 1588,
we find the passage, " Though men do determine the
gods doo dispose, and oft times many things fall out
betweene the cup and the lip." The first portion of this
passage is almost invariably cited in French—" l'homme
propose et le Dieu dispose "—giving the impression that
the saying is of Gallic origin. How far back into the ages
this proverb goes we cannot trace. We find it in the
"Imitation of Christ " of Thomas à Kempis as, " Nam
homo proponit sed Deus disponit." It is possible that
the French rendering became current in our midst
because the " Imitation," when first translated from the
original Latin, was rendered into French. The book
at once sprang into notice and esteem, and the passages
under our consideration would be noticeable not only
from its declaration of a great truth but from its rhythm
—a rhythm that was well preserved in its French
rendering. The French translation of the " Imitation
of Christ " appeared in 1488, while the first English
version was not produced till the year 1502. In the
" Vision of Piers ploughman," written somewhere about
the year 1360, we find the saying given in Latin, while
George Herbert, who died in 1633, introduces it as
" Man proposeth, God disposeth."

* We need scarcely point out that any reference to the use of any proverb
is not intended to imply that this is the only use of it by that writer. " Yet
gold is not that doth golden seem " is equally Shakespeare with the quotation given above. One passage will ordinarily suffice, but not because it is
the only one available.

The possibilities that may exist in the short interval of time between raising the cup to the lips and setting it down again are made the subject of a warning proverb that is of immense antiquity. The Samian king, Ancæus, while planting a vineyard was warned by a diviner that he would not live to take its fruits. Time passed on and the vineyard prospered, until at length one day the king, goblet in hand, was to taste for the first time the wine it had yielded. He recalled the prophecy, and derided the power of the seer as he stood before him. At this moment a messenger arrived with the news that a wild boar was ravaging the vineyard, and Ancæus, hastily putting down the cup, seized his spear and rushed out to slay the boar, but himself fell a victim to the onslaught of the furious beast.* Thus, to quote a considerably more modern authority, Jonson's "Tale of a Tub," "you see the old adage verified—many things fall between the cup and lip."

It is a wise rule of conduct to bear in mind that great offence may be given by comparing one thing with another, as the process is almost sure to end to the more or less detriment of one or the other, or possibly, when the spirit of criticism is rampant, in the depreciation of both. Hence Lydgate writes in 1554, "Comparisons do oftimes great grevance," and in More's "Dial" the idea recurs — "Comparysons be odyouse." Gascoigne, in the year 1575, declares in his "Posies," "I will forbear to recyte examples by any of mine owne doings, since all comparisons are odious." Dr John Donne in an "Elegy" has the line, "she and comparisons are odious," and we find the same idea in Burton's "Anatomy of Melancholy," in Heywood's play, "A Woman Killed with Kindness," in "Don Quixote," and many other works.

* The story is told by Pausanias : "Multa cadunt inter calicem supremaque labra."—*Horace.*

Shakespeare, in his "Much Ado about Nothing," puts into the mouth of Dogberry the variation "comparisons are odorous." Swift, in his "Answer to Sheridan's Simile," writes:

> "We own your verses are melodious,
> But then comparisons are odious."

Lilly, in the "Euphues," seems to think that comparisons may at times be an offence when the objects of such a scrutiny are incomparable in their excellence; that each is so perfect that any suggestion of comparison becomes necessarily a depreciation and a dethronement. Hence he writes—"But least comparisons should seeme odious, chiefly where both the parties be without comparison, I will omitte that," and he returns to this idea in his "Midas," where he distinctly lays down the proposition that "Comparisons cannot be odious where the deities are equall."

The picturesque adage, "a rolling stone gathers no moss," is still popular amongst our people. In Turner's "Five hundred pointes of good husbandrie," a book written between three and four hundred years ago, we find the same precept:

> "The stone that is rouling can gather no mosse;
> Who often remoueth is sure of losse.
> The rich it compelleth to paie for his pride;
> The poore it vndooeth on euerie side."

Marston, in "The Fawn," written in the year 1606, has an allusion to this proverb:

> "Thy head is alwaies working: it roles and it roles,
> Dondolo, but it gathers no mosse."

In the "Vision of Piers Plowman" we appear at first sight to have a quaint and interesting variant—"Selden mosseth the marbelston that men ofte treden." But it will be seen that in thus altering the wording from the type-form we have also varied its significance; it is, in

fact, a new saying, and of different application.   To
point out to a restless and aimless ne'er-do-well, throwing up one position after another, that no moss will
be found growing on the doorstep of some busy office
would be an entirely pointless proceeding not tending
to edification.

Another familiar proverb is "well begun is half
done."   We find its equivalent in Horace and the
severer Juvenal.   Many of our proverbs were as
familiar to Horace as to ourselves.   "Money in purse
will always be in fashion," and to "harp on the same
string" are expressions, for instance, that were very
familiar to the ancient Romans, and which are quite
as intelligible to-day.

In the "Confessio Amantis" of Gower we find :

> "A prouerbe I haue herde saie,
> That who that well his worke beginneth,
> The rather a good ende he winneth."

This proverb has historic interest, as its use on one
fateful occasion was the final cause of desolating civil
war that long ravaged Tuscany.   When Boundelmonte broke his engagement with a lady of the family
of the Amadei, and married into another, the kinsmen
assembled in council to consider how the slight should be
avenged, and atonement made for their wounded honour.
Some of the more impetuous demanded the death of
the young cavalier as the only possible reparation ; but
others hesitated, not from any particular regard for the
traitor, but because of the great issues involved—consequences which in the after-event proved so disastrous to
the Florentines.   At length Mosca Lamberti, tired of
this hesitation, sprang to his feet, and declared that
those who talked were not likely to do anything else
but talk, that the consideration of the matter from
every point of view would lead to no worthy result, and

make them objects of contempt, and then quoted the adage familiar to them all—"Capo a cosa fatta"—well begun is half done.   This sealed the fatal determination, the die was cast, Boundelmonte was murdered, and thus was Florence at once involved in the strife between Guelph and Ghibelline, and the fair land of Tuscany became the battlefield of those contending factions.

The incident is referred to by Dante in the " Inferno." Amid his wanderings in these gloomy shades he presently arrives where

> " One deprived of both his hands, who stood
> Lifting the bleeding stumps amid the dim
> Dense air, so that his face was stained with blood,
> Cried—' In thy mind let Mosca take a place,
> Who said, alas ! " Deed done is well begun,"
> Words fraught with evil to the Tuscan race.' "

It is a widely recognised principle that those who live in glass houses themselves should be very careful how they throw stones at others, as retaliation is so fatally easy.*   In a collection of " Proverbes en rimes," published in Paris in 1664, we find—

> " Qui a sa maison de verre
> Sur le voisin ne jette pierre."

In the "Troilus" of Chaucer we find the same prudent abstinence from stone-throwing advocated, but in this case it is the stone-thrower's head and not his house that is in danger of reprisals.

> " Who that hath an hede of verre
> Fro caste of stones war hym in the werre."

The use of the word " verre " instead of glass seems to suggest that the French version was so far current in England that all would know it, and that it was immaterial whether the rendering was in French or in English.   When James of Scotland succeeded, at the

---

* " Stones and idle words are things not to be thrown at random."

death of Elizabeth, to the English throne, one of the first results was that London became inundated with Scotchmen, all anxious to reap some benefit from the new political position. This influx caused a considerable amount of jealousy, and the Duke of Buckingham organised a movement against them, and parties were formed for the purpose of breaking their windows, and in a general way making them feel the force of an adverse public opinion. By way of retaliation, a number of Scotchmen smashed the windows of the duke's mansion in St Martin's Fields, known as "the Glass House," and on his complaining to the king His Majesty replied, "Steenie, Steenie, those who live in glass houses should be carefu' how they fling stanes." The story is told in Seton's "Life of the Earl of Dunfermline," and it will be appreciated that the quotation by our "British Solomon" of this ancient adage was very neatly put in.

Those who pride themselves on a certain blunt directness of speech, and who declare that they always speak their mind, further define the position they take up by declaring that they call a spade a spade. There certainly are occasions when such a course is the only honest one, when a man has to make his protest and refuse to connive at any circumlocution or whittling away of principle. There are other occasions when a regard for the feelings of others makes such a proceeding sheer brutality, and it is, we believe, a well-established fact that the audience of those who pride themselves on speaking their mind ordinarily find that they are the victims of a somewhat unpleasant experience. Baxter declares, "I have a strong natural inclination to speak of every subject just as it is, and to call a spade a spade, so as that the thing spoken of may be fullest known by the words. But I unfeignedly confess that it is faulty because imprudent." "I am plaine," we read in Marprelate's "Epitome," "I must needs call a spade a spade," and Ben Jonson advises to "boldly nominate a spade a spade."

In the year 1548 Archbishop Cranmer was busily engaged on a design for the better unity of all the Protestant churches by having one common confession and one body of doctrine drawn out of Holy Writ, to which all could give their assent. Melancthon, amongst others, was consulted by the archbishop, and was very favourable to the idea, but he strongly advised him, if the matter were to be carried to a successful issue, "to avoid all ambiguities of expression, call a spade a spade, and not cast words of dubious meaning before posterity as an apple of discord." Wise and weighty words that never fructified.

John Knox, who was not by any means the man to go out of his way to prophesy smooth things or palliate wrong-doing by any euphuism or a prudent turning away of the head, declares, "I have learned to call wickedness by its own terms, and to call a fig a fig and a spade a spade"; while Shakespeare, in his "Coriolanus," goes equally straight to the mark: "We call a nettle but a nettle, and the faults of fools but folly." Erasmus writes: "Ficus ficus, ligonem ligonem vocat" of a certain man.

Boileau in like manner writes, "J'appelle un chat un chat"; and Rabelais, "Nous sommes simples gents, puisqu'il plaist à Dieu: et appellons les figues figues, les prunes prunes, et les poires poires."

In the pages of Plutarch we read that Philip of Macedon, in answer to an irate ambassador, who complained to him that the citizens on his way to the palace had called him a traitor, replied: "My subjects are a blunt people, and call things always by their right names. To them figs are figs, and they call spades spades." The adage is one of unknown antiquity, and may be found in the writings of Aristophanes, Demosthenes, Lucian, and other classic authors. Erasmus, in his "Apophthegmes," published in 1542, tells the story of the discomfiture of the embassy to the Macedonian court very quaintly: "When those persons that were at Lasthenes found themselfes greued and toke fumishly that certain of the traine of Phillipus called theim traitours, Phillipus answered that the Macedonians were feloes of no fine witte in their termes, but altogether grosse, clubbish, and rusticall, as the whiche had not the witte to cal a spade by any other name than a spade, alluding to that the commen vsed prouerbe of the Grekes calling figgues figgues, and a bote a bote. As for his mening was that they were traitours in very deede. And the fair flatte truthe that the vplandishe or homely and play-clubbes of the countree dooen use, nameth eche thinge of the right names."

In Taverner's "Garden of Wysdome," published in 1539, the Macedonians are described as "very homely men and rudely brought vppe, which call a mattok nothing els but a mattok, and a spade a spade" — a very right and proper thing for Macedonians or anyone else to do on most occasions, but sometime a little too much like the unconscious brusqueness of children, who have in such matters no discretion, and who forget, or have never been taught, the more cautious precept that "all truths are not to be told on all occasions."

Those who, avoiding one difficulty, rashly run into a still greater dilemma, are warned, as in More's "Dial," that "they lepe lyke a flounder out of the fryenge panne into the fyre." Tertullian, Plato, and other early writers vary the wording to "Out of the smoke into the fire," but the pith of the matter is the same. Fire and smoke play their part in several adages. One of these, "If you will enjoy the fire you must not mind the smoke," recalls the days when the domestic arrange-

ments were somewhat cruder than in those more lux-
urious days, but it still remains a valuable reminder
that whatever advantages we may enjoy we must also
be prepared for certain drawbacks. The Latin "Com-
modatis quævis sua fert incommoda secum" covers the
same ground ; and the French, "Nul feu sans fumée"—
no fire without smoke, no good without some inconvenience—echoes the same idea. On the other hand,
"Where there is smoke there is fire," the appearance of
evil is a warning that the evil exists, the loose word
implies the loose life. As the effect we see cannot be
causeless, it is a danger-signal that we must not ignore.
The present whiff of smoke, if disregarded, may be the
herald of half an hour hence a raging conflagration,
spreading ruin on every side.

When a strong comparison, the expression of a
marked difference, is called for, we may, in the words
of Shaclock, in his "Hatchet of Heresies," published in
1565, exclaim, "Do not these thynges differ as muche
as chalcke and chese?" or, turning to the "Confessio
Amantis" of Gower, find for our purpose, "Lo, how
they feignen chalk for cheese!" while Heywood
hath it :

"That as well agreeth the comparison in these,
   As alyke to compare in tast, chalk and cheese."

Another popular proverb of our ancestors was "Fast
bind, fast find." Hence, on turning to the "Merchant
of Venice," we find the admonition, "Do as I bid
you. Shut doors after you : fast bind, fast find—a
proverb never stale in thrifty mind"; and the counsel
is found repeated in the "Jests of Scrogin," published
in 1565 : "Wherefore a plaine bargain is best, and in
bargaines making, fast bind, fast find"—a certain business shrewdness, a legal document, even the turning of
a key in a door, will at times preserve to us unimpaired
property that carelessness would have lost to us.

F

"The more the merrier" is an adage that has a
pleasantly hospitable ring about it, though we are
reminded in addition that the multiplicity of guests
may lead to a certain pinching in the supplies. Heywood reminds us how

> "The more the merrier we all day here see,
> Yea, but the fewer the better fare, sayd he";

while Gascoigne, in his "Poesies," while he quotes with
approval the old adage, "Store makes no sore"—no
one is the worse for having a little reserve laid by—
yet "Mo the merier is a proverbe eke" that must
not be overlooked. "More the merrier" is the happy
title of a book of epigrams published in 1608, and we
may come across the sentiment in two or three of
the plays of Beaumont and Fletcher, and in many
other directions.

Our readers will recall Spenser's eulogium on

> "Dan Chaucer, well of English undefyled,
> On Fame's eternal beadroll worthie to be fyled."

The proverb-seeker finds in his picturesque pages
abundant store. The "nonne preeste" exclaims,
"Mordre wol out, that see we day by day," and in
the Reve's prologue he reminds us that "Yet in our
ashen cold is fire yreken"; or, as a later writer hath
it, "E'en in our ashes live our wonted fires." Chaucer
again reminds us that "The proverbe saith that many
a small makith a grete"; or, as it is sometimes given,
"Many a little makes a mickle." The French tell us
that even the drainage of the great deep is possible if
only there be sufficient patience : "Goutte à goutte la
mer s'egoute."* Every heart knows its own bitterness,
knows all about that skeleton in the cupboard that the
world has no suspicion of, knows just where the shoe

---

* "Petit à petit l'oiseau fait son nid."

pinches. Hence Chaucer exclaims, "But I wot best when wryngeth me my scho"; * and in his "Testament of Love," where he writes, "Lo, eke an old proverb, he that is still seemeth as he granted," or, as we should say now-a-days, "Silence gives consent." † Another well-known adage and piece of worldly wisdom is, "Of two ills choose the least," a proverb found in the "Imitation of Christ" of À Kempis, in Hooker's "Polity," and elsewhere. Chaucer is to the fore with the saying, "Of harmes two the lesse is for to cheese." The saying appears as "E duobus malis minimum eligendum" in the pages of Cicero, so that it is not by any means an adage of yesterday's creation. It was, doubtless, a venerable saying long before Cicero employed it. When the idea got compacted into a recognised wisdom-chip, who can say? The rule of conduct is so clear and so in accordance with common-sense that we may well believe that the practice, if not the precept, would date from about the year one.

A "nine days' wonder" appears in the pages of the "Troilus" of Chaucer, as "Eke wonder last but nine daies never in towne." A thing makes a great sensation for a few days, and then something else arises, and the former matter is quite forgotten. Chaucer's addition to the adage of the limitation to town is curious, though on consideration a good deal can be said for it, since in towns incidents succeed each other quickly, and aid this obliteration of the past. Sometimes the proverb is extended into "A nine days' wonder, and then the puppy's eyes are open"—in allusion to

---

* " What cloke for the rayne so ever yee bring mee,
    Myselfe can tell best where my shoee doth wring mee."—*Heywood.*
† In "Cymbeline" Shakespeare writes—
"But that you shall not say I yield, being silent, I would not speak."
It was a proverb of Ancient Rome, "Qui tacet consentire videtur," and in Modern Italy it reappears as "Chi ta ce confessa." In France it is "Assez consent qui ne dit mot."

the fact that dogs, like cats and several other animals, are born blind. One may read this as referring to those who make a wonder of an ordinary thing; the blindness of these little new-born puppies, or, in somewhat less literal sense, the puppies whose eyes are presently open, are those people who are blind and puzzled over some incident which they presently see through and unravel, and then lose all interest in.

As an encouragement to those who seem to be the victims of one misfortune after another, of continued ill fortune, the ancient saw is quoted, " 'Tis a long lane has no turning." The expression is a picturesque one, and no doubt carries comfort and teaches patience. In the pages of Chaucer it appears as " Som tyme an end ther is on every deed." The only time we knew it absolutely to fail was in the case of an old man named Lane, who had his full share of the worries of life, and to whom one kindly well-wisher after another quoted this well-worn saying. Each thought that he had hit upon a happy idea, and applied it there and then, in full faith that it would be of soothing efficacy, but as, in the aggregate, the old fellow had had it fired off at him some hundreds of times, it acted instead as a powerful irritant! It was one trouble the more to carry through life.

One might, in the same way, though we have by no means exhausted the Chaucerian wealth of proverb-lore, hunt through the pages of Shakespeare, Milton, Pope, and other writers, and should reap an abundant harvest. It may be somewhat of a shock that Milton's name should appear in such a connection, since the stately dignity of his work would appear entirely alien to the general tone of the popular adage; but one sees in this passage from " Comus "—

"Was I deceived, or did a sable cloud
Turn forth her silver lining to the night?"—

a beautiful allusion to a well-known proverb. The plays of Shakespeare abound with these proverbial allusions. In the " Taming of the Shrew," for instance, we find, " Now, were I a little pot and soon hot," a proverb applied to short-tempered people who on slight cause wax wroth. The homely pot plays its part in homely conversation. The man whom Fortune has thwarted " goes to pot," waste and refuse metal to be cast into the melting-pot. The man on hospitable thoughts intent may invite his neighbour to pot-luck, to such chance repast, good or bad, as the " pot au feu " may yield. People who deride or scorn others for matters in which they are at least as much concerned are compared to the pot that called the kettle black,* while the rashness of those who, insufficiently pro-vided with this world's goods, seek to rival others better provided and come to grief in the experiment, are reminded how the brazen and earthen pot swam down together on the swirling flood and collided to the detriment of the pitcher.† In " King Henry VI." we have " Ill blows the wind that profits nobody,"‡ and " Smooth runs the water where the brook is deep." In " Hamlet" the familiar adage, " Murder will out," appears as " Murder, though it have no tongue, will

---

* Or, to quote another expressive and homely English proverb, " The chimney-sweep told the collier to go wash his face." In France they say " La pêle se moque du fourgon," the shovel makes game of the poker.

† " Burden not thyself above thy power, and have no fellowship with one that is mightier or richer than thyself. For how agree the kettle and the earthen pot together? For if one be smitten against the other it shall be broken."—*Ecclesiasticus* xiii. 2.

‡ " An yll wynd that blowth no man good."—HEYWOOD, *Song against Idleness*, 1540.

> " It is an old proverb and a true,
> I sware by the roode,
> It is an il wind that blows no man to good."
>
> —" Marriage of Wit and Wisdom," 1570.

speak." " Every dog has his day " ; we say : every man
his chance, so in " Hamlet " we find—

> " Let Hercules himself do what he may,
> The cat will mew, and dog will have his day."

In "Othello" we come across an equally well-known
proverb, " They laugh that win," so quaintly curtailed
by Heywood into " He laugth that winth." Another
familiar adage is that " Use is second nature," and this
Shakespeare, in the " Two Gentlemen of Verona,"
refines into " How use doth breed a habit in a man ! "
In " As You Like It " another well-known saw presents
itself in the lines, " If it be true that good wine needs no
bush, 'tis true that a good play needs no epilogue."
The bush in question was an ivy-bough, the emblem of
Bacchus, and the custom of marking the wine-shop by
this dates from Roman days. " Vino vendibili hedera
non opus est." The custom was continued throughout
the Middle Ages ; but a good article, the proverb tells
us, needs no advertisement, or, as the French proverb
hath it, " Au vin qui se vend bien il ne faut point de
lierre."

In the days of our forefathers the streets were narrow, and there were no pavements ; while discharging
pipes and running gutters by the sides of the walls
made the centre of the road the more agreeable place
for the traveller. Wheeled conveyances of divers sorts
passing and repassing forced the foot-passenger to the
side of the road, and any tumult or street fight would
drive the conquered pell-mell to take refuge in the
houses or to the shelter of the wall out of the rush.
Hence the proverb, " The weakest goes to the wall."
In " Romeo and Juliet " Sampson and Gregory are
found in the market-place of Verona, and the former
declares, " I will take the wall of any man or maid of
Montague's " ; to whom the latter unsympathetically

replies, "That shows thee a weak slave, for the weakest goes to the wall."

The wisdom of our ancestors discovered that "He who is born to be hanged will never be drowned," and our readers will recall how in the "Tempest" Gonzalo comforts himself in the contemplation of the villainous ugliness of the boatswain. "I have great comfort," he says, "from this fellow : methinks he hath no drowning mark upon him ; his complexion is perfect gallows. Stand fast, good fate, to his hanging! Make the rope of his destiny our cable, for our own doth little advantage! If he be not born to be hanged our case is miserable."

To make our list of quotations exhaustive, and therefore probably exhausting, is by no means necessary; we give but samples from the bulk, and in conclusion of our present chapter give some few of our commoner saws and one, or at most two, references to some old writer's work where it may be encountered. Naturally, the wording of some of the more ancient quotations is not always quite that of to-day.

"The potte may goo so longe to water that atte the last it is broken" we found in a manuscript of about the year 1545, entitled, "The book of the Knight of La Tour." The very ancient proverb, familiar to us in its Biblical garb, about the folly of the blind leading the blind, will be found in Gower's "Confessio Amantis"—

"As the blinde another ledeth,
And, till they falle, nothing dredeth."

The constant dropping that wears at length away a stone we found referred to in a manuscript of the time of Henry VIII. "So long may a droppe fall that it may perse a stone."

"The common proverb, as it is read,
That we should hit the nail on the head,"

is a couplet in a little book, "Wit Restor'd," issued
in 1568, and we also find Skelton writing, "He hyt
the nayle on the hede."

A caution to those who try and steer a deceitful
course between those of opposing interests, treacherously allowing each to think they have exclusive
support, has duly been crystallised into a proverb,
and Lily introduces it in the following passage :—
"Whatsouer I speake to men, the same also I
speake to women. I meane not to run with the
Hare and holde with the Hounde." "By hook or
by crook" will be found in Spenser's "Fairie Queene."
"Diamond cut diamond" is in Ford's play of "the
Lover's Melancholy." "Every tub must stand upon
its own bottom" occurs in the "Pilgrim's Progress."
"He must have a long spoon that would eat with
the devil" is found in Chaucer and Shakespeare,
amongst other writers. That "The moon is made
of green cheese" is re-asserted by Rabelais and in
the pages of "Hudibras."

In Swift's "polite conversation," proverbs are thickly
strewn. We find the old statement that "You must
eat a peck of dirt before you die," the well-meant
impertinence of "teaching one's grandmother to suck
eggs," the communistic doctrine that "Sauce for the
goose is no less sauce for the gander," and many
other well-worn scraps of ancestral belief and practice.
The wisdom of suiting your position to your circumstances, of cutting one's garment according to the
material available, is emphasised in a "Health to the
gentlemanly profession of Serving-Men," a brochure
issued in 1598, where these worthies are warned,
"You, with your fraternitie in these latter dayes
cannot be content to shape your coate according
to your cloth." In Marston's play of "What you
Will," written in 1607, we have a familiar and

homely caution borrowed from the experience of
the kitchen—" Faith, Doricus, thy braine boils ; keele
it, keele it, or all the fatts in the fire," a proverb
employed when by some inadvertence a man brings
against himself a sudden blaze of wrath.

Proverb-hunting is a very pleasant recreation. We
have left a vast field practically untrodden. We
cannot do better than conclude in the quaint words
of a little pamphlet that we once came across—"a
collection of the Choycest Poems relating to the
late Times" (1662). "Gentlemen, you are invited
here to a feast, and if variety cloy you not, we are
satisfied. It has been our care to please you. These
are select things, a work of time, which for your
sake we publish, assuring you that your welcome
will crown the entertainment. Farewell."

CHAPTER IV

WHILE we find a striking similarity existing between
the proverbs of various peoples, many being absolutely
identical, and others teaching the same truths under
somewhat different external guise ; there is also in
many cases a certain local and individual colouring
that gives added interest.

We see, too, national idiosyncrasies coming to the
front in the greater prominence given to proverbs
having a bearing in some particular direction. Thus,
a poetic and imaginative people will specially dwell
on proverbs of a picturesque and refined type, while
a thrifty and cautious race will hold in especial
esteem the inculcation of saving, of early rising, of
steady labour, the avoidance of debt and suretyship.
A more impulsive people will care but little for such
thraldom, and will teach in its sayings the delights

of the present, the pursuit of the pleasures rather than the duties of life, and the wild doctrine of revenge against those who thwart their desires ; while an oppressed and downtrodden race will very faithfully reflect the oppression under which they lie by the sayings that find most favour amongst them.

Our English proverbs, like our language, have come to us from many sources ; and while we have some little store that we may claim as of home-growth, the greater part has been judiciously borrowed. We may fairly ascribe to our changeable climate such a warning adage as the advice to " Make hay while the sun shines "; and when a settler on the prairies of the West clothes the excellent doctrine that every man for himself should perform the disagreeable tasks that come in his way, and not seek to transfer them to other people, in the formula, " Every man must skin his own skunk," we feel the sentiment to be redolent of the soil of its birth. The picture it presents to us is so entirely American that it is quite needless to search for its origin in the folk-lore of Wessex or on the banks of the Indus.*

The greater number of the proverbs of ancient Greece were fraught with allusions to the mythology, poetry, and national history of Hellas, and thus form a valuable testimony to the general high level of intellectual training of this wonderful people. The " Adagia " of Erasmus contains, as the result of the search of many years amongst the literary remains of the classical authors, some five thousand of these ancient sayings. Many that, from their Latin dress we ascribe to the Romans, were really derived from Greek or still earlier sources.

---

* The warning, " We know not under which stone lurks the scorpion," could not, for example, have had its birth in England, as it points to a peril from which we are wholly exempt.

It will be recalled that those who, from their pre-eminent wisdom, were entitled, the Seven Sages of Greece, each inscribed in the Temple of Apollo one sentence of concentrated wisdom. The best known and most freely quoted of these was the "Know thyself," the contribution of Solon of Athens; and the more we reflect on this the more we realise its profundity. To know thyself—to know, for example, thy possibilities of health and strength for strenuous bodily or mental labour, to know thy worldly status, and what of influence is there open to thee or closed against thee; to know thyself, not as the crowd regards thee, but in all the secret workings of thy heart, controlling thy actions, biassing thy thoughts, influencing thy motives; to step aside out of the bustle of life and quietly take stock of thyself; to know how thou standest in view of eternity—that is wisdom. The maxim of Chilo of Sparta was "Consider the end," and that of Bias of Priene the sad indictment, "Most men are bad." Thales of Miletos declared, and the yet greater and wiser Solomon was in accord—"Who hateth suretyship is sure." Periander of Corinth sang the praise of honest work in "Nothing is impossible to industry";* and Pittacos of Mitylene warned his hearers and pupils to "Seize Time by the forelock." The seventh, Cleobulos of Lindos, pinned his faith on the golden mean, "Avoid extremes." These maxims passed into general circulation and adoption, and thus became of proverbial rank. They do not strike one as being of at all equal value, but there is no doubt that a man who was fortified, not only by the knowledge of these precepts, but, more important yet, by their practice, would be equipped to face unscathed all the possibilities of life.

In our ordinary English word "laconic" is preserved

---

* Or in less classic phrase—" It's dogged as does it."

a curious little allusion. The Lacones or Spartans were noted amongst the other Greeks for their brusque and sententious speech, the practice of expressing much in little. Hence our word laconic, meaning concise, pithy. Plato wrote that "If anyone desires converse with a Lacedæmonian he will at first sight appear to him wanting in thought, in power of utterance, but when the opportunity arrives, this same man, like a skilful hurler of the javelin, will hurl a sentence worthy of the greatest consideration." A good example of this trait of the Spartans will be seen in their reply to Philip of Macedon when he threatened them, "If I enter Laconia I will level your city to the dust." Their rejoinder was, "If"!

The prostrate Saul was warned that it was hard for him to "kick against the pricks," to resist the Higher Power, to rebel against the guiding goad, and the utterance was a very familiar one in his ears. It will be found in the Odes of Pindar, the tragedies of Euripides and Æschylus, and in the writings of Terence. Another familiar Biblical text is that "One soweth and another reapeth." * This, too, would appeal at once to the hearers as a piece of their own proverbial lore. It is at least as ancient as Hesiod, who wrote his "Theogony," and introduced this proverb therein, some nine hundred years before the Christian era.

It is in all countries an accepted belief that the Higher Powers, under whatever name worshipped, help those who help themselves. Thus, the Spaniards say, "Pray to God and ply the hammer," while the

---

* "The preaching of the Word is in some places like the planting of woods, where, though no profit is received for twenty years together, it cometh afterwards. And grant that God honoureth not thee to build His Temple in thy parish, yet thou mayest, with David, provide metals and materials for Solomon, thy successor, to build it with."—THOMAS FULLER, *Holy State.*

Greeks taught, "Call on Athene but exert yourself as well." Another very expressive Greek proverb was "A piped-out life," as applied to one who, in rioting and dissipation, in feasting and drunkenness, had carried out that grim ideal, "A short life and a merry one," who to lulling siren song, the harp, the tabret, and the viol, sailed swiftly down the stream of Time. A graphic picture again is this—"You have burst in upon the bees," applied to one who causelessly, needlessly meddled with matters that were no concern of his, and thereby brought swift retribution on himself.

The proverbs born on Roman soil were considerably fewer in number than those of Greek birth, and this is a result that we should naturally anticipate, since the Romans had not the strong religious feeling, nor the poetic afflatus, nor the subtle thought of the Greeks. The Romans in this, as in much else, were borrowers rather than producers. At the same time the sterling common-sense and energy of the Roman people is seen in their proverbs. They are business-like and practical, inculcating patience, perseverance, independence, and frugality ; dealing in a wise spirit with the affairs of life, marriage, education, agriculture, and the like. How true, for instance, to all experience is the "Aliquis in omnibus est nullus in singulis," while in some, heathen as they were in origin, a high moral sense is reached, as, for example, "Conscientia, mille testes."

How expressive is "Res in cardine est." The matter is on the hinge, it must soon now be settled one way or the other, for, as another proverb hath it, "A door must be open or shut"—there can here be no middle course of procrastination and uncertainty. How good, again, the oft-quoted "Qui cito dat bis dat"—"He giveth twice that giveth in a trice," as an old English version rhymingly renders it, or the "Quot homines tot sententiæ." "I see

wel the olde proverbe is true," quoth Gascoigne in his
"Glasse of Government," which saith, "So many men
so many mindes." The French reading is "Autant
d'hommes, autant d'avis."

Our old English proverb about the difficulty of getting
blood out of a stone is paralleled in the "Aquam a
pumice postulare" of ancient Rome, and the saw,
"Extremis, ut dicitur, digitis attingere"—to touch, so to
speak, with the tips of the fingers—is of special interest to us, as it will be recalled that it is quoted in
the New Testament, and applied to the Pharisees who
laid on others burdens that they themselves would
not touch with one of their fingers.

Our adage, "Opportunity makes the thief," is but the
old Roman "Occasio facet furem."

The brief "Latum unguem" is expressive of those
who cavil and split hairs* over trifles, when not the
breadth of a nail of difference exists between them, and
yet sharp contention is stirred up.

It is needless to dwell at any length on these proverbs
of ancient Rome. Their character and tone of thought
are very English, and therefore many of them we shall
find incorporated in English guise in our midst, while
others find a place in our literature in their original
setting. Amongst these latter we may name, by way
of illustration, "Ab ovo," "Ad captandum vulgus," "Dum
vivimus vivamus," "Ex cathedra," "Facilis est descensus
Averni," "Humanum est errare," "De mortuis nil nisi
bonum," "Carpe diem," "Argumentum ad hominem,"
"Ars est celare artem," "Petitio principii," "Per fas et
nefas," "Ne sutor ultra crepidam," "Vox populi vox Dei,"
and "Festine lente." †

---

* "But in the way of bargain, mark ye me,
  I'll cavil on the ninth part of a hair."—"Henry IV."
† "Festina lente, not too fast;
  For haste, the proverb says, makes waste."—"Hudibras."

While many of the proverbs of Scotland are identical in significance with our own, and only vary from them by some slight dialectic influence, there are not a few that are the special possession of the Scottish people. These have a very distinct individuality. There is rarely much grace or tenderness in them, but they contain abundant common-sense. There is scarcely one that is pointless, while in most the point is driven home mercilessly. As maxims of prudence and worldly morality they are admirable, and have a certain roughness of expression that is often taking. They are distinctly canny, and not uncommonly have a strong touch of saturnine humour.

Many examples are easily recognisable as identical in spirit with the parallel English adages, the slight differences of setting giving them an added interest. One gets so used to things when always presented to us the same way that their value gets dulled, and a new reading then comes very opportunely. The Scottish version, " A bird in the hand is worth twa fleeing bye " * is, we think, a good example of this. The leading idea in both this and the English declaration that "A bird in the hand is worth two in the bush " is the greater value of a small certainty than a larger possibility ; but, while the twittering of the free birds in the bush may be provoking, there is at least the possibility of their capture, while the Scottish version gives a still greater value to our possession, seeing that even as we grasp it the possibility of increasing our store is rapidly passing away. In a collection, gathered together in 1586, we find " It is better to haif ane brede in hand nor twa in the wood fleande."

Other examples of this practical identity are these : "Before you choose a friend eat a peck o' saut wi' him ";

---

* The Portuguese is identical : " Mais valle um passaro na mao do que dous voando."

" It's no easy to straucht in the oak the crook that grew in the sapling." The "sour grapes" of our English proverb are at once suggested in this northern version : " Soor plooms, quo' the tod, when he couldna' climb the tree " ; " Ill weeds wax weel."

The value of this change of diction as an aid to appreciation is also felt still more when it arises from some little antiquity. Our most familiar adages, for instance, seem to possess an added charm when we find them embedded in the quaint English of the poems of Chaucer and others of our earlier writers, and in like manner many of the proverbs given in this collection of the year 1586 have a special interest. The mere setting is a very secondary point, though not without importance, since we readily see that what we need is, in the first and foremost place, the sterling truth, and then this truth enhanced in value by the happy way it is presented to our notice. The following extracts from this collection, gathered together over three centuries ago, will be of interest :—" The fische bred in durtie pooles will taiste of mude," " Whane the sunne schyneth the lyt of the starres ar not seene," " All the praise of wertew consisteth in doing," " Wit is the better gif it be the dearer bocht," " The foull taide hath a faire stoine in his hede," " The sweite kirnell lyeth in the harde schell," " The glass anes crazed will wt the leist clap be crackt," " The fairest silke is soonest soylede," " He quhilk walde gather frwite sould plant treis," " Bargaines maid in speid are comonlie repented at leasure," " Thair is no smoke but quhair thair is sum fyre," " In grettest charge ar grettest cares," " A kyndome is more esilie gotten than keipit," " Quhen the sone schyneth the cloudis wanish away," " The fyne golde must be purified in the flamyng fyre," " Greiwous woundes must have smarting plasters," " Many thingis happen betwene the cupe and the

G

lyp,"* " Thair is no clayth so fine bot mothes will eit it,"
" He that lepeth or he looke may hap to leip in the brook."

Scottish proverbs, despite the assertion that the only
way to get a joke into a Scotchman's head is by a
surgical operation, have a strong vein of humour in
them—a feature that is much more characteristic
of them than of those of any other nationality the
wide world over.   What could be happier than this
caution to those whose presence is not desired : " A
weel-bred dog goes out when he sees them going to
kick him out ! "   " They're keen o' company that tak'
the dog on their back," " Friends are like fiddle-strings,
they maunna be screwed ower tight."

The national shrewdness and mother-wit is naturally
reflected in the national proverb-lore.   A very quaint
example of this is seen in the warning that " Ye'll
no sell your hens on a rainy day."   Drenched and
wretched-looking, no one will look at them ; it is not
at all making the best of things.   How excellent is
this hint against avarice : " Greed is envy's auldest
brither, scraggy wark they mak thegither " ;† or this :
" Ne'er let your gear o'ergang you " ; or this : " A
greedy e'e ne'er got a gude pennyworth."

How shrewd such adages as : " Changes are light-
some and fools like them " ; " He that gets gear before
he gets wit is but a short time master of it " ; " He is no
the fool that the fool is, but he that with the fool deals";
" Oft counting keeps friends lang thegither," the English
equivalent being, "Short reckonings make long friends";
" A wise man gets learning fra' them that hae nane i'

---

* In French : " Entre la bouche et le verre, le vin souvent tombe à
terre."

† Yet it must be remembered that—

> " When I hae saxpence under my thumb,
>   Then I get credit in ilka toon,
>   But when I hae naethin' they bid me gang by,
>   Hech ! poverty parts gude company."

their ain"; "Better a gude fame than a gude face";
"He that seeks motes gets motes";* "Ill payers are
aye gude cravers"; "He speaks in his drink what he
thinks in his drouth." Prosperous people can afford to
listen to envious remarks, for "A fu' sack can bear a
clout in the side," and be never the worse for it.

There is a sharp touch of sarcasm in many of these
northern adages: "The deil's journeyman ne'er wants
wark." How true to life the feeling, yet how deftly pointed
the satire, "They are aye gude that are far awa," or this
very similar utterance, "They're no a' saints that get the
name o't." A valuable lesson, too, to people consumed
with a sense of their own importance is this: "The king
lies doun, but the world runs round." The point
becomes sharper yet in the statement that a "Green
turf is a gude mother-in-law"—that is to say, this particular member of the family is best in the churchyard.

An old Engish proverb says that "Almost and very
nigh save many a lie"; but the Scotch say, "Amaist
and very near hae aye been great liars." The two dicta
are in direct opposition, yet both may be accepted.

The power of money to make money is very pictur-
esquely expressed by "Put twa pennies in a purse and
they'll creep thegither." Down south we say that
"Experience is a dear school, but fools will learn in
no other"; but the Scottish method is wiser, if practicable, though there is a touch of selfishness in it:
"Better learn frae your neebor's skaith (misfortune)
than frae your ain."

It is very true that "His you are whom you serve,"†
and "They that work i' the mill maun wear the
livery." How full, too, of wise teaching: "When you

---

* He who mixes with unclean things becomes unclean.

† "Quien sirve no est libre," say the Spaniards—"He who serves is
not free"; while an old English proverb reminds us that "He who rides
behind another does not saddle when he pleases."

dance ken who you tak' by the hand," and realise what
the association involves. The mighty power of influence, and the responsibility that rests on us for our
actions, the impossibility of arresting the ever-widening
circle is well seen in the hint: "If the laird slight the
lady sae will the kitchen boy." The saying, "Ye hae
gude manners, but ye dinna bear them about wi' ye,"
is a very delicate way of saving the *amour propre* of the
reproved while indicating evident shortcomings. How
quaintly picturesque the adage, again, "Like a chip
amang parritch, little gude, little ill," to describe some
wholly immaterial thing.

The proverbs of the three great Latin races—French,
Italian, and Spanish—are naturally very similar, and
are practically interchangeable, all having sprung from
the same stock, and thrown into one great store-house.
We cannot too distinctly bear in mind that, because a
proverb greets us in French, or Italian, or Danish, we
must not at once class it as a French, an Italian, or a
Danish utterance alone. The inner idea is probably
cosmopolitan, and its outer garb is of very little importance; yet, as we have already said, the idiosyncrasy
of each people affects their borrowing from the common
store, and greatly influences any additions they may
make. Instead, therefore, of classifying certain proverbs
as French or German, which ordinarily they are not, we
should really think of such a gathering as merely French
or German individualism, selecting to taste from the
general hoard. An old writer says: "The Spanish and
Italian proverbs are counted the most Curious and Significant—the first are remarkable for Gravity and fine
Instruction, the Latter for Beauty and Elegance, tho'
they are a little tinctured with Levity and have too
much of the Amour. This last Variety is the Imper-
fection of many of the French, tho' otherwise they are
very Fine and Bright, and solemnly Moral as well as.

Facetious and Pleasant." This verdict, though somewhat quaintly worded, is a very discriminating and just
one : we should be inclined to add to it in the case of
the typically French proverbs a rather characteristic
touch of conceit and gasconade. The Frenchman
ordinarily studies effect a good deal.

Despite a certain unpleasant sneering at women, as in
the proverb, " A deaf husband and a blind wife make
the best couple," and others that affect to hold feminine
virtue, constancy, truthfulness and the like in poor
esteem, the Frenchman appears to preserve a perennial
spring of affection for his mother and a fervent belief in
its reciprocity on her part. Hence, in all proverb-lore,
dramatic representation, poetry, oratory, this special
relationship is a sacred one, and we get in an arid desert
of cynicism so sweet an oasis as, " Tendresse maternelle
toujours se renouvelle."

Such proverbs in common use in France as " A cheval
donné il ne faut point regarder à la bouche," " Les
murailles ont des oreilles," " Il n'y a que le premier pas
qui coute," " Il ne faut pas parler de corde dans la maison
d'un pendu," are but cosmopolitans in French garb. In
England we find that " A bad workman finds fault with
his tools," but in France this is softened down a little
and becomes, " Mechant ouvrier jamais ne trouvera bons
outils." Our picturesque declaration that it is sometimes advisable to " Throw away a sprat to catch a
herring," loses somewhat in " Il faut hazarder un petit
poisson pour prendre un grand." The Gallic " A
beau jour beau retour," is a very pleasant variant of
our saying, " One good turn deserves another." There
is in the English version a somewhat unpleasant
suggestion of barter and bargain in this exchange of
help, " Nothing for nothing, and not much for a halfpenny." * On the other hand, our " Diamond cut

* " Donner est mort et prêter est bien malade."

diamond" is pleasanter in expression than the cruder "Ruse contre ruse."

We have already seen how an English playwright once wrote a comedy in which he introduced English proverbs *ad nauseam*, and we find, in like manner, in France, a French author, Adrien de Montluc, writing in the year 1615 or thereabouts, a play called the "Comédie des Proverbës," where we find strung together dialogue-wise all the most familiar adages then current in France.*

The proverbs of Spain are very numerous, and are often distinguished by a stately sententiousness, much thoughtfulness, a strong sense of chivalry and honour, and very frequently, with these good qualities, a very happy dash of humour or irony. Ford declares that this abounding proverb-lore "gives the Spaniard his sententious dogmatical admixture of humour, truism, twaddle, and common-sense." A proverb aptly intro-duced is a decisive argument, and is always greeted with approval by high and low, an essentially national characteristic. It will be recalled how Sancho Panza has an adage for every emergency. The Don uses his own words, being a man of fine fancy and good breeding, to express his own ideas, but the vocabulary of his Squire is almost entirely composed of the well-nigh inexhaustible proverbs of his country. The Arabs, whose language is rich in such wisdom, doubtless furnished numerous contributions to this very marked feature of the national literature.

Many of the Spanish proverbs are of very great antiquity. One interesting example to the historian is connected with an incident that happened at the

---

* Those interested may turn for fuller treatment of the proverbs of France to the "Six mille proverbes" of C. Cahier, published in Paris in 1836, to the "Livre des proverbes Français" of Le Roux de Lincy, 1859, or the "Petite Encyclopédie des proverbes Français" of Hilaire le Gais, 1860.

beginning of the twelfth century. It is very rarely that one can trace the actual birth of a proverb, but in the present example, "Laws go where kings please to make them," the origin is known. The Church of Spain was in these early days greatly disturbed by a contest as to whether the Roman or the Gothic liturgy should be adopted, and at last the king, Alfonso VI., gave orders for a decisive test and definite settlement. A fire was lighted and duly blessed by the Archbishop, and then a copy of each of these liturgies was dropped into it, it being decided that whichever escaped destruction should be recognised as the true rite. The Gothic text emerged unconsumed from this fiery test, but the king, displeased at the way things had gone, tossed it back again into the fire, and thus arose the proverb, "Alla van leyes adonde quieren reyes." Many proverbs again will be found in the "Chronica General," one of the oldest Spanish books.

The Marquis of Santillana collected some 700 proverbs —"such," he says, "as the old women were wont to use in their chimney-corners." These were published in the year 1508. The "Cartas" of Blasco de Garay appeared soon after this, and went through many editions. The author was one of the cathedral staff at Toledo, and his book was thrown into epistolary form, almost every sentence being a popular adage. The "cartas" concluded with a devout prayer that his labours might tend to edification.

In the year 1549 we have an alphabetical collection of over 4000 adages compiled by Valles, while a famous scholar and professor at the University of Salamanca, Hernan Nuñez de Guzman, accumulated over 6000. These were published in 1555, by a brother professor, two years after the death of Nuñez. While acting as literary executor he somewhat ungraciously declared that respect for his friend and not for the dignity of the task was his motive. In 1568, Mal Lara selected from the compilation of Nuñez 1000 of the best examples, added some explanatory or appreciative comments to each, and sent them out into the world under the title " The Philosophy of the Common People."

Cæsar Oudin published in Paris in 1608 the " Refranes o Proverbios Castellanos." These were translated into French, and form a very interesting and valuable book.

While the gleanings of Mal Lara were especially intended to foster a practical working philosophy of life, Juan Sorapan de Rieros, in his " Medicina Española en Proverbios Vulgares," took up the medical side, dealing alone with such utterances of popular wisdom as bore on the healing art.

Bartolomé Ximinez Paton, in the year 1567, published a collection of over 1000 Greek and Latin proverbs, with a translation into Spanish, and, where practicable, the addition of a parallel or illustrative Castilian proverb. The book passed through many editions. The translations into the vernacular were in terse rhymes. Other collections, needless to particularise, though good to see, are those of Palmerino, Juan de Yriarte, and Cejudo, all of considerable antiquity, while so recently as 1815 was published in Barcelona the " Refranes de la Langua Castellana," and to this list others could no doubt be added. It will have been observed that the word, " Proverbios " is not employed, but " Refrane," a term derived from *a referendo*, because it describes a thing that is often repeated, an idea that we are familiar with in our common word " refrain."

How happily does this Spanish proverb satirise the readiness to resent what may have been, after all, a quite innocent remark, " He who takes offence has eaten garlic." The cap, as we say in English, fits. How happy again the sarcasm against awkward and inexpert helpers, " She tucked up her sleeves and overturned the kettle." The deference paid to wealth, the smoothing of the path, is graphically hit off in the adage, " An ass loaded with gold overtakes everything." The man who can perhaps scarce write his name will find many to flatter him if his coffers be full.* On the other hand how good the counsel, " Seek not for a good man's pedigree,"† or this, " Advice whispered is worthless," for anything secret may well be regarded with suspicion, and sincerity needs no veil. How happy again the saying, " I have a good doublet in France," as applied to those who boast of something that cannot be come at ; or the advice to avoid over-familiarity, " Shut your door and you will make your neighbour a good one." ‡ A somewhat similar saying is this, " When the door is shut the work improves," for gossiping means distraction and neglect of duty. " Do not go every evening to the house of your brother." There is sound common-sense in the statement that " An indolent magistrate will have thieves every market-day," since his easy-going neglect of his duties will produce a goodly crop of knaves. Those who solemnly tell as news what all can learn for themselves are happily ridiculed in the assertion that " When the spouts run the streets will be wet," or they are described as " guessing at things through a sieve,"§ making a mystery of what anyone can see at a glance.

> " Those that fly may fight again,
> Which he can never do that's slain,"

we learn in " Hudibras," and the sentiment re-appears in

---

* In France they say, " Clef d'or ouvre toutes sortes de serrures."

† " I weigh the man, not his title : 'tis not the king's stamp can make the metal better."—WYCHERLEY, *The Plain Dealer*.

‡ The Germans happily say, " Liebe deinen Nachbar, reiss, aber den Zaun nicht ein"—"Love your neighbour, but do not pull down the hedge."

§ The sieve re-appears very graphically again in this : " A grain does not fill a sieve, but it helps its companion to do so."

the Spanish adage, " It is better they should say, here he ran away, than here he died." The English dictum " Charity begins at home," is paralleled in this, " My teeth are nearer to me than my kindred," while our " Well begun is half done " re-appears in " A beard well lathered is half shaved." The well-known English proverb, "One cannot make a silk purse out of a sow's ear," is happily rendered in Spain by the assertion, " A pig's tail will not make a good arrow"; while our advice to the cobbler to stick to his last, to attend to what he understands, has its counterpart in "Fritterman, to thy fritters."

The temptation to quote is great, but we will, in conclusion, set down but half-a-dozen more, leaving their interpretation to the sapience of our readers. " A friend to everybody and to nobody is the same thing," " Truth and oil are ever above," " Words and feathers are carried away by the wind," " A little gall makes bitter much honey," " It is better to accept one than to be promised two," " When we have crossed the sea the saint is forgotten."

The proverbs of fair Italy are very numerous. While not a few are sound in teaching and justly extol the ways of truth and uprightness, of honour and righteous dealing, others are too often merely the advocates of unmitigated selfishness, are strongly imbued with cynicism, and teach a general distrust and suspicion and the glorification of revenge. The political condition of the country, split up for so many centuries into petty principalities and republics, in an almost constant state of jealousy and feud, has no doubt greatly influenced its proverb-lore. Thus, "Who knows not to flatter, knows not to reign," tells of a government at the mercy of cabals, while the saying, "An open countenance, but close thoughts," indicates the wisdom in an atmosphere of suspicion of a seeming content and the importance of great reticence of speech ; while the ingratitude of princes is summed up in the adage, " He who serves at court dies on straw."* Fierce insurrection and sanguinary suppression have fed the fiery Southern temperament with burning hatred. Hence we get utterances so terrible in their vindictiveness as these : "He who cannot revenge himself is weak, he who will not is contemptible"; "Revenge of a hundred years old hath still its sucking teeth "—is yet but at its commencement. What internecine strife becomes under such influence is seen in the utterance, " When war begins hell opens."

The soft Italian tongue lends itself readily to musical rhythm and pleasing alliteration, features that are ordinarily entirely lost in translation. This attractive cadence may be seen, for instance, in " Chi piglia leoni in assenza suol temer dei topi in presenza," or " Chi ha arte da per tutto ha parte." There is often, too, a pregnant brevity, as " Amor regge senza legge," and a very happy use of hyperbole.

The proverb-literature of Italy is very extensive. In the year 1591 Florio, by birth an Englishman, by extraction an Italian, published in London " Il giardino di Ricreatione," a collection of some 6000 Italian adages ; and a little later another Italian, Torriano, followed his example, he also being resident in England. Angelus Monozoni, in the year 1604, pub-lished in Italy another book on the subject, and in 1642 Julius Varini gave to the world his " Scuola del Vulgo." A much more recent and altogether excel-lent series is the " Raccolta di Proverbi Toscani " of Guiseppe Guisti, issued at Florence in 1853, and con-taining over 6000 examples.

" It is a foolish bird," we say, "that fouls its own nest," a sentiment that the Italians reproduce in their

---

* Another expressive proverb tells that, " Courtiers are shod with water-melon rind," a somewhat slippery and uncertain foot-gear, rendering one's footing not particularly safe.

adage, "Mad is the priest who blasphemes his own relics." A higher point is reached in this, "We are all clay and God is the potter," and this, "Who has God for a friend has the saints in his pocket." Their intervention is needless. Another fine proverb is found in "Who doth not burn doth not inflame"—he must himself be on fire who would kindle ardour in others. "The favour gained, the saint derided," appears needlessly strong—"neglected" would have been truer to human nature.* "Sin confessed is half pardoned" is true and good. "Everyone cannot have his house on the piazza," all cannot expect the best position, is quaint and of sound philosophy. "He who flings gold away with his hands seeks it with his feet," wandering forth in beggary and want. To such we may commend the warning, "Work in jest, want in earnest." In every nation the virtue of silence is upheld, and the Italians have many proverbs that deal with this : thus the gain of quiet listening is seen in this—"Talkers sow, the silent reap," reap rich wisdom from the words of the wise, prudence and caution from the loquacity of the thoughtless. The undignified flow of explanation, the lack of reserve in face of misfortune, are rebuked in the saying, "Words in plenty when the cause is lost."

In that mine of wisdom, the book of *Ecclesiastes*, we are warned that "He that observeth the wind shall not sow, and he that regardeth the clouds shall not reap," and the Italians in like manner declare that "He that looks at every cloud never makes the journey." The intuitive gift of womankind to realise the best course of action is the subject of proverbs the wide world over. In Italy it appears as "Women, wise on a sudden, fools on reflection." Every nation, too, appears to have some little tinge of self-righteousness,

---

* "In prosperity no altars smoke" is like unto it. This too is Italian.

some sarcasm to spare for those outside its borders. Thus we are told that if one scratches a Russian we get at once to the Tartar beneath ; and the Spaniard says, "Take away from a Spaniard his good qualities and there remains a Portuguese." The Italian in like manner has a proverbial rebuke for those who "drink wine like a German—in the morning, neat ; at dinner without water ; at supper, as it comes from the bottle " ; and says, "May my death come to me from Spain," for so it will be long in coming—a hit at the Spanish habit of procrastination and the wearisome delays that thwart the despatch of business in that easy-going land where " manana " (to-morrow) is one of the commonest of expressions.*

Many of the proverbs of Italy are, naturally, not exclusively Italian, but when the Florentine declares that " Arno swelleth not without becoming turbid," we have a distinctly local application of the broad truth that they who would acquire riches quickly may fall into a snare, and that a sudden prosperity may be achieved at the expense of a soiled conscience. " Il remedio e peggio del male " is but an Italian version of the generally-accepted adage, " The remedy is worse than the disease," and " Una rondina non fa primavera " is their rendering of a truth familiar to us in the state- ment that " One swallow does not make a summer," a proverb of wide acceptance. In France it is " Une hirondelle ne fait pas le printemps " ; in Holland, " Een swaluw maakt geen zomer " ; in Spain, " Una golondrina no hace verano." We find it, too, equally at home in Germany, Sweden, and many other lands. Its sig- nificance is repeated in another Italian proverb that tells us that " One flower does not make a garland." A very characteristic utterance is that " Summer is

* The old English proverb declares that " By the Street of By-and-by one arrives at the House of Never."

the mother of the poor," life in sunny Italy being then
less arduous to the indigent, and the problems of existence appear by no means so exacting.

The thorough-going character of German work is
itself almost proverbial, and the treatment of the
national proverbs in the "Deutsches Sprichwörter-
Lexicon" is an excellent illustration of this German
thoroughness, the editor having managed to gather
in over 80,000. Another excellent compilation is that
of Dr. Wilhelm Körte.

The proverbs, native or imported, that find most
favour in the Fatherland are ordinarily excellent in
quality and full of sterling good sense. We occasionally meet with rhyming examples, as in "Mutter treu
wird täglich neu," a mother's love is ever fresh; or the
less tender "Ehestand, wehestand," marriage state,
mournful state; or "Stultus und Stolz wachset aus
einem Holz," stupidity and pride grow on one bush;
or again, in "Wie gewonnen so zerronen"; our "Lightly
come, lightly go." But these rhyming adages do not
appear to be so characteristic a feature in German
proverb-lore as in some other nationalities. The English protest as to the absurdity of carrying coals to
Newcastle* is in Germany the equally needless task
of carrying water to the sea—"Wasser ins Meer tragen."
Another picturesque proverb is "Die süssessten Trauben
hangen am höchsten," the sweetest grapes hang the
highest. The greedy are rebuked in the adage—"The
eyes here are bigger than the stomach," and the
thoughtless and thriftless are warned that "One may
in seeking a farthing burn up three candles." The
difficulty in pleasing some people is felt as much in

* "To send you any news from hence were to little purpose, ours being
little else but the translation of English or French; and to send you our
news from England were to carry coals to Newcastle."—"Thoresby Cor-
respondence," 1682.

Germany as elsewhere and is expressed in the proverb,
"No tree will suit the thief to be hung on"; and there
is the equally true remark, "There are many more
thieves than gallows," many escape detection and
punishment. "Woman and the moon," we are told,
"shine with borrowed light," and the wife, in "die
Hausfrau soll nit sein eine Ausfrau," is advised that
her duties lie within the home and not outside it. It
is, however, evident that to treat at any length on the
proverbial lore even of Europe would mean not a
volume alone but a shelf of goodly folios, a prospect
much too overpowering. We pass then at once to a
quite different sphere, and seek in widely different
peoples some expression of their modes of thought
and principles of action, as revealed to us in their
popular dicta, and we may at once say that the search
will result in the decision that, however much the outer
envelope may differ, the inner thought will reveal to
us that man, wherever we find him, is swayed by
much the same impulses and guided by much the
same motives, as he thinks over the problems of life.
The resident in a mansion in Mayfair, in a kraal in
Zululand, in a sanpan on some Chinese river, differ
widely enough in externals and in much else, but we
would venture to say that any good collection of
proverbs, if rendered in the vernacular of each district,
might travel round the world and find appreciation in
every land. The burnt child dreads the fire in Samoa
as in Salisbury, and that prosperity makes friends,
and adversity proves them, is a piece of world-wide
experience.

Chinese proverbs do not appear to be very numerous,
but they are often very happily phrased and thought
out. "As the twig is bent so the tree is inclined,"
we say, and in China they have the same idea, "The
growth of the mulberry tree is as its youth." Filial

respect and the duties of friendship and hospitality
are often enforced in this Celestial teaching. Thus,
" At home respecting father and mother, what need at
a distance to burn incense ?" so only the heart be
right, no need of ceremonial and formal observance.
" To meet an old friend is as the delightfulness of
rain after drought." On the other hand, " If a man
does not receive guests at home he will meet with
very few hosts abroad." The upholders of the "spare
the rod and spoil the child" system of education of
which Solomon was so distinguished an exponent will
be in full sympathy with the Chinese view, " Pitying
your child, give him much cudgel."

On our journey through life we may find, as they
have done in the far East, that " If you do not entreat
their assistance all men will appear good-natured,"
but " The sincerity of him who assents to everything
must be small." " Master easy, servant lazy," is only
too true. It is again a common experience that, as
we say in England, " One man may steal a horse while
another may not look over the gate," a state of things
that they yet more forcibly express in China as " One
man may set the town in a blaze, another may not
light his lantern." What graceful lessons of trust in
a Higher Power are these : " Every blade of grass has
its share of the dews of heaven," " Though the birds of
the forest have no garners the wide world is before
them." To avoid even the semblance of evil we are
quaintly told, " In melon patch tie not shoe, under
plum-tree touch not cap," actions innocent in themselves, but possibly giving rise to misapprehensions !

The exigencies of the Chinese language make a
literal translation often scarcely endurable or possible,
while a lengthened paraphrase gives a wordiness that
is not a true reflection of the epigrammatic pithiness
of the original. Thus in Chinese "Yaou chi sin fo

sze tau ting kow chung yen" is "Wishing to know
heart's thoughts listen to mouth"—that is to say, if you
would desire to find out what most engages a man's
thoughts you have only to listen to his conversation,
for a man's words reflect his disposition, and he will
thus, surely though unconsciously, reveal himself to
you. The wisdom of knowing oneself, of offering
something more than a formal service, are admirably
enforced in these two heathen proverbs, redolent with
the teaching of the New Testament : " If a man be not
enlightened within, what lamp shall he light?" " If
a man's intentions are not upright, what sacred book
shall be recite?" " By a long journey we know a horse's
strength, and length of days shows a man's heart." How
beautiful, again, the imagery in this description of the
swift flight of the days and years of human life : " Time
is like an arrow, days and months as a weaver's shuttle."

How excellent the lesson of contentment with one's
lot, " All ten fingers cannot be of the same length," yet
all have their work to do. How good the lesson of
forethought, of prevision of coming needs in this:
" The tiles which protect thee in the wet season
were fabricated in the dry." How prudent the
advice: " He who wishes to know the road across
the mountains must ask him who has trodden it,"
must be willing to profit by the experience of the
experienced, and take counsel. There is a rich mine
of wealth for the social economist, for the agitator
who would set one class against another, in the following : " Without the wisdom of the learned the clown
could not be governed, without the labour of the clown
the learned could not be fed."

The mischief that may be wrought by evil speaking,
the impossibility of recalling a hasty word, of cancel-
ling a false judgment, is emphasised in the picturesque
declaration that " A coach and horses cannot bring

H

back a spoken word." How true the economic warning, "Who borrows to build builds to sell." How equally true the moral warning, "The forming of resentments is the planting of misery." How needful often the caution, "A single false move loses the game," a single false step may wreck a life.

Nothing can afford a better insight into the character and thoughts of a people than a consideration of their every-day utterances. If we were told a hundred things that a man had said we should have an excellent knowledge of the man, and if we read a hundred sayings that a nation accepts as guides, the nation stands revealed before us. Judged by this standard, and it is an entirely reasonable and just one, the Japanese come excellently out of the ordeal. Many suffer much in translation—the beauty of their outward presentment, as apart from their inner meaning, their manner as apart from their matter, consists often in an untranslatable play of words. Many are like ours, for God made of one blood all nations, thus : "Cows to cows, horses to horses," is practically our "Birds of a feather flock together." We append some few illustrations of the wealth and beauty of this Japanese proverb-wisdom ; and while we forbear to make any comment, we would ask our readers to ponder on each one : "The frog in the well knows nothing of the great sea"; "Overdone politeness is but rudeness"; "A famous sword may be made from an iron scraper"; "The mouth is the door of mischief"; "Impossibility is a good reason"; "More words, less sense"; "Making an idol does not give it a soul"; "To submit is victory"; "The spawn of frogs will become but frogs"; "Sword-wounds may be healed, word-wounds are beyond healing"; "Enquire seven times before you doubt anyone"; "Good medicine may yet be bitter to the taste"; "If you handle

5

cinnabar you will become red"; "Too much done is nothing done"; "Who steals money is killed, who steals a country is a king"; "Good doctrine needs no miracle."

The Arabs delight in figurative language and happy comparisons and allusions; hence proverbs are constantly in use. Many of them have a strong touch of humour and sarcasm. John Lewis Burckhardt, after a very long residence in Cairo, made a collection of these, and they were published under the title of "The Manners and Customs of the Modern Egyptians, illustrated from their proverbial sayings." In this he was greatly assisted by native helpers, and the book is a most valuable one. The examples are 999 in number, the author adopting a notion prevalent amongst the Arabs that even numbers bring misfortune, and that anything perfect in its quantity is especially affected by the evil-eye. By this means he doubtless received much valuable help from the natives that would otherwise have been withheld. Many of these proverbs are rhythmical in structure in their original form, but this feature is lost ordinarily in a translation. Long centuries of misrule have had their influence on the people, and the oppression of the strong, the insecurity of the weak, the power of bribery, the denial of justice, the imprudence of any independence of spirit, are revealed in these maxims. Such a saying as "What does heaven care for the cries of the dogs?" has a sadly hopeless ring about it, while the depth of servility is reached in this: "When the monkey reigns dance before him," in utter abasement of spirit. "If thou seest a wall inclines run from under it"—that is to say, shout ever on the stronger side, and fly from him whose rule is tottering. Another striking adage is "He strikes me, and says why does he cry out?" the surprise of the unjust overseer that anyone should presume to raise any objection to his injustice and tyranny; while the prudence of being on the stronger side is seen again in this: "If the moon be with thee thou needest not to care about the stars." We would fain hope that a brighter day has now risen on this ancient land.

We have in the adage, "Truly the sword inspires dread even in its scabbard," a further suggestion of the fear inspired by those in authority; while the depth of misery, of callous brutality, is seen in "Thou takest from the sore-footed his sandal," the man is hopelessly crippled. Double-dealing and the evil of a sham friendship inspires the idea in "He said to the thief, steal, and to the householder, take care of thy goods"; while the selfish man is warned that in the day of trouble he need look for no assistance from others, for "He who eats alone chokes alone." "Three," another proverb tells us, "if they unite against a town, will ruin it," for while "Union is strength" for good, it is no less powerful for harm.

A quaint and delightful humour, as we have said, is a frequent attribute of these Arab utterances; thus the generosity of those who only give away what they have no need for is very happily satirised in the saying that "The dogs had enough, and then made presents to each other out of their leavings." How pithily, too, the braggart is brought before us in the saying, "If they had not dragged me from underneath him I should have killed him!" The sense of supreme self-importance is capitally illustrated in the saying, "They came to shoe the pacha's horses, and the beetle stretched out his leg." The liberties that some people venture on with impunity when they think it safe are very happily brought home to us in the saying, "The captain loves thee, wipe thy hand on the sail." There is a good deal of quiet humour, too, in this, " He fled from the rain and sat down beneath the waterspout," a case of what in England we should call " Out of the frying-pan into the fire." How true, again, the proverb, " The camel has his schemes, and the camel-driver has his schemes," the interests of the driven and the driver being ordinarily very different; or this again, " The barber learns his art on the orphan's face," on the poor and the friend-less who cannot resent an indignity or adequately protect themselves from maltreatment.* Of people who receive a piece of good fortune that they neither desire nor appreciate, the proverb, " A rose fell to the share of the monkey," holds good. It is also a warn-ing against a thoughtless distribution of good things without heed to their appropriateness.

The picturesque expression, " Hunting dogs have scratched faces," is a wholesome recognition of the honour of the scars gained in honest labour; while the adage, " He walks on top of the wall and says I trust in God," is a reproof to those who needlessly and deliberately place themselves in positions of peril or temptation and then expect providence to step in and save them from the consequences of their folly. " God grant us no neighbour with two eyes " is the cry of the knave who would prefer that those around him should be a little blind to his proceedings.

" If they call thee reaper, whet thy scythe "; en-deavour so far as may be to rise to the position, and show the title deserved. Inculcating the lesson of gratitude, we read, " A well from which thou drinkest, throw not a stone into it." Our proverb that declares that " The shoemaker's wife is the worst shod " has its Arab counterpart in the adage, " She went to sleep hungry, though her husband is a baker." The mischief

---

* The French adage, " À barbe de fou on apprendre à raire " is very similar.

done by careless speech in the land of the scimitar is enforced in the saying, "The tongue is the neck's enemy." "A single grain makes the balance heavier," and when two courses of action seem of almost equal importance, a very slight difference will turn the scale in favour of one or the other. The lesson of inter-dependence, the power of the small to assist the great, is indicated in "The date-stone props up the water-jar." "He left off sinning but never asked forgiveness" very graphically describes those who think reformation sufficient, and take no heed of bygone days, make no atonement for the old wrongs, solicit no pardon from those they have injured. "It is a fire, to-morrow it will be ashes," the fierce heat of passion will have subsided, the glowing sense of wrong will have burnt itself out, and calm or apathy will take its place. The stronger the emotion the less likely is it to be lasting.

The delight in stories is a very marked feature of the Arab, and many of their proverbs are the pith and point of some narrative that their use at once recalls. Thus, when they say "Dust is good for the eyes of the wolf," it recalls the hyprocrisy of the wolf who was asked why he was following after those poor sheep? He explained that he had found that the cloud of dust they created was good for his poor eyes! When a business is found to be somewhat risky they tell how one said to the mouse, "Take these two pounds of sugar and go carry this letter to the cat." "The fee is good enough," she replied, "but the business is tiresome." The wisdom of keeping one's own counsel is seen in the dialogue between master and servant. The former said, "O slave, I have bought thee." "That is thy business," he replied. "Wilt thou run away?" "That is my business," he answered—a policy of non-committal.

Even amongst the savage tribes of Africa the proverb

is greatly esteemed, and many of the maxims in common use are abundantly shrewd, while not a few of them have a very homely ring in them. Our English experience that "Fine words butter no parsnips" runs on all-fours with the West African savage's discovery that "The best words give no food"; while our bad exchange from the frying-pan to the fire is paralleled in the saying, "He fled from the sword and hid in the scabbard." The desirability of not too hastily trusting plausible strangers is very effectively taught in "Make not friends by the way, lest you lose your knife."

Over 2000 of these popular proverbs were collected by Richard Burton and given to the world as "Wit and Wisdom from West Africa," and a very interesting collection it is. Another good store will be found in the "Dahomey and the Dahomans" by Commander Forbes, R.N., and various missionaries have added to our fund of knowledge,* so that even stay-at-home people have abundance of interesting material brought within their ken.

That unreachable date of classic folk-lore, the Greek Calends, has its quaint counterpart in the African saying, "I will pay thee when the fowls cut their teeth." A lesson on the importance of keeping up one's dignity, even in Yoruba circles, is given in the hint, "If thou husketh corn with the fowl it will not esteem thee." The animal life all around the village is naturally pressed into the service and made to contribute its share of proverb-lore. How quaintly happy, for instance, is this, "If stretching were wealth, the cat would be rich." How many a man in West Africa and elsewhere would be well content to find so easy

---

* As, for instance, "The Oji Language, with a Collection of Native Proverbs," by the Rev. H. N. Riis. The sketch of the Akra language by the Rev. J. Zimmerman, of the Efik language by the Rev. Hugh Goldie, of the Yoruba by the Rev. J. Bowen, all give many examples of proverbs.

a road to affluence. How equally happy this, "If
there were no elephant in the jungle the buffalo would
be a great animal"; or this, "One who has elephant's
flesh does not search for crickets." What a shrewd
humour again in the statement that "When the mouse
laughs at the cat there is a hole near." By continuous
effort much may be accomplished,* for "String added
to string will bind a leopard"—a lesson taught again
in this saying, "By going and coming the bird builds
its nest."† How true again the statement that "One
cannot deceive a baboon by tricks"; in all such he
is more than one's match, and the trickster must be
foiled by quite other methods. To try and outwit
a knave is a hopeless task and is, moreover, bad for
one's self-respect. It is well to see some return for
one's outlay; it is bad enough to "buy," in English
parlance, "a pig in a poke," but in Africa they carry
the idea yet further and declare that "It is not well
to buy the foot-prints of a bullock," while another
caution as to the disposal of one's property is very
aptly given in the reminder that "No one gives his
pig to the hyena to keep," this keeping being in such
case all too thoroughly seen to.

The Akra-man tells us that "The thread follows
the needle"; in other words, certain consequences will
naturally follow certain actions, and these results, good
or bad, may be confidently anticipated when we have
once set the machinery to work. He tells us, too,
that "Food you will not eat you do not boil"; people
will not willingly work at any task unless in some
way or other they see their advantage in it. Another
illustration of consequences following upon a certain
line of action is seen in the proverb, "A stick that

* The Italians say, " Piuma a piuma se pela l'occha," feather by feather
the goose was stripped.
† This recurs in the French, " Petit à petit l'oiseau fait son nid."

goes into the fire begins to burn"; a deliberate entry into any temptation will scarcely leave one unscathed. Another quaint little piece of worldly wisdom is that "If you lay your snare in company you go in company to look at it"—if you avail yourself of the help of others, they in turn will expect a share of any resulting good fortune.

The Yoruba-man warns you that "When a man says he will give you a gun, ask his name"—that is to say, when a stranger displays a quite unexpected interest in you, and develops a quite unlooked-for generosity, it would be well before you accept his gift to find out something about him, and what his motive may be for this sudden friendship. "Lay on, lay on, makes a load," a fact that the man or beast that has to carry it realises sooner than the person packing. The repeated addition of small things soon mounts into a considerable burden. "A canoe is paddled on both sides,"—no half-measures, no want of unanimity, will suffice when some joint task has to be formed ; it must be "a long pull, a strong pull, and a pull altogether," if any good is to come of it. We see the sudden impulse, the overmastering temptation, forcibly expressed in this, "When gold comes near you it glistens"; the eye and the desire are strained and dazzled, the desire to possess it is overmastering and "opportunity makes the thief." Another very characteristic utterance is that "A slave does not show the timber." This at first sight is enigmatical, but Burton in his comment on it explains clearly enough that if the slave points out suitable trees that he knows of in the dense forest, his only return would be that on him would fall the labour of felling them and dragging them to where they were wanted ; he therefore maintains a discreet silence. Another woodman proverb is that "The split tree still grows," calamity is not so crushing but that much good may yet be done in the life.

The importance of being on good terms with the ruler is as great in West Africa as elsewhere ; hence we get the happy saw, " To love the king is not bad, but to be loved by the king is better." In the last that we shall quote, though the temptation to extend our list is great, we find ourselves quite in the opposite scale of savage society, in the touching proverb, " When a poor man makes a proverb it does not spread." This is Oji experience, but it is certainly not Oji alone. The man is poor and friendless, overridden and despised. The writer of *Ecclesiastes* saw the matter as clearly, for he tells us that " There was a little city and few men within it, and there came a great king against it and besieged it, and built great bulwarks against it. Now, there was found in it a poor wise man, and he by his wisdom delivered the city, yet no man remembered that same poor man. Then said I, wisdom is better than strength ; nevertheless the poor man's wisdom is despised, and his words are not heard." As it was in Palestine in the days of old, so it is in Oji-land to-day, and so in all lands will it ever be. The jokes of the judge will convulse the court and his wisdom enthral it, but no meaner authority therein, either as humorist or sage, will be heard, under pain of expulsion.

Another valuable store of proverb-philosophy will be found in the pages of the Talmud. The teaching is excellent : " A myrtle among nettles is still a myrtle " ; " He who prays for his neighbour will be heard for himself " ; " Prepare thyself in the hall, that thou mayest be admitted into the palace " ; so pass through these things temporal that a welcome may be thine in the presence of the King. If offence must come, " Be thou the cursed, not he who curses," and

"Let the honour of thy neighbour be to thee as thine own."

Scorn ingratitude and "Throw no stone into the well whence thou hast drunk," and bear ever in mind the difficult lesson, "Teach thy tongue to say I do not know." He who professes to know all things shuts himself out of much opportunity for gaining knowledge. "In two cabs of dates is one cab of stones," much that is profitless will ever be mixed with the good. How true too the caution, "He who is suspicious should be suspected." To the pure all things are pure, and the honest man thinks no evil, but the man of evil heart lives in a beclouded atmosphere and sees all things through a distorted medium. How wise and charitable, how just, the counsel, "Do not judge thy neighbour until thou hast stood in his place." The Arab proverb about standing on the wall and trusting to Allah is re-echoed in this Talmudic precept, "Do not stand in a place of danger, trusting in miracles."

Others, and these we must simply put down without comment, are—"One thing acquired with pain is better than fifty with ease"; "When the thief has no opportunity of stealing he thinks himself honest"; "Let the grapes pray for the welfare of the branches"; "Who is strong? he who subdues his passion"; "If I had not lifted the stone you had not found the jewel"; "Whosoever does too much does too little"; "In his own house the weaver is a king"; "Iron sharpens iron, and scholar scholar"; "The way man wishes to go, thither his feet will carry him." It will, we trust, be seen from these examples that our commendation of the Talmud as a mine of proverbic wealth has full justification.

CHAPTER V

THOUGH in the great majority of cases the significance of a proverb is more or less apparent on consideration, and when discovered is more or less helpful
to the conduct of life, we from time to time encounter
adages that have achieved some considerable popularity and yet are quite misunderstood, or are entirely
unsound in teaching. Comparatively few proverbs
reach the highest plane ; they are mostly content to
supply good work-a-day maxims for a man's prosperity
and easy passage through this life, but occasionally
self-interest is carried to a point where principle is
lost sight of, and the result is wholly evil.

The proverbs that are misunderstood are ordinarily
sound enough in their teaching, and are freely used
by all—a meaning, not the correct one, having been

tacked on to them and found to be a good working one. This is a philological principle that we meet with in all directions. Asparagus, for instance, is so called from the Greek word to tear, many of the species being armed with spines that lacerate,* but the coster-monger knows nothing of this, so he drops the word that has no meaning to him and calls it sparrow-grass, a much more meaningless word really. A somewhat common expression amongst a certain class is " That's the ticket," meaning "that is the proper course to pur-sue." Why it should carry this significance is not on the face of it obvious, but the whole matter is cleared up when we find that it is a corruption of " C'est l'etiquette." Another popular expression of approval takes the form of " That's the cheese." Familiarity makes such an expression accepted without demur, but one moment's consideration suffices to convince us that what it says cannot really be what it means.†
If we turn it, for instance, into " C'est le fromage," and so get rid of the old formula, we realise this better. What we are to put in its place is quite another matter. One authority suggests that cheese is really the French word " chose," and would bid us accept " C'est le chose " as the true rendering. Another informs us that " chiz " is Bengalee for "thing," and that the expression has been imported from the East ; while a third, and he is the man that we would personally pin our faith on, reminds us that "choice" was in Anglo-Saxon times "chese." In the " Vision of Piers Plow-man," for example, we read—

---

* A South African species of this genus is called by the settlers and natives, " Waht en beetje"—wait a bit, because its crooked thorns catch their clothes as they journey.

† A quaint and true old proverb that says cheese and means it too is this, " The king's cheese goes half away in parings," so many dependants being ready to help themselves to a share of it.

" Now thou might chese
How thou cal me, now thou knowst al mi names."

"That's the cheese," then, if we accept this explanation, is "That's the choice," the satisfactory result that one would have chosen to happen.

Another misconception is the familiar saying, "Raining cats and dogs." Such a meteorologico-zoological phenomenon never really takes place; no instance of it has ever been known, and yet people go on using the expression as though the experience was of very ordinary occurrence. The word we want is "catadupe"—κατα δοῦπος. Δοῦπος is a word used by Homer to express the crash of falling trees, and it is applied, too, to certain falls of the Nile. Thus Pliny writes: " Here and there, and ever and anon, hitting upon islands, and stirred as it were with so many provocations, and at last inclosed and shut within mountaines, and in no place carrieth he (the Nile) a rougher and swifter streame, while the water that he beareth hasteneth to a place of the Æthiopians, called Catadupa, where in the last fall amongst the rockes that stand in his way he rusheth downe with a mightie noise."* Catadoupe is also a French word for waterfall, though it is now obsolete; and Ralph Thoresby, is his " Diary," describes Coldwarth Force in the Lake District as "a remarkable catadupa." When, then, we say that it is "raining cats and dogs" we mean that there is a tremendous downpour, a perfect catadoupe.

Another old country proverb, "Hurry no man's cattle, you may have a horse of you own some day," appears on the face of it a protest against over-driving, but the first word is a corruption of harry or steal.

To carry a thing through "to the bitter end" seems to imply that, come what may of opposition, the matter shall be forced through, no matter whose heart breaks

* Holland's translation.

in the process, but nothing so terrible as this is involved. The expression is a nautical one. Bite is a turn of a cable, and the bitter end is that part of the cable which is wound round the bitt. The bitter end is therefore the extreme end. We read, for instance, in " Robinson Crusoe," that during the storm his vessel encountered, the cables were "veered out to the bitter end "; and, if we turn to Admiral Smyth's " Sailors' Word Book," we find the bitter end defined as "that part of the cable which is abaft the bitts, and therefore within board when the ship rides at anchor. When a chain or rope is paid out to the bitter end no more remains to let go." The popular expression, therefore, that we are considering implies a determination to carry a thing through to a finish, but no bitterness of feeling is a necessary element in the process.

The expression " By hook or by crook" has grown into the idea of a dogged determination to effect a certain purpose—honestly, it may be—but at all events to effect it ; but its origin carries no such idea, the most that is involved being a choice of alternatives. Those who by ancient manorial privilege had the right to collect wood for burning were allowed a hook and a crook, the former cutting the green wood, and the latter breaking off the dry ; hence, one way or the other, by hook or by crook, they effected their purpose.

In Ray's collection of proverbs we find, " Reckon right, and February hath thirty-one days." What the significance of this can be utterly baffles us. " A little chink lets in much light," but this necessary chink is not as yet forthcoming. " They are well off that have not a home to go to " is another enigma. It sounds distinctly silly. Denham, we see, in his collection of proverbs, has the boldness to declare it " an apposite remark, often quoted by those who, sitting comfortably by their 'ain ingleside,' hear the pelting of the pitiless storm without."

We would fain hope, for the credit of human nature, that this adage is not quite so apposite as this Denham would have us believe.

Bad-hearted proverbs are, fortunately, not very numerous in proportion to the sound ones, but there are yet too many of them when we remember how the clinching of a matter by a proverb is to some people almost equivalent to supporting it by a text. In some cases an evil meaning that is not justified is read into a proverb; thus, to declare that "Charity begins at home" is to enunciate a great truth, for he that careth not for his own flesh, we are told, is an infidel. Too often, however, this adage is made the excuse for withholding any wider sympathy, a meaning that it really gives no warrant for. "Honesty is the best policy" is an oft-quoted saying, and it is, as far as it goes, a true one, but it fails because it puts the matter on too low a footing. Honesty for the sake of right, one's duty to God, to one's neighbour, and to one's own conscience and self-respect, is a right worthy aim, but honesty because on the whole it pays best is an ignoble thing. The man whom such a maxim helps is a poor creature, and one whom we should be unwilling to trust very far. The saying, "Every man for himself, and God for us all," while it clothes itself in sham invocation to Providence, is at heart bad—a mere appeal to selfishness—the weakest going to the wall and trodden under foot, or what is more deftly called "the survival of the fittest." The French put it more unblushingly as "Better a grape for me than a fig for thee." How scoundrel a maxim is the declaration that "It is not the offence, but the being found out, that matters"; and how mean a view of integrity and uprightness is shown in the statement that "Every man has his price"—only bid high enough, some perhaps requiring a little more than others, and truth and honour and righteousness become mere merchandise. " As well be hung for a sheep as a lamb " is an utterance equally unsound.

Such proverbs are found in all lands, human nature being what it is. The Bengalis say, " He that gives blows is a master, he that gives none is a dog," whole centuries of tyranny, of cringing to the strong, being revealed in these few words. The Spaniard says, " Draw the snake from its hole by another man's hand "—throw upon another the danger. The Dutchman says, " Self is the man for me." The German says, " Once is never "—some little sin may be allowed to all and never be counted. The Italian says, " At the open chest the righteous may sin "—the opportunity given to theft being a sufficient justification for availing oneself of it. Thus might we travel round the world, finding in every land some maxims of evil import.

To " look at home " is, however, a sufficient task, for no amount of depravity in a Swede or a Zulu will mend matters in Sussex or Yorkshire. " Necessity has no law " is one of the utterances quoted as though gospel truth, but it is a doctrine that will not bear investigation, and " Better a bad excuse than none at all " is not much better. The slovenly housekeeper gravely declares, as a palliative of her untidiness, that " Everyone must eat a peck of dirt before they die," and, indeed, appears to feel somewhat virtuous that her operations are assisting this great natural law! " To accept an obligation is to sell your liberty " is a double-edged adage.* If we consider it as encouraging self-reliance it is good, but if we take it as a churlish disinclination to accept a kindness, it cuts at the root of all kindly mutual help and sympathy.

The proverb that " The wholesomest meat is at another man's cost " is despicable, but the adage " Up the

* The Italians have it, "Chi prende, si vende"—"He sells himself who accepts a gift."

I

hill favour me, down the hill beware thee" is atrocious, diabolical. That a man should be willing to accept every possible help in his upward struggle, and then, when he has attained success, trample on those who befriended him, and that a proverb approving the proceeding should pass from mouth to mouth, seems almost impossible of credence. Another atrocious saying is, "If I see his cart overturning I will give it a push"; and yet another runs, "Better kiss a knave than be troubled with him." A fair parallel in abominable teaching to these may be found in the saying, "A slice off a cut loaf will not be missed";* and for a flat denial of all honourable and manly action it would be hard to beat the teaching, "One must howl with the wolves"—make no protest against evil, take no stand for righteousness, but band oneself with the powers of evil in craven fear of them.

Not fiendish, like some we have quoted, but lamentably weak as a rule of life, is the old adage, "For want of company, welcome trumpery," and this motto of the idler, "If anything stay, let work stay." One could not imagine a very noble character to be built up on such nutriment as this. Another adage that "Good ale is meat, drink, and cloth" must be taken with considerable limitations. Good ale, *instead* of the good food, the warm clothing, has much to be said for it as a corrected reading, as the sad experience of thousands of empty homes can testify.

Some proverbs have a strong touch of sarcasm in them, and this, when not too bitter and uncharitable, is a quite legitimate feature, as it may drive in a home truth where a gentler treatment would fail, while others have a touch of wit that helps to impress them on the memory. The line between the wit that makes us

---

* " Easy it is
Of a cut loaf to steal a shive."—" Titus Andronicus."

laugh and that which makes us wince is often rather a fine one. We propose to give some few examples of proverbs on these lines, and we may very well commence our series with the two adages that "Wise men make proverbs, and fools repeat them," and that "The less wit a man has the less he knows he wants it."

The fool, from the days of Solomon, and probably long before them, has supplied the basis of many a proverb; how happy, for instance, the hit at pompous self-conceit * is this : "A nod from a lord is a breakfast for a fool"; or the suggestion of the utter hopelessness of his condition, for "Heaven and earth fight in vain against a fool"; † or his recklessness and want of prevision, for "The chapter of accidents is the bible of the fool"; and his want of brains, for "A wager is a fool's argument." The only ray of hope for him is in the French saying, "Tous sont sages quand ils se taisent" —fools are wise, or may at least be so reputed, when they are silent.

It is for the help of the fool that such a maxim as this canny Scotch proverb is floated—"Dinna gut your fish till ye get them." As these unfortunate people appear to be cosmopolitan, the Dutch have very similar advice for them, "Don't cry your herrings till they are in the net." The Italians warn them not to "Sell the bird on the bough," nor "Dispose of the skin before the bear is caught"; while even the sensible German appears to need the caution that "Unlaid eggs are uncertain chickens." The lamentable condition of the fool being only too obvious, "What good can it do an ass to be called a lion?" ‡

---

* "Every man has just as much of vanity as he wants understanding."

† Another old English proverb says, "Send a fool to market and a fool he will come back." The Italians have it, "Chi bestia va à Roma bestia retorna," and the ancient Romans made the discovery that "Cœlum non animam mutant qui trans mare currunt."

‡ "The man that once did sell the lion's skin while the beast lived, was killed with hunting him."—SHAKESPEARE, *Henry V.*

The selfishness and scheming of certain people has been made the target for many shafts. The Romans had the adage, " Ficos dividere," to satirise those who strove too cheaply to gain credit for their liberality by cutting up a fig into portions and distributing these. An old English proverb says of such a man, " He would dress an egg for himself, and give the broth to the poor." How true, again, " He that is warm thinks all are so," and is careful not to raise the question. Have we not all seen, too, how the weak are imposed on, and that " The least boy always carries the greatest fiddle," and that " Those who can deny others everything often deny themselves nothing." The Italians have found out that " He who manages other people's wealth does not go supperless to bed." The way these artful people hang together (not, unfortunately, in a literal sense)* has not escaped attention, the old Roman declaring : " Ait latro ad latronem "—another rogue always being ready to say " Yes " to what the first rogue says. On the other hand, it is some little comfort to know that " When the cook and the maid fall out we shall know what has come of the butter "! How true, again, is the assertion that " We confess our faults in the plural, but deny them in the singular," and many a man who calls himself a miserable sinner would warmly repudiate any assent that others might make to this assertion of his.

A happy sarcasm is that " He refuseth the bribe, but putteth out his hand "—seeking to save appearances, and yet anxious not to lose in the process. "A bribe enters," we are told, "without knocking," no special publicity in the matter being desirable, and " He that bringeth a present findeth the door open," no obstacle being

* " Kleine Diebe henkt man, vor grosser zieht man den Hut ab "— " Petty thieves are hanged," say the Germans, " but people take off their hats to great ones."

placed in his way. It must, however, be remarked that "Favourites are like sun-dials." Why? Because no one regards them any longer when they are in the shade. "Those that throw away virtue must not expect to save reputation," and "None have less praise than those who hunt after it." The Spaniards have a severe proverb on the corruption of the law-givers: "To the judges of Gallicia go with feet in hand"—a delicate way of advising the law-seeker to bring with him a brace of pheasants or some poultry to help his cause.

Things that all may well remember for their guidance are, that "Form is good, but not formality"; that "Respect is better secured by deserving than by soliciting"; that "Candour is pleasant, rudeness is not"; that "Popularity is not love"; that "Desert and reward seldom keep company"; that "Many suffer long who are not long-suffering"; that "Good reasons must give place to better"; that "Favour is no inheritance"; that "He who sets his timepiece by everyone's clock will never know the hour"; that "Things intended are not of the same value as things done"; that "Many complain of want of memory and few of lack of judgment"; that "Too much learning hinders knowledge." The Spaniards say that "A fool, unless he know Latin, is never a great fool"—a severe hit on pompous pedantry. A room may be so full of furniture that one can hardly find a chair to sit down upon, and a man's brain may be so stuffed with recondite lore that common work-a-day knowledge is crowded out.

The direct appeal to religion is, naturally, not often met with in proverb-lore, such appeal being somewhat outside its functions, and on a higher plane than is ordinarily reached. The wisdom of proverbs concerns itself more with time than with eternity, though the advocacy of truth and honour, the exposure of knavery, the importance of a right judgment, and many other points that make for the right, are contributory to the higher life. The beacon light for those steering for the Celestial City must, nevertheless, be sought elsewhere. The old and beautiful adage, "The grace of God is gear enough," is very striking, and is, furthermore, interesting from the Shakespearean reference to it in the "Merchant of Venice," where Launcelot Gobbo says to Bassanio : "The old proverb is very well parted between my master, Shylock, and you, Sir ; you have the grace of God, Sir, and he hath enough."

To "Tell the truth, and shame the devil," is one of our well-known popular sayings. Though often quoted lightly enough, it is a noble advocacy for standing up for the right at all hazards. The French proverb tells us that "Truth, like oil, must come to the top," and the Swiss, in like spirit, declare that "Truth cannot be buried." The old Roman adage also affirms, "Great is the truth and it shall prevail." This, in turn, reminds us of the old saw : "A lie has no legs." Nevertheless, unfortunately it has, and may travel gaily enough for awhile, but it contains within itself the seed of its own dissolution, and sooner or later its vitality has gone, and it perishes discredited ; for "Truth," as the Spanish proverb beautifully has it, "is the daughter of God," and its final victory is thereby assured. Forgiveness of injuries is the lesson taught in the Bengali proverb : "The sandal-tree perfumes the axe that fells it" ;* and an equally beautiful Persian saying is this : "Cast thy bread upon the water, God will know of it if the fishes do not." Another non-Christian proverb is the Greek saying : "Many meet the gods, but few salute them"—borne down by the cares of time, fail to recognise their presence, and suffer them to pass unheeded, or receive blessing at their hands, yet thank them not.

* Or again : "If you crush spice it will be the sweeter."

It is often too true that " The vow made in the storm is forgotten in the calm," for promises made readily enough in the time of trouble require a better memory than people ordinarily possess, and gratitude seems to be one of the most short-lived of emotions. Another old saying is also too painfully true : " Complaint is the largest tribute heaven receives "—the sincerest part of our devotion—and to this we may add, " If pride were an art how many graduates should we have."

The value of Time is appreciated in such sayings as " He that has most time has none to lose"; " Time is the stuff that life is made of." Our ancestors counsel us that we " Use the minutes wisely, then will not the hours reproach," for " Like as the waves make toward the pebbled shore, so do our minutes hasten to their end," nad " Every day in thy life is a page in thy history." An ancient adage warns us : " Take time while time is, for time will away " ; or, as we find it in " The Notable and Antient Historie of the Cherrie and the Slae ' (1595) :—

> " Yet Wisdom wisheth thee to weigh
> This figure in Philosophie,
> A lesson worth the lear,
> Which is, in time for to take tent,
> And not, when time is past, repent,
> And buy repentance dear."

In Howell's " Old Sayed Sawes " it is given as " All time's no time when time's past." Hence we are warned to take Time by the forelock. Life is a loan to man, and, while we complain that our days are few, we act practically as though there could come no end to them. " The shortest day is too long to waste," therefore " Do not squander time, for that is the stuff life is made of." The French say : " Il n'est si grand jour qui ne vienne à vespre." So that it becomes us well, in the words of a fifteenth century poem, to

> "Thinke on the end or thou begyn,
> And thou schalt never be thral to syn." *

The Italians very graphically and poetically say:
"La notte è la madre di pensieri"—night is the mother
of thoughts, a quiet resting time, a pause in life when
we can honestly take stock of ourselves.†

Death hath its special proverbs and warning saws:
thus one warns the young and careless that "The
churchyard graves are of all sizes," while another dwells
on its inevitableness, declaring that "Death is deaf and
takes no denial," and that all, fit or unfit, must face
the fact, for "Death is the only master who takes his
servants without a character." The Romans had the
proverb, "Finis coronat opus," and an English proverb
hath it: "'Tis not the fight that crowns us, but the end."
The Italians say: "A ogni cosa è remedio fuora qu'alla
morte"—there is a remedy for everything save death;
but "Men must endure their going hence, even as in
their coming hither; ripeness is all," and what death has
of terror is what the life has made to be terrible. A
well-known proverb will be recalled as to the folly of
waiting to step into dead men's shoes. Thomas Fuller,
in his essay on "Marriage," very happily says: "They
that marry ancient people, merely in expectation to
bury them, hang themselves, in hope that one will
come and cut the halter" — a sufficiently painful
position.

* A poem full of suggestive thoughts, as, for instance :—
> "He that in southe no vertu usit,
> In age alle honure hym refusit."
> "Ever the hiere that thou art,
> Ever the lower be thy hert."
> "Deme the best of every doute,
> Tyl the truthe be tryed out."

† "'Tis greatly wise to talk with our past hours, and ask them what
report they bore to heaven." "Think nought a trifle, though it small
appear, sands make the mountain, moments make the year, and trifles
life."

Though it seem impossible that the place of some great philanthropist or statesman could ever, on his removal, be adequately filled up, we soon learn that no one is really indispensable. The torch is handed on: "God buries his workman, but carries on his work."

The trials of life are many, and their lessons have their place in the proverbial wisdom of our forefathers, and we learn thereby how best to face them, and to see in them not evil but good. "The worse the passage the more welcome the port," and "Bitter to endure may be sweet to remember." How excellent, too, the advice: "Make a crutch of your cross"—no longer a thing to harass but to support and help. It is well, too, to remember that, in any real and high sense, "'Tis not the suffering but the cause that makes the martyr." *

The deliberate offender is warned that "He who thinks to deceive God has already deceived himself," and "That sin and sorrow cannot long be separated." He is reminded that "He that sins against his own conscience sins with a witness," and that "Trifling with sin is no trifling sin." How true, again, that "Few love to bear the sins they love to act." He who offends against Heaven hath none to whom he can plead. In ancient days it was held that in such a case Nemesis was inevitable, and a proverb in use before the Christian era declared that "Fate moves with leaden feet, but strikes with iron hands"—that punishment might be long in coming, but was no less sure—a later proverb, in like manner, teaching that "The mill of God grinds slowly but it grinds exceeding fine." The mere hypocrite—one of the most despicable of mortals—has a special adage for his warning, that "Religion is the

---

* "To wilful men the injuries which they themselves procure must be their schoolmasters"; or, in more colloquial phrase, "Experience is a dear school, but fools learn in no other."

best armour in the world, but the worst cloak"—an altogether excellent utterance.

Proverbs cast their nets far and wide, and gather in materials from many sources of inspiration. Speech and silence, wisdom and folly, truth and falsehood, friendship and enmity, wealth and poverty, industry and idleness, youth and age, moderation and excess, are all pressed into the service; even the divers occupations of life have their varying lessons, and to these we now give attention.

All who, even in the most amateur way, have tried their hands at carpentry will at once understand the point of the saying, "To go against the grain," when a task that has been undertaken is in some way distasteful; and carpenters, like other handicraftsmen, have opportunity of testing the truth of another very common remark, "A bad workman finds fault with his tools," or yet another happy criticism, "A man is known by his chips."

The loquacity of the barber has grown into a generally recognised feature of his calling. He is the "middle man," the cause of much dissemination of news, receiving and imparting it freely during the day's business. This is no reputation of yesterday; in ancient Rome the citizens said, "Omnibus notum tonsoribus," and we see in the old English adage, "Every barber knows that," that some few centuries afterwards the matter was as much in evidence as ever, and it is by no means out of date to-day.

The occupation of the tailor, as he sits all day cramped up in some room, has been held to be so enfeebling that it has been thought to justify the adage that "It takes nine tailors to make a man." This certainly is a great number. In a poem of the year 1630 we read—

" Some foolish knave, I thinke, at first began
The slander that three taylers are one man."

Nine, however, is the generally accepted figure, and
the poet shows such a strong animus that we can
scarcely accept his counter-statement. Nine would
have suited the requirements of his metre as well as
three, and we can only conclude that the fraction
he took was one of his own devising. " The three
tailors of Tooley Street " achieved lasting fame, it will
be remembered, by sending a petition to Parliament
commencing, " We, the people of England."

The cobbler, and eke his wife, share in the im-
mortality that popular proverbs go far to confer. It
will be remembered how, as an illustration of the
general inconsistency and unexpectedness of things,
" The cobbler's wife is the worst shod." " She goeth
broken shoone and torne hoses," says a mediæval
bard, " but," as may be expected from the general
unaccountableness of such matters, " Who is worse
shod than the shoemaker's wife, With shops full of
new shooes all the days of her life ? " Cobblers
pursue a steady and somewhat monotonous business
which seems to favour reflection, and the followers
of the craft have supplied from their ranks not a few
famous men. It will be remembered, however, how in
one case a rebuke became necessary, when the cobbler
in question criticised adversely a shoe-latchet in one
of the pictures of Apelles. The great painter accepted
the criticism and repainted the fastening, whereupon
the critic extended his self-imposed functions, and
objected to the drawing of the foot. Apelles felt
the time had come to put down his own foot, and
advised the cobbler to stick to his trade. The
ancient proverb that this little incident evoked has
its modern counterpart in the saying, " Let the cobbler
stick to his last," a proverb as valuable to-day as it was

of service in the studio of Apelles, when people will insist in talking about what they do not understand.

The brewer would find a dictum after his own heart in the old lines—

> " He that buys land buys many stones,
> He that buys flesh buys many bones,
> He that buys eggs buys many shells,
> But he that buys ale buys nothing else."

The kitchen realm has supplied a very expressive proverb in " The fat is in the fire," and such sayings as " Sweep before your own door "; " The pitcher goes oft to the well, but is broken at last "; " If you enjoy the fire you must put up with the smoke "; " A watched pot never boils " — all suggested by the service of the house ; while even the breakages so common in these regions are found, by those who do not have to pay for them, to have a bright side, for " Were it not for breakage there would be no potter's trade." It is so fatally easy to be generous at another person's expense.

Ready though people be to avail themselves at need of the skill of the physician, when they are in, shall we say, rude health, they regard him as very fair game for banter. " He that wants health wants all," but while they are enjoying this happy condition of rampant well-being they cry cheerfully enough, " Throw physic to the dogs, I'll none of it." * Another proverb, however, declares that " Physic always does good—if not to the patient then to the doctor." This is a bit of German sarcasm ; and this Spanish saying, " The earth covers the mistakes of the physician," is equally unappreciative and—dare one say it?—equally true.

---

* This side of the question may be seen somewhat forcibly put in John Halle's "Historick Expostulation against the beastlye Abuses of Chyrurgerie and Physicke," 1565.

The issues of life and death are not the physician's to control. One proverb on the faculty, " Physician, heal thyself," has a special interest, being quoted in one of His discourses by our Lord ; while another biblical reference, that of the woman who had spent all her living on doctors and was no better, but rather the worse, is sometimes rather maliciously quoted against our medical practitioners. A proverb for the patient's benefit will be found in " Much meat, many maladies," or in the statement that " Englishmen dig their graves with their teeth," a genial way of asserting that the Briton eats and drinks too much, which in many cases is probably true. He is also reminded that " If pills were pleasant they would need no gilding." *

The man of law has always been the subject of satire and his work derided, the difference between law and justice being often too conspicuous. A man who flourishes on the dissensions of others can scarcely expect to be a very popular member of society. Their clients are warned that " Better is a lean agreement than a fat lawsuit," and that " In a thousand pounds of law there is not an ounce of love." We are instructed to mark that no lawyer ever goes to law

---

* " Aske Medicus counsell ere medcine ye make,
　　And honour that man for necessitie's sake,
　　Though thousands hate physick because of the cost,
　　Yet thousands it helpeth that else should be lost."

" Five hundred pointes of good husbandrie," by Tusser, 1573. It will be noted that it is "ye make"; nowadays it would have to be written "ye take." The verse is from a section on " Good huswifelie physicke." The farmer's wife herself cultivates a goodly store of

　　" Cold herbes in her garden for agues that burne,
　　That ouer strong heate to good temper may turne,"

such as " Endiue and Suckerie," " Water of Fumentorie, liver to coole." " Conserve of the Barbarie, quinces as such, With Sirops that easeth the sickly so much," must also be provided, to say nothing of " Spinnage ynough."

on his own account, and as a warning to their victims we are invited to take note that "Lawyers' gowns are lined with the wilfulness of their clients." A thing may be entirely lawful and yet not honourable, technically right and wanting in all else. In Swaffam Church we find an epitaph commencing—

> " Here lieth one, believe it if you can,
> Who, tho' an attorney, was an honest man ;
> The gates of heaven shall open wide,
> But will be shut 'gainst all the tribe beside."

Another lawyer was the subject of the following couplet :—

> " Here lieth one who often lied before,
> But now he lies here he lies no more."

The ecclesiastic is the subject of many proverbs, and these mostly of an unfavourable character. It is said, " Woe to those preachers who listen not to themselves," and the caution is a very just one, but we have to realise that while the message from God to man is beyond all criticism, " we have this treasure in earthen vessels " that may be very much open to criticism, and yet not necessarily hypocrites, knaves, fools, as some would have us believe. " He who teaches religion without exemplifying it loses the advantage of its best argument," a criticism again most just. An epitaph that may be seen in Wallesley Churchyard, on the tomb of one of the vicars of the church, shows a lofty ideal fully attained :—

> " Led by Religion's bright and cheering ray,
> He taught the way to Heaven, and went that way ;
> And while he held the Christian life to view,
> He was himself the Christian that he drew."

It is not those who talk righteousness but those who live righteously who are the light of the world, while

those who are false to this incur a tremendous responsibility when they assume the position of guides
and bring discredit on their mission. The Spanish
proverbs are of especial bitterness: "Do by the friar
as he does by you"; "A proud friar requires a new
rope and a dry almond tree," in other words, deserves
hanging. Again we are warned that "A turn of the
key is better than the conscience of a friar"; what, then,
of honour, reputation, or possession is held of value
must be protected from his malign influence. Again,
we are warned to "Take care of an ox before, an ass
behind, and a monk on all sides." Their greed is
satirised in such popular sayings as these: "Priests
eat up the stew and then ask for the stewpan"; "The
covetous abbot for one loaf loses a hundred"; "The
abbot gives for the good of his soul what he cannot
eat." In like manner the Russians say, "Give the
priest all thou hast, and thou wilt have given them
nearly enough"; and the Italians declare that "Priests,
monks, nuns, and poultry never have enough"; while
in England we have the adage, "As crafty as a friar."
We are warned, too, that "It is not the cowl that makes
the monk." Appearances may be deceitful: "They
should be good men," writes Shakespeare in "Henry
VIII.," "their affairs are righteous; but all hoods make
not monks." It was in mediæval England a common
expression, "The bishop hath blessed it," when the food
was burnt in preparation; a reminder of the days of
fiery persecution. Tyndale, for instance, writes in his
"Obedyence of a Chrystene Man," "When a thynge
speadeth not well we borow speache and say, 'The
byshope hath blessed it,' because that nothynge
speadeth well that they medyll withall. If the
podech be burned or the meate over rosted, we
say, 'The byshope has put his fote in the potte,'
because the byshoppes burn who they list and whoe-

soever displeaseth them." The Marian persecutions appear to us mere ancient history, but they were real enough when this sarcasm on the episcopal benediction passed from mouth to mouth.

The French attack the craftiness that has too often been a characteristic of the ecclesiastic in the saying: "Le renard prêche aux poules"; while in England we find the adages, "Reynard is reynard still, though in a cowl," and "When the fox preacheth then beware of your geese," and to these many other sayings of like import might be added.

The miller was the target for considerable adverse comment. An epitaph in Calne churchyard over one of the fraternity reads—

> "God worketh wonders now and then,
> Here lies a miller, and an honest man,"

and this would appear to be about the popular view of the craft. Thus Chaucer writes of his "Wel cowde he stele, and tollen thries," and he describes him as having "a thomb of golde," in itself a proverbial expression. The miller tests the fineness of the grinding by taking up a portion of the meal and rubbing it between his thumb and fingers, in itself a most harmless and necessary operation. Another well-known proverb is, "All is grist that comes to his mill," good or bad, all is used and turned to advantage; while an Italian proverb declares that "Millers are the last to die of famine"—the process of grinding the corn of other people leading, it is suggested, to a considerable quantity being transferred from the bag of the farmer to the bin of the miller, no question of mutual consent arising.

Army service suggested as a proverb based on experience and observation, "The blood of the common soldier makes the glory of the general," an adage not yet out of date; while such proverbs as, "Two strings to one's bow," "To draw the long bow," and "A fool's bolt is soon shot"* recall the days when archery was the national defence and recreation. To "Draw not your bow till your arrow is fixed," is another old English proverb; it is tantamount to another wise saw, "Look before you leap."

The pursuit of the angler appears to those not of the craft so dreary and monotonous that one hesitates to call it a recreation. It is at least an excellent school for patience and such virtues as may be taught by hope deferred. The French say, "Still he fishes, that catcheth one"; while an English proverb bluntly declares that "An angler eats more than he gets." For everything in this world a price has to be paid, and the fisherman is warned that "He who would catch fish must not mind a wetting." A very familiar saying that derives its inspiration from the pursuit of the fisherman is that "All is fish that comes to the net," a parallel saying to the one that has just been referred to concerning the grist of the miller.

The innings of the cricketer supplies the saying, "Off his own bat," to describe the results in any direction achieved by a man's own exertions, while the chess-player's board suggests the moral, "At the end of the game the king and the pawn go into the same bag," one lot befalls all; and to this we may add, "The die is cast," when the irrevocable step is taken—

"I have set my life upon the cast
And I will stand the hazard of the die."—"Richard III."

---

* In Shakespeare's "Henry V." we read how the Constable of France and the Duke of Orleans thus bandied proverbs : " *Orl.* Ill will never said well. *Con.* I will cap that proverb with—there is flattery in friendship. *Orl.* And I will take that up with—give the devil his due. You are the better at proverbs, by how much ?—a fool's bolt is soon shot."

K

The busy pursuits and pleasant recreations of life would doubtless yield much more material for the searcher after proverb-lore thereon. We are content but to indicate something of the interest that the subject may be made to evolve, and leave it to the reader to amplify, if he so will.

Maxims that apply equally to all callings are to be found in abundance. Of these we may instance, as examples: "A useful trade is a mine of gold," "Sell not thy conscience with thy goods," "He that thinks his place below him will certainly be below his place," "Mind what you do and how you do it." To these we would add, "Nothing is little," a proverb of far-reaching significance and deep import; for we need at times to consider how, from actions small in themselves, from a few words hastily spoken, from the pressure of a hand when hearts are breaking, from the neglect of a little duty or precaution, how great may be the outcome.

Personal proverbs are very numerous: a list of over a hundred could readily be compiled. Many of these we cannot now really attribute to any particular individual. They often refer to some local circumstance, some story that has been forgotten. In some cases, as in "Hobson's choice" or "the case is altered, quoth Plowden," we are dealing with real individuals; in other cases we may reasonably assume that we are, though we cannot prove it; while, in a third section, the matter is considerably more doubtful. Proverbs, for instance, that deal only with Christian names probably do not allude to any particular individual, and it may be assumed that these names are there to give a concrete realism such as the rustic loves, and are of no more definite existence than "Tom, Dick, and Harry," or "Tag, Rag, and Bobtail"—all representative of the units forming some gathering. In some cases it is a passing skit on some local character who has laid himself open in some way; while in others, such as " Madam Parnell, crack the nut and eat the kernel," or " Mock not, quoth Mumford," the things owe all the brilliancy they possess to the attraction of rhyme or alliteration. The " Jack Sprat, who could eat no fat " was doubtless a myth, created to gratify the poetic instincts of the creator of the character. The well-known nursery characters, " Jack and Jill, who went up the hill " supply, no doubt, another illustration. It would be quite hopeless to search for their baptismal registers. " As wise as the Mayor of Banbury " is an example of a local proverb. These civic authorities were often made the butt of a good deal of banter. What particular mayor was thus honoured it is, of course, impossible to determine; his individuality has been absorbed in his mayoral dignity. Small local jealousies between one village or town and a neighbouring one are often responsible for this sort of thing, the provincial mind loving to score over the people in the next parish or the next county.

Where no real option is given to a person the proverb " Hobson's choice " is suggested. One Tobias Hobson was an innkeeper and carrier at Cambridge, and a man of considerable local influence. He was said to be the first man in England that made a business of letting out horses for hire. However this may be, his custom, a custom that supplies the material for the adage, was that when anyone wanted a horse he was led into the stables, where some forty animals were ready for use, but the inexorable rule was that there should be no picking and choosing, a necessity being laid upon the customer that he took the horse which stood nearest the stable door. He had Hobson's choice and no other. This procedure placed all on an equal level and ensured a rough justice for the horses themselves, as the last horse entering from a journey was put at the far end and was only again liable for service when all the others had first done their turn.

"The case is altered, quoth Plowden," was a very popular adage with our ancestors, and especially in Shropshire. Edmund Plowden was an eminent lawyer in the reign of Queen Elizabeth, born at Plowden, a little village in Shropshire. The following circumstance is said to have given birth to the adage :—A neighbour asked him what remedy he had in law against a person whose hogs had broken into his field, and he was assured that the law would amply protect his rights. Whereupon the farmer replied that they were his (Plowden's) hogs. "Nay then, neighbour," quoth Plowden, "the case is altered." We learn hereby that it is hardly well for a man to be both defendant and judge, but it is due to Plowden's memory to add that in choosing the name of some lawyer to tack on to the proverb they merely took the name of one exceptionally well known. He was by a distinguished contemporary writer described as "A man second to none in his profession for honour and integrity." Plowden or no Plowden, the adage points to the duty of doing as we would be done by, and is a fair satire on the general readiness of lawyers to argue on either side at short notice, and to take very special care of "number one."

The old saying, "As coy as Croker's mare," may refer to some incident of which all knowledge is now lost; but as we sometimes find it rendered, "As coy as a crocker's mare," it has been, with great reason, suggested that this crocker is simply a crock-dealer, a retailer of earthenware round the country, to whom the possession of a restive animal would mean the smashing up of his stock and his consequent ruin. In a play of the year 1566, where a widow of somewhat flippant mood appears, we are told that "Of auncient fathers she took no cure nor care, She was to them as koy as a croker's mare."

A proverb that has a curious history is, "Two heads are better than one, said Weymark." Three-fourths of this is of great antiquity, and, we may take it, rank in significance with "In the multitude of counsellors there is safety," and other proverbs of that type. Whence, then, came the added fourth, and why? One theory is that it is a mere accretion, but this probably everyone, except the broacher of the idea, will feel to be very unlikely. Weymark is a distinctly peculiar name, and there must surely be some allusion to some one so called. It has been suggested that we should read it as way-mark,* a mark to guide the traveller: that we should understand that two heads are better than one to guide us on our earthly journey, but in this case why the word "said"?

In the "Anglorum Speculum," A.D. 1684, we get on to firmer ground; we there read that "One Wiemark was called to account for saying the head of Sir Walter Raleigh (beheaded that day) would do very well on the shoulders of Sir Robert Naunton; and having alleged in his own justification that two heads were better than one, he was for the present dismissed. Afterwards Wiemark being, with other wealthy persons, called on for a subscription to St Paul's, first subscribed a hundred pounds at the Council Table, but was glad to double it after Mr Secretary had told him two heads were better than one." We can readily understand that this jeering addition to the old saw

* Set thee up waymarks."—*Jeremiah* xxi. 21.
  " Is this the path of sanctity? Is this
  To stand a waymark in the road to bliss ?"
  —COWPER, *Progress of Error.*

quickly found acceptance when the incident got abroad.

The expression, " Backare, quoth Mortimer to his sow," has an extended range over our old literature, but its meaning is very enigmatical. Heywood writes, " Backare, quoth Mortimer to his sow, Went that sow back at that bidding, trow you?" In John Grange's " Golden Aphroditis" (1577) we read, " Yet wrested he so his effeminate bende to the siege of backwarde affection, that both trumpet and drumme sounded nothing but baccare, baccare." Wherever we find this baccare—in " Roister Doister," " The Dial," " Repentance of Mary Magdalene," the " Scourge of Folly," " Mydas," or elsewhere—its significance is always " Stand back." Its spelling is very variable.* Who Mortimer was, it is hopeless to conjecture, or on what occasion he found it necessary to curb the impatience of his sow.

The expression, " As wise as Dr Doddipol," is of sarcastic significance. The name of this doctor is spelt in many ways, but in all its variations the saying preserves its depreciatory character. Skelton in " Colin Clout" has Dr Daupatus and Doddypatis. Hoddypoule, Huddypeake, Dotypoll, Noddipole, are other readings one encounters in old plays and the like. In Fox's " Book of Martyrs" we have, "I will contemne these dastardly dotipoles." Latimer in his sermons used the plainest language. In preaching before King Edward, he said, " But some will say our curate is nought, an asshead, a dodipoll, a lacklatine," while in another of his discourses he breaks out, " Ye brainsicke fooles, ye hoddy-peakes, ye doddy poules." We may perhaps explain that these epithets were not applied to his audience ; they were words put by the preacher into

* In some cases it is " backer," as though the comparative, " more back."

the mouths of the Pharisees in their disgust at the
flocking of the common people to the teaching of the
Messiah. In the works of Sir Thomas More, 1557,
we find him declaring of something that, concerning
it, " a verye nodypoll nydyote might be ashamed." *

Sterne in " Tristram Shandy " is quite Latimeresque.
He writes : " Here, without staying for my reply, shall
I be called as many blockheads, numsculls, doddy-
poles, dunderheads." Thompson uses the expression
" doddering mast " in his description of a storm, while
Dryden writes of a rotting " doddar'd oke " falling
piecemeal to the ground. The idea all through is
clearly weakness, feebleness, physical or mental.

Another proverb, "Bate me an ace, quoth Bolton," has
a certain historic interest. A collection of proverbs was
presented by its compiler to Queen Elizabeth, with the
declaration that it contained every proverb in the English language. To test the matter, she asked if he had
this one, and he was obliged to confess that he had not.
Without the surname appended it may often be found
in various old authors ; in Beaumont and Fletcher's
" Prophetess," for instance, we find the passage, " Nor
bate ye an ace of a sound senator." We are told that
this Bolton was one of the courtiers in attendance on
Henry VIII., who, in card-playing with his Sovereign,
was discreet enough to beg to be allowed an ace, or
some such considerable advantage, that he might have
some little chance against so skilful a player. The
proverb was ordinarily used as an appeal for some
little advantage, or, ironically, as a hint to some one
whose statements were held to be a little beyond
credence to abate them somewhat.

It will readily be noted that most of these name-
proverbs are obsolete, but one of them, " What will Mrs

* " Nydyote " is really an idiot, even as " naddere " in old books is really
an adder.

Grundy say?" is still in use. It is found in the old play of "Speed the Plough," and was thence transported into general service. A Mrs Ashfield was there represented as always in terror of the opinion of this old lady, until at length her husband, a bluff old farmer, can stand it no longer, and bursts out: "Be quiet, wool ye? Always ding, dinging Dame Grundy into my ears, What will Mrs Grundy say!" The influence of the old lady is yet strong in the land.

In the west of England we encounter the adage, "He will live as long as old Ross of Potterne." Potterne is a village near Devizes, and this venerable Ross was probably a genuine centenarian, though all clue to him is now lost. The proverb is sometimes rather unkindly amplified into, "Who lived till all the world was a-weary of him," a very unhappy state of things for all parties.

A proverb long current in Shropshire and the adjoining counties is, "Ahem! as Dick Smith said when he swallowed the dishcloth." The moral here clearly is that troubles should be borne bravely and with as little fuss as possible. Another old saw is, "My name is Twyford; I know nothing of the matter"—a statement that would mean, "I object to enquiry; I decline to be bothered." A sarcastic saying on pretentiousness is seen in, "Great doings at Gregory's; heated the oven twice for a custard." The futility of attempting to stop proceedings after they had got to a certain point was illustrated in the adage, "Nay, stay, quoth Stringer, when his neck was in the halter." One can imagine the depth of scorn that might be thrown into "Don't hurry, Hopkins," when fired off at some notorious laggard; but the legend goes that a certain, or uncertain, Hopkins gave a creditor a promissory-note, having previously written on it, "The said John Hopkins is not to be hurried in paying this amount." Of course, in all these explanations we have to wonder whether some incident led to the adage, or whether the process has been reversed—the popular saying, its real origin forgotten, having a fictitious explanation tacked on to it. "Credit is dead ; bad pay killed him," is a popular adage with those who believe in ready-money trans-actions *—a sentiment that the creditors of the late John Hopkins would readily appreciate.

Locality proverbs, like personal proverbs, are natur-ally more in vogue in the places named than of general usage, though some of them travel far outside their place of origin. Others of them, and those generally of a derisive cast, do not originate in the place itself, but are conferred on it by outsiders. "Go to Bath," for instance, was a reference to the fact that lunatics used to be sent there for the benefit of its waters, and the inference was that the person addressed was a fit subject for a stay there. Had the proverb origi-nated in the city, it would have been "Come to Bath." "Cheshire bred, strong in the arm, weak in the head," is a saying that scarcely originated in that county. Another county saying is, "You were born at Hog's-Norton." This was a reproof to a boorish person, but there is no such place ; the village referred to is that of Hock-Norton, in Oxfordshire, rustic humour readily making the change of spelling to fit it for its purpose. Such saws as, "Grantham gruel, nine grits and a bucket of water," or "Like Banbury tinkers, that mend one hole and make three," we may be sure did not originate in the places designated. If the adage be complimen-

---

* "Many, when a thing was lent them, reckoned it to be found, and put them to trouble that helped them. Till he hath received he will kiss a man's hand ; and for his neighbour's money he will speak submissively : but when he should repay he will prolong the time, and return words of grief, and complain of the time."—*Ecclesiasticus*, B.C. 200.

An old English proverb declares that "Lent seems short to him that borrows money to be paid at Easter."

tary, it probably arose in the place, as, for instance, " True as Coventry blue," an allusion to an excellent dye for which the town was noted ; or " Diamond cut diamond, I am Yorkshire too," a testimony to the Yorkshireman's brilliancy and keenness.

The allusion is sometimes topographical. Thus, " Crooked as Crawley brook" is suggested by a little stream in Bedfordshire that has a course of twenty miles between two points that are actually five miles apart. " When Dudman and Ramhead meet "—in a word, never. These are two conspicuous headlands in Cornwall, miles apart. In Norfolk is a saying, " Arrested by the bailiff of Marshland," when the un-acclimatised stranger succumbs to the ague, the product of the local aqueous surroundings.

Rustic humour is responsible for the somewhat blunt point of many of these local sayings. A play upon words is very popular. Thus Beggar's Bush, near Huntingdon, suggests that a man " Goes home by Beggar's Bush" when his means are dwindling away. " On the high road to Needham," a place in Suffolk, is of similar import, the idea of need being the point of the adage. Tusser, for instance, writes :

" Toiling much and spoiling more, great charge smal gains or none,
Soon sets thine host at Needham's shore, to craue the begger's bone."

On the contrary, if he would prosper, let him " Set up shop on the Goodwin sands," a most unpromising locality, one would imagine, until we realise that the saw-maker means " good win." " As plain as the Dunstable road" sounds straightforward enough, especially when we recall that Dunstable is on Watling Street, one of the noble main roads of the Romans ; but the humour (save the mark!) of the thing is in the play

on the idea of "dunce." In "Redgauntlet" we read :
"If this is not plain speaking, there is no such place
as downright Dunstable"—*i.e.* the meaning of the remark is so plain that even a mere fool, the veriest
dunce, could not fail to grasp it.

In Lincolnshire, when anyone is not over - acute,
they delicately say, "He was born at Little Wittham,"
hence the cause of his having so little wit : the actual
spelling is Witham. On the decease of anyone it is
said, "He is gone to Deadham." In Sussex, if a man
were slow over his work, they would say, "He is none
of Hastings," the idea of haste being somehow involved.
The dwellers in the little town of Ware were pleased
to say that it was "worth all London." Fuller, who
wrote a delightful folio on the counties of England,
says : "This, I assure you, is a masterpiece of the
vulgar wits in this county, wherewith they endeavour to
amuse travellers. The fallacy lieth in the homonymy
of Ware, here not taken for that town so named, but
appellatively for all vendible commodities." In the
fen districts the frogs are called "Cambridgeshire
nightingales." At night, and especially before rain,
the frogs make a tremendous croaking. At Ripley,
in Surrey, where there is a pond near the village, we
have heard them called "The town band."

To be "stabbed with a Bridport dagger" was a
delicate way of saying that a man had been hanged.
The best hemp used to be grown round this Dorset-
shire town, and the place was famous for its manufacture of rope ; in fact, an ancient statute was long
in force requiring that the cables for the royal navy
should be made there.

To be "As thin as Banbury cheese" was a favourite
simile with our ancestors. Bardolph, it will be recalled,
in the "Merry Wives of Windsor," compares Slender to
a Banbury cheese. In "Jack Drum's Entertainment,"

1601, we find: "Put off your cloathes and you are like a Banbury cheese, nothing but paring"; while, in a pamphlet issued in 1664, on "The Sad Condition of the Clergy," we read, "Our lands and glebes are clipped and pared to become as thin as Banbury Cheese."* Another cheese that became proverbial was that of Suffolk. It was locally called "Bang" or "Thump."

> "Unrivall'd stands thy county cheese, O Giles!
> Whose very name alone engenders smiles,
> Whose fame abroad by every tongue is spoke,
> The well-known butt of many a flinty joke;
> Its name derision and reproach pursue,
> And strangers tell of three times skimm'd sky-blue."
> —*Blomfield.*

"Hunger will break through stone walls, or anything but Suffolk cheese," was one depreciating proverb, and Mowbray says that "It is only fit to be cut up for gate-latches, a use to which it is often applied." Other suggestions for its use are the making of millstones or grindstones or the wheels of barrows. The mention of a wheelbarrow reminds us of the saying, "A Coggleshall job." The residents in Coggleshall were the butts of the country round, and one of the tales against them is that a mad dog running through the place snapped at a barrow, and the people, fearing it might go mad as well, chained it up in a stable till they saw how things would go with it. "The wise men of Gotham," in Nottinghamshire, were similarly made the victims of many stories reflecting on their sagacity. A Gothamite, Andrew Boyde, wrote the "Menye Tales of the Wise Men of Gotham," wherein many of the follies that have been fathered on them are duly set forth. Men

---

* This thinness would appear to have been of bulk, not of quality. "Some preferre Cheshire Cheese, and others also commend the cheese of other countries; but Banbury Cheese shall goe for my money."— COGAN'S *Haven of Health*, 1612.

in all ages have made themselves merry with singling
out some place as the special seat of stupidity; thus
the Phrygians were accounted the fools of all Asia,
and the anvil for other men's wits to work upon.
The men of Gotham were so enamoured of the singing
of a cuckoo, we are told, that a number of them joined
hands round the hawthorn bush in which it was perched
to prevent its escape; while, on another occasion, they
endeavoured to divert the course of their river by
putting a line of hurdles across.

Local products sometimes figure in these proverbs:
thus "a Yarmouth capon" is a bloater,* and "Col-
chester beef" is a dish of the sprats that are caught
abundantly in that neighbourhood, while the language
of "Billingsgate" is a local growth that has attained
to proverbial fame. Dryden refers to it in the line,
"Parnassus spoke the cant of Billingsgate."

When a man of Newcastle-on-Tyne suspected his
companion of anything doubtful he would say, "Let's
have no Gateshead," marking the popular local opinion
of the folks in the sister town—a case of "the pot
calling the kettle black," and no doubt duly resented
by a Gateshead sarcasm of equal strength.

The "fair maids of Suffolk" and the "Lancashire
beauties"† were recognised, by their respective counties
at least, as worthy of proverbial recognition for their
special charm; while the men of Essex, doubtless
unfairly, were dubbed "As valiant as an Essex lion,"
these lions being the calves for which this county is
famous. "As wise as a Waltham calf" was another
ironical reference to the Essex folk. In a book

* "Few capons, save what have more fins than feathers, are bred
in Yarmouth. But to countenance this expression, I understand that
the Italian Friers, when disposed to eat flesh on Fridays, call a capon
'piscem e corte,' a fish of the coop."—*Fuller.*

† A Doctor of Divinity, fearing, we may presume, that such high
praise might turn a head here and there, improved the occasion for

written in 1566 we find a man called in to mediate between man and wife declaring—

"Ye will me to a thanklesse office heere,
And a busy officer I may appeare,
And Jack out of office she may bid me walke,
And thinke me as wise as Waltam's calf to talke."*

In "Dyet's Dry Dinner," 1599, after dispraise of veal as an article of food, the author says that "Essex calves the proverb praiseth, and some are of the mind that Waltome calfe was also that countrey man."

A common proverb in Yorkshire is, "A Scarborough warning," equivalent to "a word and a blow and a blow first." Several explanations have been given of this adage. One explanation was that if ships passed the castle without saluting it a shot was fired into them, but in an old ballad another theory is started—

"This term, Scarborow warning, grew, some say,
By hasting hanging for rank robbery theare,
Who that was met, but suspect in that way,
Strait he was trust up, whatever he were."

We need scarcely point out that when several reasons are given for anything it is an indication that nothing very satisfactory is forthcoming.

That "Tenterden Steeple is the cause of the Goodwin Sands" is a proverb that was at one time often brought forth when any ridiculous cause was assigned as an explanation of anything. We have already

the benefit of these ladies—"I believe that the God of Nature, having given fair complection to the Women in this County, Art may spare her pains in endeavouring to better them. But let the Females of this County know that, though in the Old Testament express notice be taken of the beauty of many Women—Sarah, Rebekah, Rachael, Abigail, Thamar, Abishag, Esther—yet in the New Testament no mention is made at all of the fairness of any Woman, not because they wanted, but because Grace is chief Gospel-beauty, and this is far better than skin-deep Fairness."

* A proverb of like import is this, "He talks in the bear-garden tongue."

seen how very colloquial Bishop Latimer could be on occasion, and he tells us that a "Mr Moore was once sent with commission into Kent to try out, if it might be, what was the cause of Goodwin's Sands which had stopped up Sandwich Haven. Thither cometh Mr Moore, and calleth all the country before him, such as were thought to be men of experience, and men that could of likelihood best satisfy him of the matter. Among the rest came one in before him, an old man with a white head, and one that was thought to be little less than a hundred years old. When Mr Moore saw this aged man he called him unto him and said, Father, tell me, if you can, what is the cause of the great arising of the sand here about this harbour, which stops it up, so that no ships can arrive here. You are the oldest man I can espy in all the company, so that if any man can tell the cause of it you in all likelihood can say most of it. Yea, forsooth, good Mr Moore, quoth the old man, for I am well-nigh one hundred years old, and no man in this company anywhere near my age. Well then, quoth Mr Moore, how say you to this matter, what think you to be the cause? Forsooth, sir, I think that Tenterden Steeple is the cause of Goodwin's Sands. I remember the building of Tenterden Steeple, and before that was in building there was no manner of talking of any flats or sands that stopped up the haven, and therefore I think that the Tenterden Steeple is the cause of the decay and destroying of Sandwich Haven." This was the tale as the bishop told it, and the explanation seems particularly far-fetched; but one story is good until another is told, and though this as it stands supplied the material for the proverb, there is really a supplement. Time out of mind money was constantly collected to fence the eastern shore of Kent against the

inroads of the sea, and such sums were deposited in
the hands of the Bishop of Rochester. For many
years, the work being so well done, no irruption took
place, and the bishop diverted some of the money
to the building of a steeple to Tenterden Church.
People dwelt in a false security, and the dykes were
gradually growing weaker, until at last the catastrophe came. The old man's tale was quite rational,
had he been allowed to finish it, but the audience,
impatient of his garrulousness, and ready for a laugh
at his expense, did not give him an opportunity to
do so. It was not the ignorance of the speaker but
the impatience of the auditors that supplies the true
moral of the story.

Any extended reference to old collections of proverbs, to county histories, to old plays, and such-like
sources of information would readily yield a large
harvest of these local allusions, but enough has been
brought forward to illustrate the nature of them, and
for our purpose a specimen twenty is as satisfying
as an illustrative hundred.

CHAPTER VI

THE animal life around him has always been an object of interest to man. Some creatures, like the horse, the dog, or the camel, he has trained to minister to his wants—for man is at his lowest level of sympathy and intelligence, the lowest type of savage, when we find him absolutely alone—while others, like the fox or the wolf, have necessarily become of concern to him in their power of molestation, disturbing his peace and thwarting his interests. In either case the very varying nature of the animals amidst which he dwelt has attracted his notice, since the fidelity of the dog, for example, the cunning of the fox, the sagacity of the elephant, could not fail to impress themselves upon his mind. Far away in the mist of a great antiquity the Old Testament has numerous allusions to the lessons that may be derived from the observation of

L

animals, while Æsop and many other writers have made the various creatures the subject of their writings and evolved lessons for the benefit of mankind from their varying dispositions. We are, therefore, entirely prepared to find that in proverb-lore also the animal kingdom has been largely drawn upon, and we propose to give some few examples of this.

We are told that "It is a good horse that never stumbles," a proverb that reminds us to make allowance for others and to take heed to ourselves. We are warned, too, that "Boisterous horse must have boisterous bridle," that those who incline to resist authority have no cause for complaint if the hand of authority press somewhat hardly upon them. A fairly analogous adage is that "Mettle is dangerous in a blind horse." That "A horse is neither better nor worse for his trappings" teaches us to look below the surface in forming our judgments, and then again there is the well-known and excellent warning that "One may take a horse to the water but you cannot make him drink," a hint that one cannot always have one's own way, and that the co-operation of the other party in the arrangement is an essential point. To "Get upon the high horse" is to take up a needlessly dignified position, and make oneself somewhat unpleasant in the process; while "Putting money on the wrong horse," a saw suggested by the race-course, implies that one has supported the wrong side and helped on, through folly or ignorance, a matter that we had much better have left alone.* The caution, "Do not lash a willing

---

* This is sometimes rendered "saddling the wrong horse." Cicero, before the Christian era, thus quoted it. His writings and orations teem with proverbs—the foolishness of trying to kill two birds with one stone, the undignified spectacle of a tempest in the classic equivalent of a tea-cup, the statement that while there is life there is hope, and many other such adages familiar to ourselves being introduced.

horse," is often necessary, and the hopelessness of "Flogging a dead horse," endeavouring to infuse life into a defunct cause, sometimes needs a reminder; while the "Working for a dead horse" is almost as disheartening a process. The Spaniards in such a case say, "When the money is paid the arms are broken."

That "One must not look a gift-horse in the mouth" is a lesson in the proprieties of immense antiquity; we find it, for instance, in the writings of St Jerome in the fourth century. A mediæval writer tells us that "A gyuen hors may not be loked in the tethe." Rabelais says it must not, and the author of "Hudibras" says it must not; in fact there is an abundance of testimony to this effect, extending over centuries. The Frenchman says, "A cheval donné il ne faut pas regarder aux dens"; the Portuguese says, "Cavallo dado nao se repara a idade"; and the Spaniard says, "Caval donato non guardar in bocca"; and all over the world we find this delicacy of feeling advocated. In the proverb, "He is a proud horse that will not carry his own provender," we have a good lesson quaintly put. In Puttenham's "Arte of Englishe Poesie," 1589, we are instructed that "When we misplace our wordes and set that before which should be behind, we call it in English proverbe, 'The cart before the horse.'" The unequal way in which Fortune appears to work is borne home to us in the strong, yet scarcely too strong, statement that "One man may steal a horse while another may not look over the gate"; or, as Lily, in his "Endimion," hath it, "For as some man may better steale a horse than another looke over a hedge." In the "Paradise of Daynty Devices," 1578, we find this couplet—

> "To whom of old this proverbe well it serves,
> While grasse doth growe the silly horse he sterves."

In the more modern guise this is "While the grass is growing the steed is starving." It may at first sight appear a little hard to brand the horse as silly, since he can in no way be held responsible for the backward condition of the meadow, but we must remind our readers that "silly" is one of the words that has greatly changed its significance—it originally meant harmless or innocent.

"Money," we are told, "will make the mare to go," and the finding of "a mare's nest" is a feat that is still now and then performed.

> "Why doest thou laugh?
> What mare's nest hast thou found?"
> —BEAUMONT AND FLETCHER, *Bonduca.*

In France it is the rabbit's nest, "nid le lapin," that people sometimes discover.

It is a curious thing that the fidelity and affection of the dog get little or no recognition in proverb-lore. This may possibly arise from the fact that in the East, the original source of many of our proverbs, the dog is held in no esteem. He is an outcast, the scavenger of the streets. "Him that dieth in the city shall the dogs eat"; and "Is thy servant a dog that he should do this thing?" was the indignant outburst of Hazael. In classic days it was said of a morose, ill-conditioned person, "A black dog has walked over him," and at the present day such a person is said to have "the black dog on his back." The dog of the fabulist that dropped the substance for the shadow was held up as a warning in his greed and folly, and "to dog" a person is not to lavish canine affection on them by any means; while a favourite piece of nursery teaching was, and perhaps still is, that "Dogs delight to bark and bite." "Every dog," we are told, "has his day," and "Love

me, love my dog," has sometimes been made a
stipulation. Latimer puts it more pleasantly, "Whosoever loveth me loveth my hound"—from his regard
for me he will for my sake look kindly on what he
knows to be dear to me.

To him who is hungry any food is welcome—"À
la faim il n'y a point de mauvais pain," and therefore "Hungry dogs will eat dirty pudding." "Let
sleeping dogs lie" is excellent counsel ; the precept
is not in the interest of the sleepers but of those
injudicious enough to disturb their slumbers. "It is
nought goode," writes Chaucer in his "Troylus and
Cryseyde," "a sleping hound to wake," and again in the
"Frankeleine's Tale," "Wyf, quod he, lat slepen that is
stille"; while Shakespeare writes, in "Henry VIII.":—

> "This butcher's cur is venom-mouth'd, and I
> Have not the power to muzzle him ; therefore best
> Not wake him in his slumber."

In Italy and Germany we have the same proverb, but
it becomes in France "N'as tu pas tort de reveiller
le chat qui dort," a much less formidable proceeding ;
and in Spain we find the variant, "When sorrow is
asleep do not awaken it." Another Spanish proverb,
and one of excellent wisdom, is "Though your blood-
hound be gentle do not bite him on the lip." It is,
by the way, remarkable how gentle big dogs are, mas-
tiffs, retrievers, Newfoundlands, and the like, while
being mauled and hauled by small children. Little
Bessie, aged five, might venture to any extent on
her great companion's forbearance and magnanimity,
while we, reader, must exercise much more discretion.

"Give a dog a bad name and then you may as
well hang him"* is a true and very oft-quoted adage.

* "Give a dog an ill name and hang him, and it may be added, if
you give a man, or race of men, an ill name, they are very likely to

One less well known is " He that would hang his dog gives out first that he is mad." * He who is about to do something dubious first bethinks himself of some plausible excuse that appears to justify his action, and when this is accepted he is free from all fear of interference. The Greeks say that " He who keeps another man's dog shall have nothing left but the line." If he endeavour to keep it dishonestly — in fact, to become a dog-stealer—he cannot complain if such care as he has bestowed comes to nought and nothing is left to him but the cord and the food-bill. One old commentator would tell us that the meaning is that " He who bestows a benefit upon an ungrateful person loses his cost." This is a common enough experience, but it scarcely appears to be a moral springing from this proverb. The dog, stolen, tied up, amongst strangers, has no particular reason to feel grateful ! The following proverb, " Wash the dog and comb the dog, still the dog remains the dog," indicates that externals do not affect the real nature.

Other doggy sayings are : " Two dogs agree not well over one bone," " Brawling curs have torn ears," " A scalded dog dreads cold water." Those who, having a good staff of assistants, find that much of the burden and responsibility yet weighs on them, will appreciate the point of the adage, " What, keep a dog, and bark myself ? " a proceeding that certainly seems unreasonable. The Turks have a happy proverb that " The dog barks, but the caravan passes," its fussy interference being simply ignored. The Spaniards declare,

do something that deserves hanging."—WALTER SCOTT, *Guy Mannering*. The French say, " Le bruit pend l'homme."
 " *Clown*. Oh, Maister, you are half-hanged !
 " *Nobody*. Hanged. Why, man ?
 " *Clown*. Because you have an ill name : a man had almost as good serve no master as serve you."—" Nobody and Somebody," 1606.
 * " Qui veut noyer son chien, l'accuse de rage."

in like manner, that "More are threatened than are stabbed," while the Dutch with equal wisdom advise us that "No one dies of threats." The Danes very happily warn us against judging too hastily in the hint that "An honest man is none the worse because a dog barks at him."

The cat takes its place in our proverb-literature. The "Kilkenny cats" that fought so desperately have often been quoted as a warning to warring factions, and tenacity of purpose gone mad and self-destructive. The old belief that a cat has nine lives has also got embalmed in an adage, and the question will be recalled, in "Romeo and Juliet," "What wouldst thou have with me?" the reply being, "Good king of cats, nothing but one of your nine lives."* Yet "Care," we are told, "will kill a cat." While we may accept this saw on its moral side, and learn from it a lesson against despondency, its zoological side is open to grave question. A cat dying of anxiety may fairly be bracketted off with the broken-hearted oyster crossed in love. The "Grinning like a Cheshire cat," in a continual state of mirthful good humour, suggests a quite opposite phrase of feline nature. To "let the cat out of the bag" is another old saying that will at once occur to the reader; a less known, but very good one, Scotch in its birth, is, "He that puts the cat in the pock kens best how to tak' her oot." Another good proverb of like nature is, "Who will carry the cat to the water?"—*i.e.* who will endeavour to carry the plan through, undeterred by the difficulty of its accomplishment? To be made "a catspaw of" is also a very expressive saying; it arose from

---

* A school-boy, writing an essay on the cat, put down that it was said to have nine lives, but he added that he did not now need them, because of Christianity. This, quaint as it is, has a great truth wrapped up in it—the love of mercy, including kindness to animals, that is one of the points of the teaching of Christ.

the old fable of the monkey using the cat's paw instead of his own to rake out chestnuts from the glowing embers. To live "a cat-and-dog life" is to lead such an existence of strife and snarl as one ordinarily sees in the aversion felt by these two animals for each other. The old saw, "A cat may look at a king," has, too, ordinarily been used as an impertinence.* In France its equivalent is "Un chien regarde bien l'évêque."

> "Where window is open cat maketh a fray,
>   Yet wilde cat with two legs is worse, by my fay." †

The cat utilised as an excuse for other people's shortcomings has always been a favourite subject. Thus—"How can the cat help it if the maid be a fool?" On the other hand, the cat's larcenous propensities must be reckoned with, so we have the disheartening thought for the thrifty housekeeper, "What the good wife spares the cat eats," and "It's easy learning the cat the way to the churn." The Arabs say, "He trusted the keys of the pigeon-house to the cat," but on the other hand, "Honest is the cat when the meat is on the hook." Of him who declines to be turned aside by trifles, the Scottish proverb may be quoted, "He's ower auld a cat to draw a strae before." The man whose affairs, big and little, run smoothly, and whose ventures, however speculative they may be, are successful, may be said to be "Like a cat, he always falls on his feet." This power of falling on her feet from any height is a most valuable gift for pussy, and saves her from many a mishap.

The cat has her enthusiastic admirers, but as a friend of man she is ordinarily held in no great

---

* John Dunton, for instance, wrote in the year 1705, "A cat may look on a Queen, or a Satyr on her present Majesty."

† Tusser. "Fray" may be taken as foray, while "fay" is faith—*i.e.* by my faith.

esteem. "Make much of the cat, and she will fly in your face." She is too commonly treacherous, selfish, and unreliable. We have more than once seen, and our experience cannot be unique, a cat fondled and stroked and made much of, suddenly savagely bite or scratch the hand that has been caressing it.

Pussy as a follower of the chase has suggested the proverb, "The cat that is always crying catches nothing," and the better known saw, "A cat in mittens catches no mice." "Fain would the cat fish eat, but she's loath her feet to wet"; and in Chaucer's "House of Fame" we find an interesting reference to this—

> "Ye be like the slepie cat
> That would have fish ; but wost thou what ?
> He will nothing weate his clawes."

The "slepie cat," dormant on the hearth-rug, is, of course, like its confrères of the jungle, a nocturnal animal, and in the hours of darkness often becomes a little more wakeful than is altogether appreciated. As a songster of the night, instead of receiving merely barren compliments on its performance, it often gets the much more tangible reward of a boot, lump of coal, cake of soap, or such-like little token of appreciation as the auditor may find most readily come to hand.

A very venerable proverb indeed tells us that "The ass and his master do not always think alike." Phædrus, living nearly nineteen hundred years ago, had a fable in his collection to illustrate this. He pictures to us a man resting by the road-side, and his ass grazing near him. The man, suddenly catching sight of an advancing enemy, says that they must at once decamp that they be not captured, whereupon the donkey asks, "Will they clap on me a double load?" and the man can only reply that he does not suppose that they will. "Then," said the donkey, "what matters it to me to whom I belong?"

"He that makes himself an ass must not mind if men ride him," truly says the old English proverb, and another is like unto it, "When all men say you are an ass it is time to bray." It is no less true that "If an ass goes travelling he will not come back a horse." The locality changes, but under every sky the traveller remains much as he started. The ancient Romans declared that "One ass rubs another," a lesson in mutual help. When a coward boasts what great things he will do, or a fool assumes the philosopher, "An ass in a lion's skin" is suggested—from the fable that an ass once decking himself in the skin of the lion, was so elated at the terror he created that he could not forbear braying his delight, a performance which entirely altered the whole complexion of things and the animal stood revealed, the mere ass that he really was.* "The ass is wagging his ears" is a hit at those who, understanding little or nothing of the matter in question, assume a grave demeanour and an attitude of close attention. Two German proverbs may be quoted here, as they are both good: "The ass dreams of thistles," and "One ass nicknames another, Long-ears." The Spaniards have a very expressive adage, "The ass knows well in whose face he brays," a warning against too great a familiarity with unsuitable companions, or we shall infallibly find ourselves exposed to great liberties and a free-and-easy "Hail fellow, well met" manner that give us cause for repentance.

The Arabs have a happy reflection on those who, when we are in an intricate business, raise additional

---

* The Germans vary this into, "Wenn der Esel auch eine Löwenhaut trägt, die Ohren gucken vor"—"Even when the donkey wears the lion's skin its ears peep out and betray it."

difficulties instead of smoothing our path, " A narrow
lane and the ass kicking."

A lesson of contentment is found in this homely saw :
" Better the head of an ass than tail of a horse "—to
be valued in a low position is far preferable to being
the fag-end of a higher. We once heard a man of
some considerable influence in a country town declare
that he was there a whale amongst the minnows, but
that if he moved to the metropolis, as his family were
desiring him to do, he should be but a minnow amongst
the whales. Such a man would entirely appreciate this
proverb. Another lesson of very similar import is seen
in this : " Better an ass that carries us than a horse that
throws us." A very quaint and shrewd utterance is :
" Now I have got a donkey, everyone says, Good
morning, John." Things are looking up, and friends
are beginning to come in.* Finally, the Spanish
caution : " He who wants an animal without fault
may go afoot," that particular kind not often coming
into the market.

The Sermon on the Mount and other discourses of
our Lord afford us numerous examples of the national
Jewish proverbs.† " Sufficient unto the day is the evil
thereof," is one illustration of this kind of popular folk-
lore, and "Cast not your pearls before swine," is another;
and in the old Greek proverb, " A scorpion for a perch,"
we have practically, " If he asks a fish will he give him
a serpent ? "

The Spaniards say, " Echar magaritas a puerco s,"

---

* " As long as I am riche reputed
    With solemn voyce I am saluted ;
    But wealthe away once worne,
    Not one wyll say ' Good morne.' "
                —*Harleian MS., sixteenth century.*

† " Jesus did vouchsafe to aunswere by a riddle and a prouerbiall saying : teaching that it was an other manier of kyngdome whereof the
prophetes had spoken."—*Udall.*

and this throwing of pearls before swine re-appears in English proverb-lore, and, indeed, much further afield.

To "buy a pig in a poke" is to make a purchase without knowing really what one is buying. The alliteration has, no doubt, given the saying an added popularity. In France it is, "acheter chat en poche," or "acheter le chat pour le lièvre," a cat being palmed off as a hare on the incautious purchaser. We see now, too, how a determination to see for oneself would "let the cat out of the bag," and expose the trickery of the proceeding.

When a man has heedlessly made a bad bargain he is said, ironically, to have "brought his pigs to a pretty market"—the advantageous sale of his pig being a very important matter to the country cottager, meaning the payment of his rent, the clearing of the score at the village shop, and his general rehabilitation in the ranks of the solvent.* The generally unsympathetic and unsociable nature of the pig and his human counterparts is expressed in such sayings as : " Feed a pig and you will have a hog," and " What can you expect from a hog but a grunt ? " while its " wallowing in the mire," and being well content to have it so,† has also been utilised as a warning.

A bit of homely advice, quaintly put, is found in this —" Do not drive black hogs at night." " Much cry and no wool " is the result of shearing swine, a hopeless task. The adage is often met with. In Fortescue's treatise on " Absolute and Limited Monarchy," written over four hundred years ago, we find a reference to " the man that scheryd his hogge, moche crye and no

---

* A quaint old English proverb warns us that " A hog upon trust grunts until he is paid for," a very discomposing habit.

† " For thilke verrei prouerbe befelde to him—The hound turnyde agen to his castyng, and a sowe to waischen in walewing in fenne."— 2 *Peter*, chap. ii. Wyclif's translation.

wull." In a book published in 1597 it runs: "Of the shearing of hogges there is great crie for so little wolle," and we find the saying again in "Hudibras" and many other books, and in old plays.

In "Hudibras," too, may be found the equally familiar expression, "wrong sow by the ear," a proverb of great antiquity that occurs frequently in the old dramas. We are told by some etymologists that the sow in question is not porcine at all, but is a large tub with handles. Sowsed meat is meat that has been in pickle in one of these sows. To have got the wrong sow (by the ear or handle for facility of moving) is to have brought the wrong vessel. To confirm this view they quote the old Latin proverb, "Pro amphora urceolus"—instead of the great amphora you have brought me a small pitcher. Either reading will serve the turn, and is of like significance in application — the warning against getting hold of an entirely wrong idea and hammering away at it.

To "cast sheep's eyes" on one is to snatch a hasty glance, looking askance with sheep-like timidity on some fair object whose regard has not been won or as yet appealed to. The idea that "One black sheep infects the flock and poisons all the rest" has, we need scarcely say, no warrant in actual fact, though, morally, a black sheep is a dangerous addition to any flock, a something to be promptly eliminated from regiment, workshop, school, or whatever other body he may be infecting or exposing to risk of contagion. A much more attractive adage is the well-known declaration, "God tempers the wind to the shorn lamb." The French say, "À brebis tondue Dieu mesure le vent," and the English proverb, as we find Herbert using it in 1640, is a repetition of this—"To a close-shorn sheep God gives wind by measure." This shearing process suggested eighteen hundred years ago, or possibly long before this,* the proverb, " Boni pastoris est tondere pecus, non deglubere" — " It is the duty of a good shepherd to shear his sheep, not to skin them." This note of warning is repeated in the reminder that "The orange that is too hard squeezed yields a bitter juice," both proverbs teaching moderation.

It is a pleasant little saying that " He who has one sheep in the flock will like all the rest the better for it." In these happy islands the fear of the wolf has long been extinct, but in other lands the sheep and the wolf are often bracketted together in their proverbs; thus in France one is warned against a too self-effacing humility in this world in the words, " He that maketh himself a sheep shall be eaten of the wolf"; while another lesson of worldly prudence is taught in the Italian proverb, " It is a foolish sheep that makes the wolf his confessor." The Spaniard says, " Oveja que bala bocada pierde"—" The sheep loses a mouthful when it bleats," a proverb which seems to encourage mere greediness at the expense of social converse, but which we may take more favourably to imply that it is better to stick steadily to one's work than break off for useless interruptions and, possibly, querulous complaints.

A "bull in a china shop" calls up a picture of tremendous uproar and devastation. The ancient Greeks substituted " An ass peeping." Menander, three hundred years before the Christian era, refers to it, as do Lucian and others. The story upon which it is founded is, that an ass, being driven along the road, put its head into the shop of a potter. This potter was a great lover of birds, and had many of them in his shop, and the sudden appearance of the ass's great head frightened them and led to a big

* The date we have given is that of Suetonius, from whose writings we quote it. It was probably an ancient saying in his day.

smashing up of the crockery. The moral may be found in another ancient saying—"A mad beast must have a sober driver." The Latin "Bovem in lingua habet"—"He has an ox on his tongue"—is a hint that the man has been bribed to silence or false speech, an ox being a favourite device on the coins. Another saying of like significance is that, "The man has a bone in his mouth." A valuable lesson to the discontented, a warning that necessary troubles must be endured, that duties may not be shirked, is this—"To what place can the ox go where he will not plough?"

That the malicious cannot do all the harm they would is happily suggested in the adage, "Curst cows have curt horns." This proverb is centuries old, and is merely a translation from an ancient Latin* original— if indeed it be safe to suggest any date when this proverb sprung into birth—for it is quite possible that Noah quoted it as a bit of the good old wisdom of his forefathers.

It is scarcely necessary to remind our readers of, and much less to expound for their benefit, so familiar a saying as, "A regular John Bull."

The goose appears in several adages, one rather severe one being, that "If all fools wore white we should look a flock of geese." One could readily acquiesce in this if the adage said "they"; it is the "we" that is so painful. It is held that the goose is a foolish bird,† but how much more foolish was he

* "Dat Deus immiti cornua curta bovi."

† Pliny, in speaking of the goose, says that "It may be thought there is visible in the creature some sparks of wisdom, for Lacydes, the philosopher, is said to have had one of them attached to him as a constant companion, which would never leave him night or day, neither in the open street nor in the baths." One does not quite see where the wisdom comes in. It appears either to suggest that the bird showed great fidelity, or, as some might think it, became an intolerable nuisance. However that may be, Pliny points to a remedy for the latter when he adds quaintly—"But our countrymen are wiser, who

who, having a goose that laid him a golden egg each day, cut the bird open to get at once the whole store. "Much would have more, and so lost all." The man who cannot say "Bo! to a goose" is rightly regarded as a poor creature. A very sarcastic adage is that which satirises the man who, having gained great wealth by dubious means, endeavours to buy over Heaven and his own conscience by a little cheap almsgiving in the words — "He steals a goose and gives away the giblets to the poor." We must not overlook, either, the great charter of freedom and equality enshrined in "What is sauce for the goose is sauce for the gander." "To shoe the goose" is now quite obsolete as a saying, though it was at one time very popular as a suggestion to those people, fussy busybodies, who will keep meddling in other people's affairs. It was a task that would take them, at all events, some little time, give their energies something to work on, and was no more useless than many of their toils. In the "Parliament of Byrdes," written about 1650, we read that he "Who wyll smatter what euery man doos maye go helpe to shoo the goose." There is a useful word of warning in the following :— "A goose-quill may be more dangerous than a lion's claw" to one attacked by it.

There is homely wisdom in the hint that "If you would have a hen lay you must bear with the cackling"; and, of course, the need or otherwise of teaching one's grandmother to suck eggs must not be forgotten. The Greeks phrased the idea as "Teach-

know how to make a dainty of their liver !" He then goes on to describe the cramming to which they are exposed. Polladius says that they were chiefly fed on powdered figs. Martial also mentions the great size to which the liver was developed—all of which goes to show that "There is nothing new under the sun," and that the equivalent of Strasburg paté has been an appreciated delicacy for many years before Derby hampers were dreamt of.

ing a dolphin to swim," while the French say: "The goslings want to drive the geese to pasture." Two useful proverbs in this connection are that "There is reason in roasting eggs," a right and a wrong way for almost everything, and "Don't carry all your eggs in one basket."

A crotchety, fanciful individual, regarded by most people as a little peculiar, has, in English proverbial phrase, "A bee in his bonnet," or "Is bitten by a maggot," while the French say, "He has a rat in his head," and the Dutchmen account for his eccentricities by crediting him with a mouse's nest in his brains.

The Italians say: "Si prendono piu mosche col miele che coll' aceto"—"More flies are caught by honey than by vinegar." To arrive at any desired result, sweetness of manner will carry matters on much more efficaciously than the reverse.

"Where there are industrious persons there is wealth," and "Where bees are there is honey." Steady industry must reap a reward. On the other hand, we find a proverb, "To poke one's hand into a hornet's nest," and receive the painful reward of indiscreet meddling thereby.

An old English proverb hath it that "It is an ill bird that bewrays its own nest." Skelton, writing in 1520, declares how

> "Rede and lerne ye may,
> Howe olde prouerbys say
> That byrd ys not honest
> That fylyth hys owne nest."

While Heywood gives it as: "It is a foule byrde that fyleth his owne nest." As a member of a family, of a trade or profession, as the citizen, or the denizen of any country, each should bear in mind this adage,

M

and beware of bringing reproach on himself or his surroundings.

The Italians say: "Ad ogni uccello suo nido è bello" —every bird thinks its own nest beautiful—and in a very old French book we found the equivalent of this: "A chescun oysel son nye li semble bel." A quaint little adage is this one from Spain: "A little bird must have a little nest"—a lesson in contentment, a warning against pretension and undue importance; while the Turkish saying, "The nest of a blind bird is made by God," is a beautiful lesson of resignation and faith.

The Italians say: "Better be bird of the wood than bird of the cage." This is rightly enough the bird's point of view; but the owner of the cage puts things rather differently, and declares: "Better one bird in the hand than ten in the wood." The Italians say that "It is better to have an egg to-day than a hen to-morrow"; but this, surely, is rather overdoing the thing. Even though present gain may outweigh future grander possibilities, the policy may be too narrowly pinched, and does away then with legitimate hope.

Those troublous little robbers, the quarrelsome sparrows, supply the material for some few proverbs. Of these we may instance a couple: "For fear of the sparrows the hemp is not sown"—a saying directed against the over-cautious, for necessary things must be done, even though there be some little risk in the doing; and "Two sparrows on one ear of corn cannot agree," though, if they would only be wise enough to let the other alone, there would be ample provision for both.

The French have a very true saying: "Chacun aime son semblable"—our English equivalent being "Birds of a feather flock together." Hence it is a saying: "Tell me with whom thou goest, and I will tell thee what thou doest." Burchardt, in his collection of Arabic proverbs, gives the following very graphic one: "He who introduces himself between the onion and its peel goes forth with the onion smell"; but, on the other hand, we have in the Spanish, "Associate with the good and thou shalt be one of them."

When some matter comes unexpectedly and inconveniently to general knowledge, the explanation of the informant as to his or her source of information sometimes takes the form of "A little bird told me." The probable origin of this will be found in the Biblical warning: "Curse not the king, no, not in thy thought, and curse not the rich in thy bed-chamber, for a bird of the air shall carry the voice, and that which hath wings shall tell the matter." Another very familiar saying, and still in use amongst our people, is that "One swallow does not make a summer,"* and yet another adage, and one equally well known, is the reminder that "Fine feathers make fine birds," almost always quoted disparagingly, but at least a hint that even externals have their value, and are worth consideration.

Another well-known adage is that "An old bird is not to be caught with chaff." The art of the bird-snarer has supplied several other useful contributions to the cosmopolitan ingathering of proverbial wisdom: thus, for instance, we are cautioned that "Drumming is not the way to catch a blackbird," and, again, that "An empty hand is no lure for a hawk"—that is to say, if we are unwilling to risk anything we shall probably also not obtain anything. There is yet again another, the warning voice against temptation and the snare, in this: "The fowler's pipe sounds sweet till the bird be caught." The Arabs declare that "A thousand cranes in the air are not worth one sparrow in the fist." This, with due

---

* "One swallow proueth not that summer is neare."—"Treatise against Dauncing," 1577.

allowance for Eastern exaggeration and hyperbole, we recognise as but over again the familiar estimate of the repective values of the so well-known bird in the hand as compared with that of the bird in the bush.

When folks are looking for some special and exceptional interposition of fortune that is going to put everything straight for them, and lead them by a delightfully lazy route to an easy affluence, we may not unfairly remind them that " When the sky falls we shall catch larks ready roasted." Only the little "when," that will call for no labour at all, and then a glorious abundance to at once follow.

The Scotch remind us that " A craw is nae whiter for being washed "; but then, on the other hand, this washing process seems needless, for another saw tells us that " The crow thinks her young ones the fairest." Elsewhere, though, we find that " The rook said to the raven, Stand aside, blackamoor " — an ornithological version of the same derisive spirit that led to the jeering pot calling the kettle black. It has been suggested that it would be a happy thing if some power would " the giftie gi'e us, to see oursel's as others see us," but we fancy it would be but a doubtful blessing after all.

An old proverb, with much good sense in it, says that " The woodpecker loses itself by its bill," the continuous tapping calling attention to its presence, and making its life depend on the gamekeeper's forbearance. The scream of the jay and the fussy cry of the blackbird often, in like manner, betray their presence in the woodlands, and thus, also, chatterers expose themselves, and are the cause of their own downfall. In many cases it is what other people are saying that works mischief to a man ; but in the case of the blatant and thoughtless chatterer he works his own woe—all that other people have to do being to let him do his own summing-up, and be his own executioner. Other bird proverbs are : " One raven will not pluck out another raven's eyes," and " He greatly needs a bird that gives a groat for an owl." We are told, too, and it is a capital saying, that " An eagle does not catch flies " ; * that " The hawk is not frighted by the cry of the crane "— greater size being not necessarily greater courage. Yet another true, too true, proverb is, that " If you breed up a crow he will pluck out your eyes "—a lesson to prepare one for the base ingratitude that may follow great kindness shown, and of the still sadder returning evil for good.

The cunning of the fox has been a never - failing subject for the writer of fables, and has supplied the material for scores of popular sayings. Of these we need quote but a few as samples of the many, since they are almost all constructed on the same lines, the subject being nearly always more or less of admiration for successful trickery. Not a very good moral this, we may say, yet if, in its outcome, it teaches to beware of putting oneself in the power of such particularly artful and shifty characters, it will not be without its use.

Absolutely the only proverb that we can recall that takes up entirely different ground is one of jubilation on the final downfall of this arch-trickster, and, curiously enough, it is of wide appreciation. In Italy, it is : " Tutte le volpi si trouvano in pellicaria." In France it is : " En fin les renards se trouvent chez le pelletier " —the fox at last finds his way to the furrier's.

When he would conceal the real object in view, " We are going for a little music, said the fox." We are told, too, that " An old fox needs not to be taught tricks," and that " He would cheat the fox must be an early riser." The Germans say : "Wenn der Fuchs Richter ist gewinnt schwerlich eine Gans den Process "—if the fox

---

* " The eagle suffers little birds to sing,
   And is not careful what they mean thereby."

be judge the goose is hardly likely to win the case.*
" Wenn der Fuchs sie todt stellt so sind die Hühner
in Gefahr " — when the fox feigns death the poultry
are in danger.

The wolf is often introduced in proverb-wisdom, but
he is, as his nature is, always a cruel, cheerless beast,
quite wanting in the debonair attractiveness of the fox
—who is as big a rascal really as he is. " To put one's
head into the wolf's mouth " is to needlessly court great
risks. The proverb is based on the old fable of the
crane putting its head down the wolf's throat to extract
a bone that had stuck there. The operation was entirely
successful, and, on asking for his reward, the wolf told
him that it was reward sufficient to have safely with-
drawn his head. " To keep the wolf from the door " is
to keep starvation at bay, and " To eat like a wolf " is to
eat ravenously.

The Italians say that " Who keeps company with
the wolf will learn to howl." Deliberate association
with evil characters will make one as bad as those they
associate with.† " Though the wolf may lose his teeth
he does not lose his inclinations "—he is at heart as
wolfish as ever. The Persians give the caution : " Keep
the dogs near when thou suppest with the wolf," while
the Romans had a saying, " Auribus lupum teneo."
This having the wolf by the ears is a most dangerous
position to be in, for the furious creature is so difficult to
hold, and yet one dare not let go on any consideration.
Thus do unfortunates at times get entangled in some
bad business—the beginnings of a lawsuit, or the like—
where advance or retreat seem equally alarming. The

* " Pheasants are fools if they invite the hawk to dinner.
And wer't not madness then
To make the fox surveyor of the fold."
—*Shakespeare.*

† On the other hand, the Portuguese warn those who do not want to be

" Wolf in sheep's clothing " is a still more objectionable beast than the wolf *in propria personâ*, since he thereby adds treachery to all his other evil qualities :

> " And by these guileful means he more prevail'd
> Than had he open enmity profest.
> The wolf more safely wounds when in sheep's clothing drest."

The bear has not so distinctive an individuality in fabledom as the fox or wolf. The best proverb that we have met with in which he figures is the declaration that "A man without restraint is a bear without a ring ; " and then there is, of course, the well-known caution to the over-sanguine, " Sell not the bear's skin before you have caught him," or, as it is also phrased, " Spending your Michaelmas rent at Midsummer noon," not consider what may arise to mock your present confidence.

In our list of wild beasts it is a considerable drop from the wolf and bear to the mouse ; but the mouse claims his place on our list, and is a much better known wild beast in England than the wolf, and therefore more in evidence in our proverbs. "The mouse that hath but one hole is easily caught," says an old adage, and we meet with it again in Chaucer's " Wife of Bath," in the couplet,

> " The mouse that always trusts to one poor hole
> Can never be a mouse of any soul " ;

or, at all events, of any great enterprise.

A very true and impressive proverb is that " A mouse may stir what a man cannot stay "—a very small commencement may lead to an incalculable ending ; a momentary slip unarrested may hurl half-a-dozen mountaineers over a precipice ; a little trickle of water unregarded may be the solvent that will melt away

taken for wolves not to wear the skin : "Quem nao quer ser loubo nao che vista a pelle."

all barriers, and sweep all living things to destruction in the swirling torrent as it breaks its bonds.

There is a note of caution in the picturesque statement, "I gave the mouse a hole, and she has become my heir." The Spanish, "Give me where I may sit down and I will make a place for myself to lie down" is like unto it, showing in each case that if we "Give an inch, they will take an ell," and that we may, too late, repent of our first assistance when it has led in the end to our effacement.

The Chinese say, with quaint common-sense, "A mouse can drink no more than its fill from a river." Beyond a certain point that is soon reached all else is needless superfluity.

The strained relations between the cat and the mouse form the subject of divers popular adages. How good is the Scottish, "Weel kens the mouse when the cat's oot o' the house," paralleled in our English version, "When the cat's away the mice will play," or in the French, "Les rats se promenent a l'aise la ou il n'y a point des chats," and there is a pleasant vein of truth and humour in the assertion that "Mice care not to play with kittens."

In the "Order of Foles," a manuscript of about the year 1450, we find the graphic declaration that "It is a hardy mouse that is bold to breede in cattis eeris"; and Skelton writes, in 1520, "It is a wyly mouse that can build his dwellinge house within the cattes eare."* Heywood and other later writers also refer to this proverb in their various works.

The query, "Who shall bell the cat?" may be called a fable abridged, for it contains the point of one. The mice held a consultation how to secure themselves from the too marked attentions of the cat, and someone

---

* "That's a valiant flea that dare eat his breakfast on the lip of a lion." —SHAKESPEARE, *King Henry V.*

uggested that it would be an excellent plan to hang
ᴜ bell round her neck, so as to give warning of her
ᴀpproach. The idea was taken up warmly, but then
the point arose—Who shall do it?

> " Quoth one mouse unto the rest,
> Which of us all dare be so stout
> To hang the bell cat's neck about :
> If here be any let him speake.
> Then all replide, We are too weake ;
> The stoutest mouse and tallest rat
> Doe tremble at a grim-fac'd cat."

The above is from " Diogenes Lanthorne," issued in
the year 1607. Heywood writes :

> " Who shall ty the bell about the cat's necke low?
> Not I (quoth the mouse) for a thing that I know."

To " smell a rat " is to have one's suspicions aroused
as to something concealed, and is suggested by the
eagerness of dog or cat to follow scent. The saying
will be found in Ben Jonson's " Tale of a Tub," in
Butler's " Hudibras," and elsewhere.

The art of the fisherman supplies material for some
few wisdom-chips. " All is fysshe that cometh to net "
we read in ' Colyn Cloute " and other old sources of
information.* " To swallow a gudgeon " is to be caught
by some designing schemer's bait, some lying pros-
pectus of the " All-England Aërated Soap Company,
Limited," in which it is shown that the profits must
necessarily warrant a dividend of sixty-five per cent.
after six hundred thousand pounds have been set
aside for working expenses. " To throw away a sprat
to catch a herring " is a popular adage and of much
good sense. " All fish are not caught with flies " is
a useful hint too—all people that we would influence

---

* As, for instance, in Gascoigne's " Steele Glas," 1575, where we read :
> " Where favor sways the sentence of the law,
> Where al is fishe that cometh to net."

are not open to the same considerations. "It is a silly fish that is caught twice with the same bait." To err is human, and to be once entrapped may easily happen, but it is mere folly not to profit by bitter experience. The French say, "C'est la sauce qui fait le poisson," and the way in which a thing is presented to one is often of great importance. The use of proper means to effect our purpose is enforced in the warning that "Fish are not to be caught with a bird-call."

It is excellent advice to "Never offer to teach monkeys to climb up trees"—another variant on instruction in ovisuction. It is very true, too, that "Monkeys are never more beasts than when they wear men's clothes" and "ape" humanity.

The laborious ant has not escaped the notice of the moralist, fabulist, and adage-employer. That they store up a mass of grain for winter service is entirely untrue, but it was at all events thought that they did ; hence Juvenal writes, "Some men, instructed by the labouring ant, provide against the extremities of want," while Ovid declares that "Ants go not to an empty granary." The Arabs say that "If God wills the destruction of an ant He allows her wings," a hint that sudden elevation above the capacity and beyond the experience of anyone will very probably cause their downfall. Another Arab proverb is, "The beetle is a beauty in the eyes of its mother." Whatever the rest of the world may think, maternal affection is all-embracing. The French adage, "Faire d'une mouche un eléphant," is a needed caution, equivalent to our reproof of those who would "make a mountain out of a mole-hill." Such exaggeration is most profitless ; it is soon detected, and thenceforth even true statements are subjected by the hearers to a liberal discount.

That "Even the worm will turn" is an oft-quoted saying to rightly justify a limit to endurance of injustice. "Tread a woorme on the tayle and it must turne agayne," quotes Heywood ; and Shakespeare, who clothes with beauty the commonest sayings of his day, writes :

> "The smallest worm will turn, being trodden on,
> And doves will peck in safeguard of their brood."

A great proverbial use is popularly made of similes or comparisons, and observation of the very varying characteristics of the animals around them soon supplied our forefathers with an abundant store of these. "All that is required," as Bland, an old proverb-collector, states, "in forming this species of adage is that the person or thing used as a comparison be generally known or reputed to possess the property attributed to it."

As examples of the sort of thing we find amongst similes suggested by various beasts : "As greedy as a pig," "as surly as a bear," "as cunning as a fox," "as quiet as a mouse," "as poor as a church mouse," "as obstinate as a mule," "as sharp as a weasel," "as fierce as a lion," "as timid as a hare," "as mischievous as a monkey," "as faithful as a dog," "as quiet as a lamb," "as playful as a kitten," "as sly as a cat," "as patient as an ox," or "as weak as a rat," and "as wet as a drowned rat." "As drunk as a rat" may have arisen from an idea that the creature imbibed too freely from the liquors often stored in the cellars it frequented. In Borde's "Book of Knowledge," 1542, we find the passage, "I wyll be dronken other whyles as a rat." These sayings sometimes refer to old beliefs that are now exploded. "As uneven as a badger" arose from an idea that the badger's legs are shorter on one side than on the other. "As melancholy as a hare" was a saying that sprang from the belief that the flesh of a hare engendered melancholy in those who partook of it, and

that this effect was naturally produced from the unhappy disposition of the animal itself.   Another saying,
and one that has come down to the present day, is,
"As mad as a March hare." *

Amongst the similes derived from bird nature we
find : "As hoarse as a raven," "as stupid as an ostrich,"
"as innocent as a dove," "as chattering as a jay," "as
plump as a partridge," "as proud as a peacock," "as
bald as a coot," "as black as a crow," "as giddy as a
goose," "as dull (or as wise) as an owl," "as blithe as a
lark," and "as rare as a black swan."   To our forefathers the idea of a black swan seemed an absolute
contradiction, and to say, as was said in classic days,
"Rara avis in terris, nigroque simillima cygno," was to
express at once the greatest impossibility the speaker
could imagine.†   Many things have happened since
then, and amongst them the discovery of Australia
and its singular fauna.

"As slippery as an eel," "as flat as a flounder," "as
dead as a herring," "as round as a roach," are other
well-used similes.   "As thirsty as a fish," "as busy as
a bee," "as blind as a bat," "as spiteful as a toad," are
also in common use.   The spitefulness of the toad arose
from an old belief in his venomous nature and his
promptitude in spitting poison on those who molested
him.   We also hear, "as merry as a cricket" or "as
a grig."   It has been conjectured that this latter
should be, "as a Greek," and in support of this the
Shakespearean passage, "Then she's a merry Greek,"
may be brought forward, and others of like tenor

---

* " Contrary to reason ye stamp and ye stare,
    Ye fret and ye fume, as mad as a March hare."—*Heywood.*
       " Thou madde Marche hare."—*Skelton,* 1520.

† " He that worse may must holde the candle, but my Maister is not
so wise as God might have made him : hee is gone to seeke a Hayre
in a Hennes nest, a Needle in a Bottle of Haye, which is as sildome
seene as a black Swan."—" Angrie Women of Abington."

might be cited. "As blind as a beetle" doubtless
arose from the way that some species have of blunder-
ing into the wayfarer in the dusk of the evening. The
common dor-beetle, the cockchafer, the stag-beetle, and
others supply us with illustrations of this. Sir Thomas
Brown, in his interesting book on "Vulgar Errours,"
writes : " Slow worms are accounted blind, and the like
we affirm proverbially of the beetle : although their eyes
be evident." Udall writes : " Proude Ierusalem deserued
not to haue this pre-eminence, which, albeit she were in
every dede as blynde as a betell, yet thought herselfe to
haue a perfect good syght, and for that cause was more
vncurable"; while in the " Mirror for Magistrates" we
find : " Say not the people well, that Fortune fauours
fooles? So well they say, I thinke, which name her
beetle-blind."

To compare a man out of his element to a fish out
of water is a well-worn and familiar simile. Chaucer
writes that " A monk whan he is cloysterless is likned
till a Fissh that is watreles." This illustration of the
unhappy condition of the monk outside his cloister is
found not uncommonly, the earliest perhaps being in a
Greek " Life of St Anthony," that is certainly not later
than the year 373. Wyclif, for instance, writes : " For
as they seyn that groundiden in these cloystris thes men
myghten no more dwelle out therof than fiss mighte
dwelle out of water." Some fish, as the tench, are
much more tenacious of life when removed from their
native element than others, and the saying that we have
already quotod, " as dead as a herring," originated from
the fact that this fish is in a marked degree unable
to survive a very short removal from the sea.

The household surroundings of our ancestors readily
supplied them with many apt similes readily understood by all. Of these we may instance : " As thin as
a rake," " as round as a tub," " as cold as ice," " as

dull as ditch-water," "as rough as a nutmeg-grater," "as hard as iron," "as smooth as a pebble," "as deep as a well," "as cool as a cucumber," "as soft as wool," "as hard as nails," "as stiff as a poker," "as light as a feather," "as flat as a pancake," "as dry as a bone," and "as fresh as paint." "As naked as a needle" occurs in "Piers Plowman," the only place we have come across it. "As dead as a door-nail" no doubt owes some of its popularity to its alliteration ; it is sometimes "as dead as a dore-tree." In "Wit Restored," 1658, we find, "As dead as a dore-nayle"; and in "2 King Henry IV." Falstaff exclaims, "What! is the old king dead?" and Pistol replies, "As nail in door." In a much older work than either of these we find, in the description of a tournament : "Thurth the bold bodi he bar him to the erthe as ded as dornayl"; while another manuscript reads : "Feith withoute fait is feblere than nought, and as ded as a dorenail"— faith without works is dead. Piers Plowman says on this, "Feith withouten the feet is right nothyng worthi, and as dead as a dore-tree." The door-tree is the door-post, once part of a living tree, but now dead ; while the door-nails are the equally moribund nails that in mediæval days studded the surface of the door.

Other similes from the furniture or other details of the house or its surroundings were, "as clear as a bell," referring to its tone, or "as sound as a bell," referring to its freedom from cracks that would destroy its sounding powers. We also have "as hot as toast," or "as crusty as a houshold loaf." "As clean as a whistle," or perhaps "as clear as a whistle." Those who have seen a country boy making a whistle from a bit of elder or other pithy or hollow wood, and then seen the final peeling of the bark and the re-vealing of the light green of the spotless underwood thereby, would give their vote probably in favour of

" clean." It has been suggested again that the word
means empty, a whaler that returns unsuccessfully from
the fishing-ground being technically called "clean." On
the other hand, the word " clear " may suggest either
the quality of the sound or the necessity for their
being no stoppage or impediment in the tube. Some
will brush aside both explanations and say that the
thing in question is not a whistle at all but a whittle,
the big knife that butchers use, and that the notion
really is that the thing in question, whatever it may
be that calls forth the comparison, is cut off as
cleanly and clearly as if it had been done by a
whittle.

To be " as like as two peas " is a very happy simile,
as all who have ever shelled peas will recognise. " As
right as a trivet " is still an expression that may be
heard from time to time. What those who use it
quite mean by it it might perhaps puzzle them to
explain, Some tell us that the trivet is a three-
legged thing and must therefore necessarily stand
firm, while we know by experience that a four-legged
article will not always do so. Others tell us that
this valuable quality of rightness depends on its
being truly rectangular, as if it be not accurately
made it will not fit the bars to which we would
attach it, and will not give a level surface to stand
pot or kettle on. Whatever the true explanation may
be the rightness of a trivet is an article of popular
faith, and no theorising will have any power to upset
our firm belief in its rectitude. " As big as a parson's barn " refers to the olden time when the minister
of the parish received his tithes in kind instead of
in cash, and had to find sufficient stowage-room
accordingly for these contributions.

Various callings were also laid under contribution
in the quest for similes. Thus are : " As hungry as a

hunter," "as dusty as a miller," "as black as a sweep," or a coal-heaver or a collier, "as sober as a judge," and "as drunk as a lord"—this latter being a relic of the old times when men of wealth and influence thought it no shame to give way to intoxication, and one of the duties of the butler, having supplied them with wine, was to loosen the cravat of any gentlemen who showed any signs of apoplexy, and to generally make their stay beneath the table as comfortable as possible. "As mad as a hatter" is really a corruption of the French, "Il raisonne comme une huitre"—he reasons like an oyster, and has no association with the gentlemen who provide our head-gear. The French proverb, we need scarcely point out, is sarcastic. The oyster when crossed in love, it will be remembered, is thus again made mock of and its feelings derided.

The various colours of the objects that meet our view are also pressed into the service of the seeker after similes; thus we have the excellent one, "as white as snow." We also find "as yellow as a guinea," a coin we rarely see, but familiar enough when this saying was to the fore. "As red as a rose" was common enough as a popular saying, but it is not so happy as many, seeing that roses are not by any means always red. "As red as a lobster" is above reproach if only we come across the creature after he has passed through the boiling stage, and "as white as a sheet" will pass muster. "As green as grass" is admirably descriptive, and "as grey as a badger" will do very well. "As brown as a berry" is more open to question, unless indeed it be a roasted coffee-bean. Berries are white, red, yellow, green, purple, orange, black, but we really cannot at this moment recall a brown one, so that it seems as though to be true we should say "as un-brown as a berry!" Black invites many comparisons. "As midnight," "as coal," "as ink," "as pitch," "as jet," are a few of these.

We were gratified to learn from a Brazilian that they have a simile, "as reliable as an Englishman." Job is of course the model of patience, Solomon of wisdom, Crœsus of wealth, and we have also "as true as Troilus," though the simile never took hold of the popular fancy. He was the Shakespearean ideal of unshaken constancy, and he declares that,

> "After all comparisons of truth,
>   As truth's authentic author to be cited,
>   As true as Troilus shall crown up the verse."

"As true as steel" is the more ordinary simile that rises to one's memory. Other qualities, good and bad, that have supplied material for the makers of similes are: "Swift as an arrow," "deaf as a post," "ugly as sin," "cold as charity," "bright as the sun," "changeable as the moon," "sweet as sugar," "sour as vinegar," "hard as a diamond," "good as gold," "changeable as a weathercock," "quick as lightning," "firm as a rock," "soft as silk," "clear as crystal," "bitter as gall," "as rosy as an apple," "as cross as two sticks," "as bright as a new pin." Our list has no pretension to be complete—doubtless many others might be recalled; we have, as we write these words, remembered that we have overlooked "as plain as a pikestaff" and "as tight as a drum." Many such omissions will be duly noted by our readers, but our full justification will be found in the fact that we have had no desire or intention to make our list all-embracing. If those we have given are sufficiently representative of the sort of thing we have had under consideration, our object is gained.

N

CHAPTER VII

The Power of the Tongue—Speech and Silence—Knowledge and Wisdom not Interchangeable Terms—Truth and Untruth—Travellers' Tales—Flattery—Industry and Sloth—Youth—Friends, True and False—Riches and Poverty—The Ladder to Thrift—The Influence of Womankind—The Good Wife—The Shrew—The Testimony of Epitaphs—The Grey Mare—Home—Hope—Forethought—Excuses —Good and Ill Fortune—Retribution—Detraction—Pretension— Self-Interest—Bribery and Corruption—Custom and Habit—The General Conduct of Life—The Weather—The Moon made of Green Cheese—Conclusion

SPEECH, wise or otherwise, and silence, under the same limitations, have supplied the material for countless wisdom-chips, the power of the tongue in what it says and how it says it being recognised as of vital importance, and this has been admitted at every period and under every sky. It has been said that "More have repented speech than silence," and the assertion has much experience in its favour. Though times arise when prompt speech is needful, and cowardice and a poor expediency prevents the words being uttered, it is, perhaps, more ordinarily the experience that one unavailingly regrets having spoken, and would give much to be able to recall the hasty and inconsiderate utterance.*

It has been truly said that he knows much who

---

* The Portuguese warn us that great talkers make many mistakes, in the adage, "Quem muito falla muito erra."

knows when to speak, but that he knows yet more
who knows when to be silent, and that the good
talker is known by what he says, and also by what
he does not say. It has been very happily declared
that "Flow of words is not always flow of wisdom,"
and that "Quality is ever better than quantity," so
that "Words should be delivered not by number but
by weight."* Another very true adage is that "Talking comes by nature, silence by understanding."

The Italians say: "Great eloquence, little conscience,"
and it is certainly true that "Great talkers fire too
fast to take good aim." Speech has been declared to
be the portraiture of the mind, so that as the man
talks to us he is quite unconsciously depicting himself. "A close mouth catches no flies" says the old
saw, and modest merit that trusts to its deserving is
likely enough to be supplanted by the boldly importunate. Many would prefer to let these others do
the impudent begging, and would surrender the flies,
but keep their self-respect. Young tells us that

> "Thoughts shut up want air,
> And spoil like bales unopen'd to the sun"—

which is very true; while Shakespeare's advice is no
less so:
> "Have more than thou showest,
> Speak less than thou knowest."

A very homely saw declares, "Least said, soonest
mended," and certainly "Speaking silence is better
than senseless speech"; but the assumption that the
speech is of such a quality that it is best left unsaid
is a little severe, and the mental atmosphere in which
the less said implied the less to be mended would be,

* "They have spent theyr tyme lesse fruitfully heretofore in ouer
runnyng a multitude of wordes with small consideracion or weyghing
of them."—FISHER, *A Godlye Treatise.*

we would fain hope, a very exceptional one. We shall all agree that "Say well is good, but do well is better," and in the value of the caution that "In lavishing words one wears out ideas." An old rhyme hath it that "A man of words and not of deeds Is like a garden full of weeds," and a grave old writer advises us on this that "The way of God's commandments is more in doing than in discourse."* "Great talkers are ill doers" is another version of the saying.

It has been said, and very justly, that "Silence often expresses more powerfully than speech the verdict and the judgment," and to one who comes beneath its sway it must be more eloquent and more crushing than any audible denunciation that can be repudiated or challenged. It is a very common saying that "Silence gives consent," but one readily sees that this is much too sweeping. Nevertheless, the adage is of venerable antiquity and of wide distribution. We find it quoted by Euripides long before the Christian era. The Romans said, "Qui tacet consentire videtur," while the modern Frenchman believes that "Assez consent qui ne dit pas mot." In Psalm L. v. 21, things are presented on an entirely different footing. "Silence," says Shakespeare, "is the perfectest herald of joy; I were but little happy if I could say how much." The tongue, "the unruly member," has been the subject of countless discourses and essays, and also of warning adages beyond number. The writer of Ecclesiasticus tells us that "The pipe and the psaltery make sweet melody, but a pleasant tongue is above them both," and a French proverb runs that "Douces paroles ne scorchent pas la langue."

---

* "There are perilous times at hande by reason of some that vnder pretence of godlynesse turne true godlynesse vp side down, and so prate boastynglye of themselues as thoughe the Christian religion consisted in wordes and not rather in purenesse of herte."—*Udall.*

Richard Taverner, writing in 1539, tells us that being
"demaunded what in a man is the worst thyng and
the best, Anacharsis answered — the tonge. Meanyng
that the selfe same parte of a manne bryngeth most
utilitie yf it be with ryght reason gouverned, and
agayne is most perylouse and hurtfull yf otherwyse."
This testimony may be accepted as being about the
truth ; but, as it is much less necessary to commend the
good than to denounce the evil, the general set of proverb teaching is strongly in the latter direction. An old
Roman proverb runs, "Lingua quo vadis?"—"Tongue,
where goest thou?" The hint, to stop a moment and
see in what direction we are being taken, the journey
and its ending, is an excellent one.

> "The first vertue, sone, if thou wilt lere,
> Is to restreine and kepen wel thy tonge," *

writes Chaucer, in the "Manciple's Tale," and he re-
peats this in "Troilus and Creseide," and refers to
this control of the tongue as part of the valuable
practice and precept of the wise men of old :

> "For which these wise clerkes that ben dede
> Have euer this prouerbed to us young
> That the first vertue is to kepe the toung."

Hence, "If you keep your tongue prisoner your body
may go free." Another old proverb of similar import
is, "Confine your tongue, lest your tongue confine you";
while the Spaniards throw even more force into their
version, "Let not the tongue say what the head shall
pay for." "Life and death are in the power of the
tongue"—self-destruction, or that of others. "A fool's
tongue may cut his throat" is a homely English saw,
and very much to the point.

A very quaint old MS. in the Harleian collection

---

* "The tunge is but a litel membre, and reiseth greet thingis. Lo
hou litel fier breuneth a ful greet word : and our tunge is fier, the
unyversitie of wickidnesse."—*St James*. Translation of Wiclif.

deals with the faults and failings to which men are liable. Thus, for instance:

> " With thy tong thou mayst thyself spylle,
> And with tong thou mayst haue all thy wylle.
> Here and se, and kepe thee stylle,*
> Whatsoever ye thynk avyse ye wele."

This call to reflection terminates each verse. The whole poem is so quaintly refreshing that we cannot forbear quoting, at all events, one more verse — the caution against insobriety; and as this particular evil has, amongst its other bad effects, that of provoking strife, angry discussion, and foul language, we may still feel that it comes within our scope—the influence of the tongue:

> " And thow goo vnto the wyne
> And thow thynk yt good and fyne,
> Take thy leve whane yt ys tyme,
> Whatsoever ye thynk avyse ye wele."

An ancient proverb reminds us that " It is good sleeping in a whole skinne," and thereupon Heywood comments and advises: " Let not your tong run at rover, since by stryfe yee may lose and can not winne." To " Teach thy tongue to say, I do not know " is also an excellent discipline. The young, especially, shut themselves off from much valuable knowledge rather than admit their ignorance.†

In a manuscript of the fourteenth century we found the following :—

* In the " Parlament of Byrdes," written somewhere about 1550, the chough, or Cornish crow, is thus admonished, in very similar strains to the above :

> " Thou Cornysshe, quod the Hauke, by thy wil
> Say well, and holde thee styll."

† The following wisdom-chips may be commended to these unfortunates : "Affectation of wisdom often prevents our being wise"; "The man who knows most knows his own ignorance "; "Knowledge is proud that he has learned so much : wisdom is humble that he knows no more."

"Wykkyd tunge breket bon, the first
Thow the self haue non"—

This is the first reference that we have come across to
a proverb commonly encountered in the form of "The
tongue breaks bones, though she herself has none." *
It is no doubt based on the passage in Ecclesiasticus,
declaring that "The stroke of the whip maketh marks
in the flesh, but the stroke of the tongue breaketh the
bones. Many have fallen by the edge of the sword,
but not so many as have fallen by the tongue." The
book of Ecclesiasticus is an overflowing treasury of
wisdom. What could be wiser counsel, for example,
than this?—"If thou hast understanding, answer thy
neighbour: if not, lay thy hand upon thy mouth.
Honour and shame is in talk, and the tongue of man
is his fall. Be not called a whisperer, and lie not in
wait with thy tongue." "Where there is whispering
there is lying" says one of our proverbs, and it is
in the main true. The honourable and straightforward thing can ordinarily be proclaimed in the ears
of all.

The Spaniards declare that "La langua del mal
amigo mas corta que el cuchillo"—"The tongue of a
false friend is sharper than a knife." "Mors et vita
in manibus linguæ": it is the arbiter of life and death,
and yet it has been necessary to remind men that "It
is better to lose a jest than a friend." A quick sense
of humour, a talent at repartee, the power of seeing
the ridiculous side of things, are dearly bought when
their display is at the expense of the feelings of
others.† A happy conceit may be the beginning of
an unhappy strife, and it must be remembered that
"He who makes others afraid of his wit had need be

* " Thou hast hearde of many a man,
Tongue breaketh bone and it selfe hath none."
—The " Parlament of Byrdes," *c.* 1550.
† " Raise not the credit of your wit at the expense of your judgment."

afraid of their memories"—the sarcastic speech, the little touch of ridicule rankling in the mind of the victim long after the utterer has entirely forgotten them.

We are reminded, too, that "A fool, when he hath spoken, hath done all"; and the Spaniard tells us that "A long tongue betokens a short head"—the braggart tells us much of what he is going to do, but the performance is not at all in proportion.*

"The price of wisdom is above rubies" we read in one of the most ancient of books, dating some fifteen hundred years before the Christian era; and Baruch, also writing in far-off time, exclaims: "Learn where is wisdom, where is strength, where is understanding, that thou mayst know also where is length of days and life, where is the light of the eyes and peace." The apocryphal books of the Bible include Ecclesiasticus and the Book of Wisdom, and in each of these the praise of wisdom is the dominant theme, as, for example: "Wisdom is glorious, and never fadeth away"; "She is a treasure unto men that never faileth"; "All gold of respect of her is as a little sand, and silver shall be counted as clay before her"; "All wisdom cometh from the Lord, and is with Him for ever"; "The parables of knowledge are in the treasures of wisdom"; "Wisdom exalteth her children, and layeth hold of them that seek her." We need scarcely stay to point out that in the book of the Proverbs of Solomon wisdom is again exalted in many striking passages full of poetry and beauty.

We are all familiar with the adage, "Experientia docet"; but the following, equally true, is less well known—"He that loses anything and gets wisdom by it is a gainer by his loss." Another very happy saying is, that "A wise man has more ballast than sail," and

* "Beaucoup de bruit, peu de fruit," as the expressive French jingle has it.

yet another is that "Wisdom is always at home to those who call." It is very true, too, that "By the thoughts of others wise men may correct their own," for a wise man gets learning even from those who have none themselves; and "He is the true sage," says the Persian proverb, "who learns from all the world"—a wide field, but not too wide for profitable service.

We must be careful to bear in mind that knowledge and wisdom are not necessarily interchangeable terms; a man may have a far-reaching knowledge, and be a perfect encyclopædia of useful and useless facts, and yet be wofully deficient in wisdom. "Learning is but an adjunct to oneself," writes Shakespeare, in "Love's Labour's Lost," a sentence luminous and golden. We see the essential difference perhaps the better if we append to each its opposite—knowledge and ignorance, wisdom and folly.

The fool has supplied material for countless proverbs. Solomon tells us that "A foolish son is the heaviness of his mother"; that "A prating fool shall fall"; that "It is as sport to a fool to do mischief"; that "The fool shall be servant to the wise of heart"; that "He that is soon angry dealeth foolishly"; that "Folly is joy to him that is destitute of wisdom"; that "He that begetteth a fool doeth it to his sorrow"; that "A fool returneth to his folly"; that "A fool uttereth all his mind"; that "Fools die for want of wisdom"; that "The legs of the lame are not equal, so is a parable in the mouth of fools";* while the writer of Ecclesiasticus says—"Weep for the dead, for he hath lost the light; and weep for the fool, for he wanteth understanding. Make little weeping for the dead, for

* "By a fole in the prouerbes is pryncypally vnderstande him that in folowynge his awne councell defendeth infydelyte and the vnknowing of God for trueth and hyghe wysdome."—*Matthew.*

he is at rest; but the life of the fool is worse than
death. Seven days do men mourn for him that is
dead, but for a fool all the days of his life." Many
other Biblical references may very readily be found.

In the domain of secular literature and proverb-lore
the material at our service is equally lavish in amount
and definite in its pity and scorn of these unfortunates.
The following may be accepted as samples from the
bulk: "Wise men learn more from fools than fools
from wise men"; "Folly, as well as wisdom, is justified in its children"; "Little minds, like small beer,
are soon soured"; "Wise men make jests, and fools
repeat them"; "He is a fool who makes his fist a
wedge"; "On the heels of folly shame treads"; "To
promise and give nothing is a comfort to a fool"; "A
foolish judge passes a quick sentence"; "A wise man
shines, a fool would outshine"; "Cunning is the fool's
substitute for wisdom"; "The fools wonder, wise men
ask"; "A fool and his money are soon parted";*
"The fool says, Who would have thought it?"; "Folly
jumps into the river, and wonders why Fate lets him";
"Wit is folly, unless a wise man has the keeping of
it"; "A fool can ask more questions than a wise
man can answer, but a wise man cannot ask more
questions than a fool is ready to answer"; "A fool
shoots without taking aim." These proverbs are severe,
but one feels, on full consideration of them, one after
another, that there is not one that is exaggerated.
They all describe people whom we have all met, and
who are still living.

There is some considerable compensation in the fact
that "The less wit a man has, the less he knows he
wants it." The French say that "Un sot trouve

* "A foole and his monie be soone at debate
Which after with sorrow repents him too late."
—Tusser's *Husbandrie*, 1580.

toujours un plus sot qui l'admire"—a fool always finds a bigger fool to admire him—and that, too, must be very comforting.* As writer and reader alike happily feel beyond any uncomfortable misgiving that these various proverbs refer to quite other folk than themselves, we may pick up a few hints from yet other proverbs as to our dealings with these unfortunate people. One point that we need to remember is that " He who has to deal with a blockhead has need of much brains." It is expedient, too, to remember that " If you play with a fool at home, he will play with you in the street "; and the caution may be given that " A fool demands much, but he is a greater fool that gives it." It is painful to know that " Knaves are in such repute that honest men are counted fools," though to be counted a fool by a knave is, after all of little moment. We must bear in mind, too, that " No one is so foolish but may give another good counsel sometimes," and the true wisdom is to value good, from whatever quarter it comes.

The value of truth and the meanness of falsehood find due place in our proverb literature. " Truth," we are told, "hath always a fast bottom," a firm anchorage. " Truth hath but one way, but that is the right way." Esdras tells us that, " As for the truth, it endureth, and is always strong : it liveth and conquereth for evermore." Even in the old classic days, before Christianity influenced the lives of men, the beauty of truth was recognised, for Plautus wrote, two hundred years before the coming of Christ, " That man is an upright man who does not repent him that he is upright "; and Seneca declared that " He is most powerful who has himself in his power." It has been beautifully said that " Truth is God's daughter," and that " It may be blamed, but it may never be shamed."

* " No creature smarts so little as a fool."—*Pope.*

The following sayings will bear consideration :—
"Truth begets trust, and trust truth," "The use-
fullest truths are the plainest," "He who respects his
word will find it respected," "Craft must have clothes,
but truth can go naked," "No one ever surfeited of
too much honesty," "A straight line is the shortest in
morals as in mathematics," "It is always term-time
in the court of conscience," "Character is the diamond
that scratches every other stone," "Truth is the
cement of society," "Sell not thy conscience with thy
goods," "Smart reproof is better than smooth acqui-
escence." Truth, then, must necessarily make enemies,
for "Honest men never have the love of a rogue,"
and "Truth is always unpalatable to those who will
not relinquish error"—to those who love darkness
rather than light.

In the Library of Jesus College, Cambridge, in a
manuscript of the fifteenth century we find the following excellent teaching :

> "Of mankynde thou shalt none sle
> Ne harm with worde, wyll, nor dede ;
> Ne suffir non lorn ne lost to be
> If thow wele may than help at nede.
>
> Be thou no thef, nor theves fere
> Ne nothing wyn with trechery ;
> Okur ne symony cum thow not nere,
> But conciens clere kepe al ay trewely.
>
> Thou shalt in worde be trewe alsso ;
> And fals wytnes thou shalt none bere :
> Loke thow not lye for frende nor foo
> Lest thow they saull full gretely dere.
>
> Hows, ne land, ne othir thyng,
> Thow shalt not covet wrangfully ;
> But kepe ay wele Goddes biddyng
> And Cristen fayth trow stedfastly."

Another writer gives the very wise advice to take
some little care of what goes into the mouth, but

much more of what comes out of it. Bacon, in his
"Advancement of Learning," speaks of "The sun
which passeth through pollutions and itself remains
as pure as before," and Milton adopts the thought
but modifies it into this : "Truth is as impossible to
be soiled by any outward touch as the sunbeam." It
has been said that "Ridicule is the test of truth,"
but one scarcely sees why, and we see that Carlyle,
referring to it in one of his books, says, "We have,
oftener than once, endeavoured to attach some
meaning to that aphorism." Another adage, which
we find in France as well as in England, is that
"All truth must not be told at all times." Expediency
is a somewhat doubtful guide, but expediency at its
best is good common-sense, and common-sense
admits the truth of this adage. A much more doubtful saying is that, "That is true which all men say,"
practically an echo of "Vox populi, vox Dei," though
in the highest and deepest sense a great truth is
involved in it. To assert that the clamour of the
mob is necessarily inspired by the wisdom of Heaven
is mere blasphemy ; self-interest, prejudice, passion,
are too evidently factors, and what all men are saying
at a certain period may be but a passing emotion
built on the shifting sand. Such a proverb so
employed may serve well enough as a plea for drift-
ing with the stream and shouting with the crowd,
but if we go deeper the proverb is profoundly true.
Man, born in the image of God, marred as that
image now is, preserves yet something of the divine,
and far below popular clamour and waves of passion
is the seed of truth and righteousness; and where
this throughout humanity blossoms into detestation
of slavery, unjust war, or other outrage against the
conscience of mankind, and the cry goes to Heaven
against the iniquity, the Spirit of God is dwelling in

the souls of men, and they become co-workers with Deity.

Falsehood, like truth, has its attendant proverbs. How true, for instance, is this, "Subterfuge is the coward's defence," or this, "Falsehood stings those who meddle with it."

> "O what a tangled web we weave,
> When first we practise to deceive."

Hence the French say, "Il faut qu'un menteur ait bonne mémoire"—"Liars need to have good memories"; while the Scotch say very happily, "Frost and fausehood hae baith a dirty wa'-gang." Other adages are: "To conceal a fault is to add to it another,"* "The credit that is got by a lie only lasts till the truth comes out," "Ill doers are ill deemers," "No poverty like poverty of spirit," "Better lose good coat than good conscience," "Half a truth is often a whole falsehood," "He who breaks his word bids others be false to him." "Almost, and very nigh, saves many a lie," is a saw that is somewhat difficult to classify; it appears to be on the side of truth, and yet it seems to suggest a way of coming nearly to the boundary-line without actually crossing into the domain of falsehood. In an old book of morals we find the precept, "In relating anything extraordinary it is better, in case of doubt, to be within rather than beyond the line of fact"—a somewhat half-hearted precept this!

"Travellers' tales" have long been under suspicion, and certainly some of the earlier explorers did expose the credence of their auditors and readers to a severe strain in some of their narrations. On the other hand,

---

* "A fault denied is twice committed,
　And, oftentimes, excusing of a fault
　Doth make the fault the worse for the excuse."—*Shakespeare.*

we must have the grace to admit that later explorers have verified many statements that were long held impossible. The Persians say that "Whoso seeth the world telleth many a lie"; while human nature is so essentially the same all the world over that in the sayings of a savage tribe in West Africa we meet with this, "He who travels alone tells lies." The common experience of mankind is unfortunately against the traveller, and he must sometimes be content to wait, years or centuries maybe, before his wonderful experiences are fully accepted.

It is a true and far-reaching proverb that "Error, though blind herself, sometimes brings forth seeing children." Thus from alchemy, with its *elixir vitæ* and *aurum potabile*, has sprung the science of chemistry; and astrology, a farrago of superstitious rubbish, had yet within it the seed that should afterwards develop into the grandest of all sciences, astronomy.

"Flattery," Swift tells us, "is the food of fools," and Gray speaks of "Painted flattery with its serpent train," while Goldsmith dwells on the

> "Flattering painter who made it his care
> To draw men as they ought to be, not as they are."

The lines in "Julius Cæsar" will also be recalled, where Shakespeare writes, "But when I tell him he hates flatterers, He says he does, being then most flattered." * These various passages sufficiently indicate that when we tag on flattery to the end of our section on falsehood, the arrangement is not far wrong. Those only are the recipients of flattery from whom some benefit may be obtained; hence "Flatterers haunt not cottages" we are told, with

---

* And again in another passage—
> "O that men's ears should be
> To counsel deaf, but not to flattery."

quaint humour. That such incense is appreciated by its objects rather than plain truths may be gathered from another quaint old adage, " Flattery sits in the parlour when plain-dealing is kicked out of doors." Perhaps this is a little the fault of plain-dealing, its directness being not always tempered with courtesy. The man who boasts that he always speaks his mind is not invariably the pleasantest of companions. There must be a happy medium somewhere between acidulated brutality of frankness and the sugared seductiveness of flattery.

The virtue of industry and the vice of sloth are factors in life that have not by any means escaped the notice of the builders-up of our proverb lore and store. The praise and inculcation of industry may very happily be seen, for example, in this gleaning : " Every man's task is his life-preserver," for rust consumes more than use wears. " He who serves well need not fear to ask his wages " ; " Those that trust to their neighbours may wait for their harvest " ; " It is better to do the thing than to wish it done " ; " A wise man makes more opportunities than he finds " ; " He that will eat the kernel must crack the nut " ; " Learn to labour and to wait, but learn to labour first " ; " Well begun is half done " ; * " God calls men when they are busy, Satan when they are idle " ; " Work provides easy chairs for old age " ; " Time wasted is existence, used is life "; " Save yourself pains by taking pains " ; " Things don't turn up, they must be turned up " ; " If you don't open the door to the devil he goes away " ; " One grain fills not the sack, but it helps " ; " Prudence is not satisfied with maybe " ; " Nothing venture nothing have " ; " It is working that makes a workman " ;

---

* In France they say, " Il est bien avancé qui a bien commencé." In both English and French versions there is a certain ring that helps the memory.

" Industry is Fortune's right hand "; * " A willing
helper does not wait till asked "; " We must not spend
all the time whetting the scythe " ; " Love labour, for
if you want it not for food you may for physic ";
" Bustle is not necessarily industry" ; " The deeper the
ploughing the heavier the reaping " ; " He that begins
many things finishes but few " ; " Good beginning
makes good ending." To these one could readily add
one hundred more.

It is a true saying that " Every man is the son of
his own works," and another good old saw is that
" The burden which one likes is not felt." The
labour is then wonderfully lightened, and those who
are fond of their calling think little of the attendant
toil, but perform as a pleasure what others consider
a weariness.

A proverb still in common use is that " Many
hands make light work " ; while sometimes one can do
better work by not working at all, for " The master's
eye will do more than his two hands," the supervision being of more value than the sharing in the
toil.

An interesting old relic and reminder of old times,
when the spinning-wheel was in daily use, is seen
in the saying, " I have tow on my distaff"—in other
words, I have work all ready to engage my attention.
Chaucer and other old writers introduce this proverb,
but now the lapse of time, or, rather, the change of
customs, has made it obsolete, a distaff being as

* " Industrie is a qualitie procedying of Wytte and Experience by whyche
a man perceyveth quickely, inuenteth freshely, and counsayleth spedily :
wherfore they that be called industrious do most craftely and depely
vnderstand in al affayres what is expedient, and by what meanes or
wayes they may sonest exployte them. Those thingis in whome other
men trauayle these lightley and with facilitie spedeth, and findeth new
wayes and meanes to bring to effecte that he deseyreth."—*Sir Thomas
Elyot.*

O

utterly out of date as a battle-axe or a pair of snuffers.

The entirely accepted, and very justifiable, belief that " Satan finds some mischief still for idle hands to do," is seen in such proverbs as, " If the devil catch a man idle he will set him to work," and its parallel, " Our idle days are Satan's busy days." It has been said, again, that " An idle brain is the Devil's workshop," and that " It is an ill army where the Devil carries the colours." Chaucer is in full agreement, and says that " Idlenesse is the gate of all harmes. An idel is like to a place that hath no walles ; theras deviles may enter on every side," while Bishop Hall declares that " The idle man is the Devil's cushion, upon which he taketh his free ease."

Amongst the many proverbs that have the dispraise of idleness as their theme we may quote the following :—" Easy it is to bowl down hill "; " He is but idle who might be better employed "; " They must starve in frost who will not toil in heat "; " Idleness is the greatest prodigality "; " Idleness always envies industry "; " Business neglected is business lost "; " He that maketh his bed ill must be content to lie ill "; " Better to do a thing than wish it done "; " More die of idleness than of hard work "; " There is more fatigue in laziness than in labour "; " Shameful craving must have shameless refusing "; " Fish are not caught in one's sleep "; " Like a pig's tail, going all day, and nothing done at night "; " Lie not in the mud and cry for Heaven's aid "; " Were wishes horses beggars would ride "; " One of these days is none of these days "; " Wishing is of all employments the poorest paid "; " Accusing the times is excusing ourselves "; " There belongs more than whistling in going to plough." Life, however brief, is made yet shorter by waste of its opportunities, and it has been very truly said that " He who will not work until he feels himself in the proper mood will soon find himself in the proper mood never to work at all." For years we have had illuminated round our study walls the stirring words : "Whatsoever thy hand findeth to do, do it with thy might ; for there is no work, nor device, nor knowledge, nor wisdom in the grave," and they have lightened for us many a burden, and given an impulse to many an undertaking.

A Spanish proverb says that "She that gazes much spins little"—the distraction caused by externals being fatal to concentration of thought on the work. "No mill, no meal," is an old English proverb, signifying that if the necessary rattle of the machinery and the supervision of it is an offence one must be content to forego the benefits. "Black will take no other colour," is to be read as a hint that vicious people are seldom or never satisfactorily reclaimed. Camden, writing in 1614, tells a story of " A lusty gallant that had wasted much of his patrimony, seeing a gentleman in a gowne, not of the newest cut, tolde him that he had thought it had beene his great-grandfather's gowne. ' It is so,' saith he, 'and I have also my great-grandfather's lands, and so have not you.'" We see that Fuller declares "Oil of whip to be the proper plaister for the cramp of lazinesse" ; while Cowper compares the idler to " A watch that wants both hands, As useless if it goes as if it stands "—a very happy idea.

One Smart, whom we may without offence class amongst the lesser poets, wrote an ode on "Idleness," in which he declares that that is the goal, and work merely its means of attainment. He thus apostrophises his ideal :

> " For thee, O Idleness, the woes
> Of life we patiently endure ;
> Thou art the source whence labour flowes,
> We shun thee but to make thee sure."

The aspirations, the temptations, the duties of youth, form the subject of divers proverbs. These we may illustrate sufficiently by a judicious selection from the great mass of material available. How excellent the advice: " Be true to the best of yourself "; or this, " Rather set than follow example "; or yet, again, this, " Take care to be what thou wouldst seem to be." How good the teaching: " Liberty is not the freedom to do as we like, but as we ought "; that " Golden age never was present age "; that " Trinkets are no true treasure "; and that " In seeking happiness we may overlook content "—the first may perhaps be ours, but the second should always be obtainable.

The very familiar adage, " As the twig is bent so is the tree inclined," remains as true as ever; therefore " Guard well thy thoughts, for thoughts are heard in Heaven." * Another writer very aptly declares that " It is better to hammer and forge one's character than to dream oneself into one "; while the old adage, " Keep good company and be one of the number," is excellent advice, pithily put.

Tusser, some three hundred or more years ago, declared that

> " The greatest preferments that childe we can giue,
> Is learning and nurture, to traine him to liue."

It has been well said that " Ignorance is a voluntary misfortune," and that " If the brain sows not corn it plants thistles." Were a farmer to leave a field a year untilled, not only would the corn supply that it might have yielded be lost, but the ground would produce in abundance useless weeds that would scatter their seed on the wind over the whole country-side;

---

* " To dread no eye, and to fear no tongue is the great and blessed prerogative of the innocent life "; " Man is a thinking being, whether he will or not—all he can do, then, is to turn his thoughts aright."

neither brain nor cornfield will remain neutral and dormant; a crop of something or other is inevitable. "If a man empties his purse," says the proverb, "into his head no man can take it from him;" and other good adages are: "Not the studies, but the study, makes the scholar"; "Inquirers who are always inquiring never learn anything"; "It is less painful to learn in youth than to be ignorant in age"; while the doctrine of plain living and high thinking was admirably foreshadowed in this: "Cater frugally for the body, but feed the mind sumptuously"—an altogether excellent precept, and we must remember that, when all is done, the best and most important part of a man's education is that which he gives himself, and which fits him in this great workshop of the world to use his tools to the best advantage, and contribute something of value to the general store.

It is a wise counsel to "Read not books alone but men, and chiefly to be careful to read oneself"—to take stock of oneself from time to time; that youth should remember what seems too difficult then to realise, that a day will come when youth has fled, when the demands of life will continue, and the power to meet them will have weakened. Such proverbs as these should be pondered over: "Reckless youth makes rueful age"; "If youth knew what age would crave, it would both get and save"; "A young man negligent, an old man necessitous." The same truth is put as clearly, but not so lugubriously, in the quainter saying: "He that saveth his dinner will have the more for his supper"—he that spares, that is, when he is young may the better spend when he is old. We have this, again, in a slightly varied and more intense form in the French, "He sups ill who eats all at dinner."

When the youth goes forth into the world his knowledge of the trials and temptations of life is small, while his faith in himself is great, and he sadly needs, far more than he knows, guidance, human and divine. What of counsel and of warning will our proverbs yield here?

The following precepts answer this weighty question, and all are rich in wisdom and guidance:—"No one is mighty but he that conquers himself"; "As we sow the habit so we reap the character"; "Let others' shipwrecks be your beacons"; "Careless watch invites vigilant foe"; "Every day is a leaf in our history"; "We live in the body, not as the servant but as the master"; "One vice is more expensive than many virtues"; "Consider not pleasures as they come, but as they go"; "Wade not where you see no bottom"; "The path of virtue is the path of peace"; "Clean glove may hide soiled hand"; "Satan promises the best and pays the worst"; "Those that would be kept from harm must keep out of harm's way"; "One bad example spoils many good precepts"; "The day has eyes, the night has ears"; "He who makes light of small faults will fall into great ones"; "He that cometh into needless danger dies the Devil's martyr." Each of these will amply repay quiet pondering over.

We give two verses of a very striking poem from a manuscript of the fifteenth century. It is entitled, "Man his own Woe," and is fifteen verses long:

> " I made covienaunte trewe to be
> When I fiyrste crystened was,
> I wente to the worlde, and turned fro Thee,
> And folowede the fend and his trace.
> Fro wrathe and enuye wolde I not passe,
> With covetyse I was bawte also,
> My flesh hadde his wyll, alas,
> I wyte myselfe myne owene woo.

"Ryche manne a thefe ys another,
That of covetyse woll not slake,
What he with wronge begyle his brother,
In blysse ful sone shall he forsake.
Byfore God for thefte hit ys take,
All that wyth wronge he wynneth so ;
But he the radure amends make
He shall wyte hymeself hys owen wo."

We have seen that rhymes are commonly used as a
means of impressing proverbs on the memory. The
four couplets—one from Gower's "Confessio Amantis";
one from Burns, from his "Tam O'Shanter"; one from
"An Honest Man's Fortune," written by John Fletcher
three hundred years ago ; and the fourth from "The
Lady's Dream" of Hood — that we now quote are
equally worth remembrance :

"Lo now, my son, what it is,
A man to caste his eyes amis."

"Pleasures are like poppies spread,
You seize the flower, its bloom is shed."

"Our acts are angels, for good or ill,
Our fatal shadows that walk by us still."

"Evil is wrought by want of thought,
As well as want of heart."

Other good proverbs for those at the commencement
of life, are : that "A man is valued as he makes himself
valuable"; "Crises form not character, but reveal it";
"He that finds it easy to repent will not find it hard to
sin"; "Wine neither keeps secrets nor carries out promises"; "Bacchus has drowned more than Neptune";
and, happy truth, "Every slip is not a fall." It must
be remembered that, while a man may have enough of
the world to drag him down, he will never have enough
to satisfy him—peace and satisfaction being found in a

quite other direction than what by a strange misnomer is called "life." "A sound conscience is a triple fence of steel," so "Better keep evil out than turn it out." "Character is property," and "A good conscience makes an easy couch"; "Complaining is a contempt upon oneself"; "Thanksgiving is good, thanks-living is better."

Friends, true and false, have made their mark on our proverb store, and counsels of encouragement and of warning are abundantly at our service. How to recognise the true friend, how to detect the counterfeit article, is invaluable knowledge, and if we could only at all times be as wise as our rich mass of proverb-lore would fain have us to be, we should in matters of friendship, and in most other things, make a very prosperous voyage on the sea of life. One seems to detect several grades or qualities of friendship in these adages. There is that, for instance, which is unfailing, which in sickness and health, poverty or wealth, is always true and real; then at the other end of the scale a sham article that soon has all the gilt rubbed off; and then in between these a less obvious failure, which has many of the marks of the real thing, and which will stand by one bravely when all is going smoothly, but which must not be put to any severe strain or it may snap. Then, again, we detect another variety of the article, who appears to be merely some one to be worked on, as, for example, "He is my friend that grindeth at my mill"—who comes to our help in our necessity, lends us money, tools, and so forth, and of whom we presently tire because he loses his yielding properties, or who presently tires of us and our multitudinous wants. Then there is the candid friend, who is theoretically such a helpmate, but who in practice grows unbearable. This by no means exhausts the types one meets with, and we soon find that "friend" is a noun of multitude and stands for many things, from pure gold down to the veriest brass or pinchbeck.

The touchy people who are easily offended are not the people to make friends, or to keep them long if they do make them. "Who would be loved must love," or, with a slightly different shade of meaning, "That you may be loved, forget not to be lovable." To love and to be lovable are both essential if you would be loved. "A man is little the better for liking himself if no one else like him," since self-sufficiency means selfishness, and love does not prosper on that. A very good hint against selfishness is found in the Spanish, "Who eats his dinner alone must saddle his horse alone," for no one will go out of their way to help curmudgeons. It is an excellent maxim, too, that "He who receives a good turn should never forget it; he who does one should never remember it."

All have not the tact of him whose praises Moore sings:

> "Whose wit in the combat as gentle as bright
> Ne'er carried a heart-stain away on its blade."

An old adage says, "Leave jesting ere it ceaseth to please"; while another warns us that "A joke never gains over an enemy, but often loses a friend." * Some folk have a bantering manner that is disastrous, and if not held sternly in check will presently turn a warm-hearted friendship into indifference and repulsion.

The part of the candid friend is a very difficult one; nothing short of transparent honesty and abounding sympathy will make it possible. "Few there are," says the adage, "that will endure a true friend"; while another runs, "I will be thy friend, but not thy vice's

---

* Similar wise counsel is found in the warning that "A jest driven too far brings home hate," and that "Jeerers must be content to taste of their own broth."

friend," but we should imagine that the recipient would scarcely take kindly to such a remark. "Better a little chiding than a great deal of heart-break," but few can bear it. On the other hand, "Toleration should spring from our charity, and not from our indifference." "Reproach is usually honest—the same cannot always be said of praise"; but the happiest proverb is, "Charity is greater than all." Those who live their lives in the light of that will need no lessons in the art of friendship, but will be already in the midst of friends, and themselves of that happy company.

Some people's notion of acquaintance seems to be what they can get out of it, and though they talk freely of "my friend," such folk have little notion of friendship. The following proverbs, though not exclusively theirs, point to this state of mind: "A friend in need is a friend indeed," "Short reckonings make long friends," "The begging of a courtesy is selling of liberty," "He is not charitable that will not be so privately," "Lenders have better memories than borrowers," "He is my friend that succoureth me, not he that pitieth me," "Promises may get friends, but performance keeps them," "He that gives his heart will not deny his money," "He loseth his thanks who promiseth and delayeth." Chaucer, in the "Romant of the Rose," writes:

> "Soth to saie
> Of him that loueth trew and well
> Frendship is more than is cattell,
> For frend in Court aie better is
> Then penny in purse certis";

while one of our old proverbs declares, "As a man is friended, so the law is ended." This seems to imply that in the case of the man who has friends on the bench Justice will be a little blinder than usual, but it is evident that an unknown and friendless culprit must necessarily start under a disadvantage.

The following proverbs we see we have classed in our rough notes as pertaining to "friends you have not proved," * and this classification may very well stand. It includes such sayings as "Friends got without desert will be lost without cause," "A friend is never known till one have need," "Before you make a friend eat a bushel of salt with him." Heywood seems to have got very near to the root of the matter in these lines of his:

> "Many kinsfolke and few friends, some folke say:
> But I find many kinsfolke and friend not one.
> Folke say it hath been sayd many yeares since gone
> Prove thy friend ere thou hast neede : but in deede
> A friend is never knone till a man have neede.
> Before I had neede my most present foes
> Seemed my best friends, but thus the world goes."

The experience, we suppose, of all men, if ever this testing time really comes, is a twofold surprise—how entirely some they had trusted failed them, and how splendidly others came out of whom it was not expected.

Seneca declares that "Our happiness depends upon the choice of our company," and we may, we suppose, take it that we all of us get about such friends as we deserve. "Our friends are the mirror in which we see ourselves." Other excellent adages pertaining to friendship are these: "Be slow in choosing a friend, slower yet in changing"; † "Friendship multiplies joy and divides grief"; "Wherever you see your friend trust yourself"; "The way to have a friend is to be one";

---

* " Myne ease is builded all on trust,
　　And yet mistrust breedes myne anoye."—*Gascoigne*.

† "I love everything that is old—old friends, old times, old manners, old books."—"She Stoops to Conquer."

"What find you better or more honourable than age? Take the pre-eminence of it in everything: in an old friend, in old wine, in an old pedigree."—"The Antiquary."

"Hearts may agree though heads differ"; "Wise and good men are friends, others are but companions"; "Search thy friend for his virtues, thyself for thy faults"; "Love sought is good, but given unsought is better"; "God divideth man into men, that so they may help each other"; "A man is valued as he makes himself valuable." The Spaniards declare that "Eggs of an hour, bread of a day, wine of a year, a friend of thirty years, are best."

> "The friends thou hast, and their adoption tried,
> Grapple them to thy soul with hooks of steel";

and in another passage Shakespeare writes of kindly

> "Words of so sweet breath compounded,
> As made the things more rich";

and it certainly appears to us that if we had reached the lowest depth of destitution we would yet rather have the gracious inability to help that some would express to us than the brusque brutality of some donors. When one would seek fine thoughts admirably presented one naturally turns in the first place to Shakespeare, but Chaucer makes an excellent second. How charming this line from "The Clerke's Tale," "He is gentil that doeth gentil dedis," and this passage again from the "Romant of the Rose":

> "Loue of frendshippe also there is,
> Which maketh no man dou amis,
> Of wil knitte betwixt two,
> That wol not breke for wele ne wo."

Tusser, in his quaint directness, says in his "Five Hundred Points of Good Husbandrie":

> "The quiet friend all one in worde and dede
> Great comfort is, like ready golde at nede
> With bralling fooles that wrall for euerie wrong
> Firme friendship neuer can continue long.

Oft times a friend is got with easie cost,
Which vsed euill is oft as quickly lost.
Hast thou a friend, as heart may wish at will?
Then vse him so to haue his friendship still.
Wouldst haue a friend, wouldst knowe what friend is best?
Haue God thy friend, who passeth all the rest."

The following sayings of warning and experience have their valuable lessons:—"Trust not new friend nor old enemy"; "Though the sore may be healed yet the scar may remain";* "Small wounds, if many, may be mortal"; "Vexation is rather taken than given"; "At the gate which suspicion enters friendship departs"; "False friends are worse than open enemies"; "He that ceased to be a friend never was a good one"; "An unbidden guest knoweth not where to sit"; "All are not friends that speak us fair"; "Every one's friend, no one's"; "A friend that you buy will be bought from you."

An old saw bluntly says, "To make an enemy lend money, and ask for it again"; and it is certainly an excellent rule to have as little to do with money matters as one can help with one's friends and relatives. To appeal for help and to be refused, to lend and to see very little chance of repayal, to receive and to be under a heavy sense of obligation, are all destructive of frank and hearty friendship. Chaucer declares that

"His herte is hard that woll not weke
When men of meeknesse him beseeke."

An excellent man, most kindly in all his dealings, told us that he never lent money. The borrower is ordinarily in such straits that he has little chance of ever repaying. If he never intends to pay he is a

* "Geflickte Freundschaft wird selten wieder ganz," say the Germans —patched up friendship seldom becomes whole again.

knave,* and if he has more honourable thought he is crushed by the burden of the debt. Anyone who came to our excellent friend with a true and touching story was sympathetically received, and his request for the temporary loan of twenty pounds promptly declined! As an alternative he was offered a somewhat smaller sum, the half or, mayhap, the quarter of this, as a free gift, which he never failed to accept joyfully. In one of the Harleian manuscripts, dating from the reign of Edward IV., the writer's experience is a very common one, and his decision sound :

> " I wold lend but I ne dare,
> I have lent and I will beware
> When I lant I had a frynd,
> When I hym asked he was unkynd.
> Thus of my frynd I made my foo,
> Therefore darre I lend no moo."

The writer was evidently a kindly man, desiring to do the best he could, and he touchingly appeals to us not to judge him harshly :

> " I pray yo of your gentilnesse
> Report for no unkyndnesse."

Some one has very wisely remarked that many of the disappointments of life arise from our mistaking acquaintances for friends, and then when some little testing incident arises they break under the strain. " Prosperity makes friends, adversity proves them." One sarcastic adage hath it that " Friends are like fiddle-strings : they must not be screwed too tight "; but the Scotch say, and justly, that " He that's no my friend at a pinch is no my friend ava." Some

---

* Tusser writes of such :

> " His promise to pay is as slipprie as ice,
> His credit much like the cast of the dice,
> His knowledge and skill is in prating too much,
> His companie shunned, and so be all such.
> His friendship is counterfeit, seldome to trust."

centuries ago, human nature being then evidently very similar to what it is to-day, a wise man wrote : " If thou wouldst get a friend, prove him first, and be not hasty to credit him. For some man is a friend for his own occasion, and will not abide in the day of thy trouble ; and there is a friend who, being turned to enmity and strife, will discover thy reproach ; again, some friend is a companion at the table, and will not continue in the day of thy affliction."

In Chaucer's " Romaunt of the Rose," we find the poet using the expression, " Farewel fieldfare," a valediction on summer friends that, like the wild and migratory fieldfare, take to themselves wings and depart. An old rhyming adage declares that " In time of prosperity friends will be plenty, in time of adversity not one in twenty " ; or, to quote Tusser :

> " Where welthines floweth, no friendship can lack,
> Whom pouertie pincheth, hath friendship as slack " ;

while Goldsmith, it will be remembered, bitterly sums all up in,

> "What is friendship but a name,
> A charm that lulls to sleep,
> A shade that follows wealth and fame,
> But leaves the wretch to weep."

Another adage declares that " Compliments cost nothing but may be dearly bought," while another candidly warns, " I cannot be your friend and your flatterer too." The flatterer has ordinarily "an axe to grind,"

> " His fetch is to flatter, to get what he can,
> His purpose once gotten, a fig for thee then."

In the "Rambler" No. 155, Johnson sapiently remarks, " Flattery, if its operations be nearly examined, will be found to owe its acceptance, not to our ignorance, but to our knowledge of our failures, and to delight us rather as it consoles our wants than displays our possessions." Swift asserts that

> " 'Tis an old maxim in the schools,
> That flattery's the food of fools,
> Yet now and then your men of wit
> Will condescend to take a bit."

Bacon tells us, however, that " There is no such flatterer as is a man's selfe, and there is no such remedie against flatterie of a man's selfe as the libertie of a friend." It has been said that " A friend's frown is worth more than a fool's smile," but a cynical writer has affirmed, with some little truth, that " Most of our misfortunes are more supportable than the comments of our friends upon them," and it was long since discovered that " Whoso casteth a stone at the birds frayeth them away, and he that upbraideth his friend breaketh friendship." The duty of remonstrance is one of the most difficult that the friend can undertake, and " Save, save, O save me from the candid friend!" is the cry of Canning in " The New Morality," a cry that many have been inclined to echo.

Our ancestors, with blunt directness, asserted that " Fish and guests stink in three days," while the Arabs have the picturesque proverb, " A thousand raps, but no welcome "—a pertinacious hammering at the closed door but no response from within ; a fruitless endeavour to thrust an intimacy on those who do not desire it.

We have seen that the friend lost is never really recovered and may become very readily an implacable enemy. Shakespeare warns us to " Trust not him that hath once broken faith," and we most of us know by experience how true are the lines of Dryden :

> " Forgiveness to the injured doth belong,
> But they ne'er pardon who have done the wrong."

The ancient Romans had a proverb that the French have adopted in the words, "Jeter de l'huile sur le feu." We have no identical English proverb, but its meaning is clearly a reference to those evil spirits who foment a quarrel, add fuel to the fire, irritate rather than soothe, and who have no part or lot in the blessing promised to the peace-makers.

The following adages are here worthy of our consideration :—" He that does you an ill turn will not forgive you"; "Pardon others often, thyself seldom "; " We are bound to forgive an enemy, but we are not bound to trust him " ; * " Better ride alone than have a bad man's company "; " Haste is the beginning of wrath, and its end repentance "; " It is wiser to prevent a quarrel than to revenge it "; " If thou wouldst be borne with, bear with others." To these we may add the oft-used saw, " The absent are always wrong," without at all endorsing its truth. The absent are often quite as right as the other people, and are merely unable through absence to protect themselves from defamation.

Poverty and riches naturally find a place in proverb-lore. " Poverty," says an old author, "is no crime, and it is no credit "; but the truth is, it is impossible to generalise quite so dogmatically as this—for poverty may be a crime when a lazy ne'er-do-well allows his wife and children to come to rags, and, on the othe hand, it may be a credit when a man has done his best and foresworn all the dirty little tricks that have enriched his trade rivals. It is sometimes too readily and sentimentally assumed that poverty is itself a benediction ; hence such sayings as " The poor are

---

* " The book sayeth that no wight retourneth safely into the grace of his olde enemie, and Ysope sayth, ne troste not to hem, to which thou hast some time hed werre or enmitee, ne telle hem not thy counseil." —CHAUCER, *The Tale of Melibeus.*

P

God's receivers and the angels are His auditors," but the real state of the case is excellently well put in the proverb, "There are God's poor, and the devil's poor."

> " Honour and shame from no condition rise ;
> Act well your part, there all the honour lies."

Everywhere in life, some one has admirably said, the true question is not what we gain, but rather what we do. "Poverty need not be shame, but being ashamed of it is," poverty of spirit being a more distressing state of things than emptiness of pocket.

Let us turn to the wisdom of those who have gone before us, and see what teaching for our edification we may find. "Nothing is to be got without pains except poverty"; "Dependence is a poor trade to follow"; "Opportunities do not generally wait"; "Enough is a plenty, too much is pride"; "The groat is ill-saved which shames its master"; "Providence provides for the provident"; "To bear is to conquer"; "Poverty craves much, but avarice more"; "Gain ill-gotten is loss"; "Poverty is the mother of all arts"; "Content is the true philosopher's stone"; "If honesty cannot, knavery must not"; "Poor and content is rich"; "Flatterers haunt not cottages"; "Thrive honestly, or remain poor."

In a manuscript of the fifteenth century we found the following excellent precepts amongst many others, the whole being much too long to quote :

> " If thou be visite with pouerte
> Take it not to hevyle
> For he that sende the adversite
> May turn the agen to wele.
> Purpose thy selfe in charite
> Demene thy worschip in honeste
> Let not nygardschip haue the maystre
> For schame that may befalle

> Faver not meche thy ryeches,
> Set not lytel by worthynes
> Kepe thyn hert from dowblenes
> For any manner thyng."

Another budget of excellent precepts will commend itself to the thoughtful reader in the following :—" He who buys what he does not want will want what he cannot buy"; "Winter finds out what summer has laid up "; " Sleeping master makes servant lazy "; " Thrush paid for is better than turkey owed for "; " Better small fish than empty dish "; " He that borrows binds himself with his neighbour's rope "; " A man must plough with such oxen as he hath "; " He goes like a top, no longer than he is whipped "; " Better half a loaf than no bread "; " Better do it than wish it done "; " He that goes borrowing goes sorrowing "; " Better say here it is, than here it was "; " If you light the fire at both ends the middle will take care of itself."

Some three hundred years ago an old writer thought out what he called " the ladder to thrift," and these were some of his hints :

> " To take thy calling thankfully
> And shun the path to beggary.
>
> To grudge in youth no drudgery,
> To come by knowledge perfectly.
>
> To plow profit earnestlie,
> But meddle not with pilferie.
>
> To hold that thine is lawfullie
> For stoutness or for flatterie.
>
> To suffer none live idlelie
> For feare of idle knaverie.
>
> To answere stranger ciuilie,
> But show him not thy secresie.
>
> To vse no friend deceitfully,
> To offer no man villeny.

To learne how foe to pacifie,
But trust him not too trustilie.

To meddle not with vsurie
Nor lend thy monie foolishlie.

To loue thy neighbor neighborly
And shew him no discurtesy.

To learne to eschew ill company
And such as liue dishonestlie."

Though quaintly put—and their quaintness is accentuated by spelling such as would not at all pass muster in these iron-bound days of examinations for high and low, rich and poor—these halting couplets contain a full modicum of excellent common-sense.

It is not really the man whose possessions are few who is poor as he whose desires are great, and it has been well said that if we help some one who is worse off than ourselves we soon realise that we are more affluent than we thought. The helping to bear another's burden does not add to our own, but lightens it.

The French say, "Vent au visage rend un homme sage," a proverb fairly paralleled in an English adage, "Adversity makes a man wise, not rich." A quaint and serviceable proverb, quoted by Ray and others, though it has now passed quite out of use, is the assertion that "A bad bush is better than the open field," whether in sultry sunshine, piercing gale, or heavy downpour. It is better to have some friends, even though they can do little or nothing for us, than to be thrown quite destitute on a pitiless world ; and it is wiser to make the best of what is than to scorn the small amount of help that it is able to give.

Wealth has its store of proverb-wisdom even in more abundance than poverty has, and it is only reasonable that this should be so, for it is a position of great responsibility, and its proper use requires all the wisdom that a man possesses, and sometimes, as we see, more than he possesses. Let us turn, then, to the precepts of the past and see what of value we can find in them for the present and the future. The following are a few of these:—" If a good man thrive, all will thrive with him ";* "Riches rather enlarge than satisfy appetite"; " Possess your money, but do not let it possess you"; " Reputation is often measured by the acre"; " Great spenders are bad lenders"; "Liberality is not giving largely, but giving wisely"; "One may buy gold too dearly"; " He gives but little who gives only from a sense of duty"; " No estate can make him rich that hath a poor heart"; " Lavishness is not generosity"; " Great receipt renders us liable to great account"; "Wealth is not his that gets it, but his that enjoys it";† " Worth has been under-rated ever since wealth was over-rated "; " Covetous people always think themselves in want"; " He is alone rich who has contentment"; " God reaches us good things by our own hands"; " Slow help is very little help at all"; "Bounty is more commended than imitated ";‡ "Spare well that you may spend well"; " The liberal

---

* " To become rich is a good thing, but to make all rich about you is better."—*V. Hugo.*

　† " They call'd thee rich, I deem'd thee poor,
　　　Since, if thou dar'dst not use thy store,
　　　But sav'd it only for thy heirs,
　　　The treasure was not thine, but theirs."

" The prodigal robs his heir ; the miser himself."

‡ " Bountifulness is as a most fruitful garden, and mercifulness endureth for ever." " Of great riches there is no real use, except it be in distribution, the rest is but conceit."

　　" Who shuts his hand hath lost his gold,
　　　Who opens it, hath it twice told."

hand gathers."* It has been said that "Some men give of their means and others of their meanness," and the statement has copious experience either way to fully justify it.

Plutarch declared "E tribus optimis rebus tres pessimæ oriuntur,"—that from three things excellent three very bad things were produced ; truth begetting hatred, familiarity contempt, and success envy. Another old Roman saying is, "An dives sit, omnes quærunt, nemo an bonus"—all want to know if a man be rich, but no one troubles to inquire if he be good ; yet "Great possession is not necessarily great enjoyment," and the moralist warns us—

"Put not in this world too much trust,
The riches whereof will turne to dust."†

"As a means of grace prosperity has never been much of a success." The Spaniards say, "Honor y provecho no capen en un saco": "Honour and profit cannot be contained in the same bag," rather too sweeping a statement. Another Spanish adage is, "El que trabaja y madra, hila oro": "He who labours and strives spins gold," reaps the reward of his industry. The French say, in praise of the thriftiness that is so characteristic of them, that "Le petit gain remplit la bourse": "Light gains make a full purse." Those who sell dearly sell little, and the small margin of profit oft repeated is the more advantageous. The Spanish proverb affirms that "He who would be rich in a year gets hanged in half a year," the pace being too

---

* "If lyberalyte be well and duely employed it acquireth pepetuelle honour to the gyuer, and moche frute and syngular commoditie thereby encreaseth."—*Elyot.*

† "A little wealth will suffice us to live well, and still less to die well." "Seek not proud riches, but such as thou mayest get justly, use soberly, distribute cheerfully, and leave contentedly."

great for honesty to keep up with. Another maxim
of thrift is that "If you make not much of three-
pence you will never be worth a groat." The moral
atmosphere, however, is getting a little stifling, and
we are reminded of the lines of Gower on the over-
frugal man :

> " For he was grutchende euermore,
> There was wyth hym none other fare
> But for to pinche and for to spare
> Of worldes mucke to gette encres."

Let us "Take care of the pence that the pounds may
take care of themselves,"* but having got the pounds
let us remember that "Judicious saving affords the
means of judicious giving," and that "The best way
to expand the chest is to have a large heart in it."
"Money is a good servant but an ill master," and
"He is not fit for riches who is afraid to use them";
"To a good spender God is treasurer."

Woman's influence on mankind is the subject of
many proverbs, some of them kindly enough in tone,
but the greater number of them characterised by satire
and bitter feeling. As a sample of the first method
of treating the subject may be instanced the testimony
borne by this old rhyming adage : "Two things do
prolong thy life—a quiet heart and a loving wife."
It has been truly said that "A man's best fortune,
or his worst, is a wife," and another excellent saying
is this : "Men make houses—women make homes."†

---

* "But then their saving pennie proverbe comes."—"Two Angry
Women of Abington," 1599.

† "Who so fyndeth an honest faythfull woman she is moch more
worth than perles. The hert of her husband maye safely trust in her,
so that he shall have no nede of spoyles. She wyll do hym good and
not euill all the dayes of her lyf. Strength and honoure is her clothynge
and in the latter daye she shall reioyce. She openeth her mouth with

Another wise old saw tells us that a man should
" Choose a wife rather by ear than eye," judging her,
not by personal charms, that are at best evanescent,*
but by the kindliness of her nature and by the testimony
of her worth that others declare.   " Beauty," we are
warned, " is but skin-deep," a truth that the old moral-
ists and painters sometimes made more of with their
paraphernalia of skulls and other symbols of mortality
than was altogether seemly.   St Chrysostom writes :
" When thou seest a fair and beautiful person, a comely
woman, having bright eyes and merry countenance, a
pleasant grace, bethink with thyself that it is but earth
that thou seest."†

Another piece of sound proverbial teaching is this :
" Choose your wife on a Saturday, not Sunday," that
is to say, be drawn to her rather by what you see of
her industry and power of management than be merely
fascinated by a triumph of the milliner's art ; choose
her rather when her sweetness of temper carries her
smoothly through turmoil and worry than when the
Sunday rest gives no test of her power to stand this
strain.   Saturday manners may be very different to
Sunday manners.

> " Good husewife good fame hath of best in the towne,
> Ill husewife ill name hath of euerie clowne."

Amongst popular proverbs we find the cautious—

wysdome, and in her tonge is the lawe of grace. She loketh well to
the wayes of her housholde, and eateth not her bred with ydelnes.
Her children aryse and call her blessed : and her husband maketh
moche of her."—" Matthew's Version of Bible," 1537.

> " La beauté du visage est un frêle ornement,
> Une fleur passagère, un éclat d'un moment."—*Molière.*

† " But admitting your body's finer, all that beauty is but skin-deep."
—" The Female Rebellion," 1682.   " All the beauty of the world, 'tis
but skin-deep, a sunne-blast defaceth it." — " Orthodoxe Paradoxes,"
1650.

"Marry in haste and repent at leisure,"* and "Love and lordship like not fellowship," and the advice—"Marry for love, but only love that which is lovely." It is very gracefully true, too, that "When the goodman's from home the good-wife's table is soon spread," while there is quaint sarcasm in this : "Next to no wife a good wife is best ";† and the value of influence is brought before us in the adage, "A good Jack makes a good Jill."

In Torrington churchyard we find the following high testimony to a wife :—

> "She was—my words are wanting to say what—
> Think what a woman should be—she was that";

while in Chaucer's "Shipmanne's Tale" we find the following quaint appeal :—

> "For which, my dere wife, I thee beseke,
> As be to every wight buxom and meke,
> And for to kepe our good be curious,
> And honestly governe wel our hous."

The following Italian proverb is a very happy one, and accords entirely with general experience :— "La donna savia è all' impensata, alla pensata è matta": "Women are wise offhand and fools on reflection"; while the advice of the Spaniard, though ungracious enough in its utterance, is valuable—"El consejo de la muger es poco, y quieu no le toma es loco": "A

---

* "Daughter, in this I can thinke none other
But that it is true thys prouerbe old,
Hastye loue is soone hot and soone cold."
—"Play of Wyt and Science," c. 1540.

† "Whosoever lives unmarried lives without joy, without comfort, without blessing. Love your wife like yourself, honour her more than yourself. It is woman alone through whom God's blessings are vouch-safed to a house. She teaches the children, speeds the husband, and welcomes him when he returns, keeps the house godly and pure, and God's blessings rest upon these things."—*Talmud.*

woman's counsel is no great thing, but he who does not take it is a fool." An old English proverb goes so far as to declare that " A man must ask his wife's leave to thrive," and there is not a little wisdom in the counsel. A very ungracious proverb, indeed, is the German—" Es giebt nur zwei gute Weiber auf der Welt : die Eine ist gestorben, die Andere nicht zu finden ": "There are only two good women in the world ; one of them is dead, and the other is not to be found."

Some would tells us that marriages are made in heaven,* but a sapient saw reminds us that " There is no marriage in heaven, neither is there always heaven in marriage."

Gossip, and the mischief-making that may too often accrue from imprudent loquacity, have at all times been so commonly attributed to the fair sex that we naturally find many such proverbs as these : "Silence is not the greatest vice of a woman "; " A woman conceals what she does not know "; " He that tells his wife news is but newly married." The words of Hotspur will be recalled :

> " Constant you are,
> But yet a woman, and for secrecy
> No lady closer; for I well believe
> Thou wilt not utter what thou dost not know."

The writer of Ecclesiasticus declares that "As the climbing up a sandy way is to the feet of the aged, so is a wife full of words to a quiet man "; while in a MS. of the time of Henry V. we find the following quaint statement :—

---

* " You see marriage is destinie, made in heaven, though consummated on earth."—LELY, *Mother Bombie*, 1594. Shakespeare, too, in the " Merchant of Venice," declares that "hanging and wiving go by destiny." In "The Cheats," written by Wilson in 1662, Scruple remarks, "Good sir, marriages are made in heaven." Many similar passages to these might be cited.

"Two wymen in one howse,
Two cattes and one mowse,
Two dogges and one bone
Maye never accorde in one."

Udall writes that " As the kynde of women is naturally geuen to the vyce of muche bablynge there is nothyng wherein theyr womanlynesse is more honestlie garnyshed than with sylence "; but a Welsh proverb declares that " A woman's strength is in her tongue," * and we can scarcely be surprised that she is at times reluctant to forego the use of this weapon.

The Spaniards sarcastically assert that " He who is tired of a quiet life gets him a wife "; and Solomon, we recall, declares that " It is better to dwell in a corner of the house-top than with a brawling woman "; while another proverb bitterly, but truly, declares that " He fasts enough whose wife scolds all dinner-time "; and yet another hath it that " He that can abide a curst wife need not fear any "; so that an old writer breaks out:

"Why then I see to take a shrew
(As seldome other there be few)
Is not the way to thriue:
So hard a thing I spie it is,
The good to chuse, the shrew to mis,
That feareth me to wiue."

This bitter feeling against womankind is seen not only in our proverbs, but very largely also in epitaphs, as for example:

" Here lies my wife, a sad slattern and shrew,
If I said I respected her I should lie too."

" Here lies my wife, and, Heaven knows,
Not less for mine than her repose."

---

* " He is a fool who thinks by force or skill
To turn the current of a woman's will."
TUKE, *Adventures of Five Hours*, 1673.

> "Here lies my poor wife, much lamented;
> She is happy, and I am contented."

> "Here rests my spouse; no pair through life
> So equal lived as we did;
> Alike we shared perpetual strife,
> Nor knew I rest till she did."

> "Here lies my poor wife,
> Without bed or blanket;
> But dead as a door nail:
> God be thanked."

At Prittlewell Church a man buried his two wives in one grave, and then placed over their remains this callous rigmarole:

> "Were it my choice that either of the twaine
> Might be restor'd to me to enjoy again,
> Which should I choose?
> Well, since I know not whether,
> I'll mourn for the loss of both,
> But wish for neither." *

On the tomb of a man at Bilston we get the other side, as the widow selected as a text the words: "If any man ask you, why do you loose him, then shall ye say unto him, because the Lord hath need of him." Those who recall the occasion on which these words were first used will see that her husband was, by implication, an ass.

* The following, from Wycombe Church, is an agreeable variation:

> " Here lies one, whose rest
> Gives me a restless life,
> Because I've lost a good
> And virtuous wife."

In Milton Abbot Church we find a memorial to one Bartholomew Doidge and Joan, his wife. The wife was buried on the 1st of February 1681, and the husband on the 12th, and the inscription goes on to say:

> " She first deceased: he a little tried
> To live without her, liked it not, and died."

Mere loquacity is satirised in the two following :—

> " Here lies, returned to Clay,
> Miss Arabella Young,
> Who, on the first of May,
> Began to hold her tongue."

> " Beneath this silent stone is laid
> A noisy, antiquated maid,
> Who from her cradle talked till death,
> And ne'er before was out of breath."

Other proverbs that deal with womankind are the following :—" He that has a wife has strife "; " Of all tame beasts sluts are the worst "; " If a woman were as little as good, a peascod would make her a gown and a hood "; " He that loses his wife and a farthing hath great loss of the farthing "; " Every man can tame a shrew but he that hath her "; " Lips, however rosy, must be fed "; " Women, wind, and fortune soon change." The feminine readiness to take refuge in tears is responsible for the following cynical adage :— " It is no more sin to see a woman weep than to see a goose go barefoot." * Another well-known proverb is that " No mischief in the world is done, but a woman is always one "; while the French say, if any inexplicable trouble breaks out, " Cherchez la femme "—in the assured belief that a woman is in some way or another at the bottom of it. Lamartine, on the other hand, declares that " There is a woman at the beginning of all great things." There is considerable truth in both statements, antagonistic as they are.

In the household where the unfortunate husband has allowed the control to slip into the hands of his

---

* " By thys tale ye may se that the olde prouerbe ys trew that yt is as gret pyte to se a woman wepe as a gose to go barefoote."—" Mery Tayls," c. 1525. Puttenham, in " The Arte of English Poesie," 1589, gives a rather different rendering, a satire on feminine gush and misplaced sympathy, " By the common prouerbe a woman will weepe for pitie to see a gosling goe barefoote."

wife, "The grey mare is the better horse." The French call this "Le marriage d'epervier"—a hawk's wedding, because the female hawk is the bigger bird. In "A Treatyse Shewing and Declaring the Pryde and Abuse of Women Now a Days," c. 1550, we find:

> "What! shall the graye mayre be the better horse,
>   And be wanton styll at home?
> Naye, then, welcome home, Syr Woodcocke,
>   Ye shall be tamed anone."

Heywood, writing in the year 1546, has the couplet:

> "She is, quoth he, bent to force you perforce,
> To know that the grey mare is the better horse,"

and in many of the old plays the saying crops up:

> "Ill thrives that hapless family that shows
>   A cock that's silent and a hen that crows;
> I know not which live more unnatural lives,
>   Obeying husbands, or commanding wives."

"The whistling maid" and "the crowing hen" are alike held objectionable, these masculine performances being considered entirely out of place and of bad omen.

The perils of matrimony would, according to the proverb-mongers, appear to be so great that we can scarcely wonder at the counsel:

> "If that a batchelor thou bee
> Keepe the same style, be ruled by mee,
> Lest that repentance all too late
> Rewarde thee withe a broken pate.
> Iff thou be yonge then marye not yett,
> Iff thou be olde thou hast more wytt:
> For yonge men's wyves wyll not be taught,
> And olde men's wyves bee good for nought."

The home-life has goodly store of proverbial wisdom associated with it. The French say: "Chaque oiseau trouve son nid bien," and the Italians, "Ad ogni uccello il suo nido é bello," while the Englishman says, "East,

west, home is best." *   Monckton Milnes very truly
says, "A man's best things are nearest him, lie close
about his feet"; and a charming old saying is this,
that "Small cheer, with great welcome, make a big
feast." Proverbs, it must be confessed, are ordinarily
very worldly wise, and much more frequently see the
worse than the better side of things, and most of
the adages about the home are very materialistic in
tone; the sweet sentiment that is associated with the
idea must be sought elsewhere. "The suit is best that
fits me best," says an English adage, and the comfort
of content is seen again in the Scottish saying—
"Better a little fire that warms than mickle that
burns." Socrates, passing through the markets, cried:
"How much is here I do not want." "He who wants
content," says an old proverb, "cannot find an easy
chair."

Prudential maxims are very numerous; thus, we are
warned that "Wilful waste makes woful want," that
"Silks and satins put out the kitchen fire," and that
"If you pay not a servant his wages he will pay
himself;" while caution in another direction is advised in the saying, "The child says in the street
what he heard at the fireside," and in this: "One
bad example spoils many good precepts." The
Germans say that "It is easier to build two hearths
than to keep a fire in one," while the Portuguese

---

* "The shuddering tenant of the frigid zone,
  Boldly proclaims the happiest spot his own,
  Extols the treasures of his stormy seas,
  And his long night of revelry and ease.
  The naked savage, panting at the line,
  Boasts of his golden sands, and palmy wine,
  Basks in the glare, or stems the tepid wave,
  And thanks his gods for all the good they gave.
  Nor less the patriot's boast, where'er he roam,
  His first, best country, ever is at home."
                          —GOLDSMITH, *The Traveller.*

advocate a judicious blending of prudence with sentiment in the adage : " Marry, marry, but what about
the housekeeping ? "—a by no means unimportant consideration.   Love in a cottage will fare the better if the
larder be not too bare.

The writer of Ecclesiasticus describes very happily
the plight of the unwelcome guest—the man or woman
who, as we say in English, is sitting all the while on
thorns.   " Better is the life of a poor man in a mean
cottage than delicate fare in another man's house.   For
it is a miserable life to go from house to house, for
where thou art a stranger thou darest not open thy
mouth.   Give place, thou stranger, to an honourable
man ; my brother cometh to be lodged, and I have
need of mine house "—a sufficiently humiliating dis-
missal.   It has, we presume, been the lot of most
people to find themselves the objects of a special
and not quite disinterested friendship ; to feel that one
is being used, and one's kindness abused.   Such people
in the end defeat their own object, since one soon
learns to avoid the risk of an invitation for a week
when we remember that the last acceptance of such
an invitation meant a two months' sojourn, and the
upsetting of all our plans.   Proverbs relating to this
state of things will be seen in " An unbidden guest
knows not where to sit " ; " Who depends on another's
table may often dine late " ; and the advice to " Scald
not your lips with another's porridge "—all warnings of
excellent value and weight.

Our readers will long ere this have discovered that
the book of Ecclesiasticus is ever at our elbow when
we would find words of wisdom, and we turn to it now
afresh in our search for caution as to the tale-bearer and
the breaker of confidences.   " Love thy friend and be
faithful unto him ; but if thou bewrayest his secrets
follow no more after him.   For as a man hath de-

stroyed his enemy, so hast thou lost the love of thy neighbour. As one that letteth a bird go out of his hand, so hast thou let thy neighbour go, and shall not get him again." And elsewhere, in the same treasury of wisdom, we read : " Whoso discovereth secrets loseth his credit, and shall never find friend to his need." In the Book of Proverbs * we find : " He that repeateth a matter separateth very friends "—loss of faith implying loss of friend.

Chaucer, it will be remembered, says that " Three may keep a counsel if twain be away." Another old writer tells us that " Curiosity is a kernel of the forbidden fruit, which still sticketh in the heart of the natural man," and this is seen almost at its worst when endeavouring to find out a matter that the person most concerned would desire to leave unknown, and quite at its worst when knowledge thus gained is made general property. " None are so fond of secrets as those who do not mean to keep them." There is no more trying person to deal with than he or she who continually punctuate their conversation with cautions that they " wish this matter to go no further," and warn us that that detail is " entirely between ourselves." They are an unmitigated nuisance.

A very quaint old proverb is that which tells us that " He was scarce of news that told that his father was hanged," and a very excellent rule of conduct is this : " Whether it be to friend or foe talk not of other men's lives." We are warned, too, that " He who chatters to you will chatter also of you," and the experience of most of us will confirm the wisdom of the adage.

Other happy sayings are these : " No one will repeat the matter if it be not said "; " Sudden trust heralds

* The Book of Proverbs is no less rich in wisdom than the Book of Ecclesiasticus, but the latter being somewhat less familiar to many readers we prefer to draw upon its pages in illustration of our English adages.

Q

sudden repentance"; "More have repented of speech
than of silence"; "A fool will neither give nor keep
counsel"; "He that tells all he knows will also tell what
he does not know"; "To tell our own secrets is folly,
to tell those of others treachery"; "Thy friend has a
friend, and thy friend's friend hath a friend"—great
discretion is therefore necessary.

Heywood warns the man who thinks himself secure:

> "Some heare and see him whom he heareth and seeth not
> For fieldes have eies and woods have eares ye wot,"

an idea that we find yet earlier in a manuscript,
"King Edward and the Shepherd," written about the
year 1300:

> "The were bettur be styll,
> Wode has erys, felde has syght."

So gracious a gift of Heaven to the sons of men as
hope must necessarily find recognition in our proverbial
wisdom. Our readers will recall the lines in Pope's
"Essay on Man," where he declares that

> "Hope springs eternal in the human breast;
> Man never is, but always to be, blest.
> The soul, uneasy, and confin'd from home
> Rests and expatiates in a life to come."

And in "Measure for Measure" we read that "the
miserable have no other medicine, but only hope";
hence the saying: "Quench not hope, for when hope
dies all dies." The Italians say: "L'ultima che si
perde è la speranza"—the last thing lost is hope,*

---

* "To speed to-day, to be put back to-morrow;
    To feed on hope, to pine with feare and sorrow;
    To fret thy soule with crosses and with cares;
    To eate thy heart through comfortlesse dispaires."
    —*Spenser.*

and the terrible words in the " Paradise Lost " recur
to us :

> " So farewell hope, and, with hope, farewell fear,
> Farewell remorse : all good to me is lost,
> Evil, be thou my good."

Lord Bacon, being in York House garden, looking
at some fishermen as they were throwing their nets
in what was then the pellucid and silvery Thames,
asked them what they would take for their catch.
They mentioned a certain price, and his lordship
offered them somewhat less, which they declined to
accept. They drew up their nets and in it were but
three small fishes, and Lord Bacon said that it had
been better for them had they closed with his offer.
They replied that they had hoped that the catch
would have been much greater, and his lordship in
response reminded them of the proverb, " Hope is a
good breakfast, but a bad supper " ;* and an admirably
true saying it is.

A pithy old adage has it that " Hope is as cheap
as despair," and it is certainly pleasanter ; while
another proverb tells us, as we lament departed
opportunities, " When one door shuts another opens,"
a comforting state of things that the experience of
many will confirm. How strong the encouragement
to look forward with courage when cares seem over-
whelming is the reminder that " When the tale of
bricks is doubled Moses comes." Philosophy, good as

* In the following passage Bacon shows us hope as a veritable life-
preserver. " Hope, being the best of all the affections and passions, is
very powerful to prolong life, if, like a nodding muse, it does not fall asleep
and languish, but continually feeds the fancy : and therefore such as
propose certain ends to be compassed, thriving and prospering therein
according to their desire, are commonly long-lived ; but having attained
to their highest hopes, all their expectations and desires being satisfied, live
not long afterwards."

it is, breaks under the strain, and is, when most wanted, but a broken reed. Goldsmith, in his play of " The Good-natured Man," says that "this same philosophy is a good horse in the stable, but an arrant jade on a journey," and Rochefoucauld equally happily declares that "Philosophy triumphs easily over past and over future evils, but present evils triumph over philosophy." We are reminded here anew of that definition of a proverb, " The wit of one voicing the experience of many," for certainly here Rochefoucauld supplies the *esprit* while the rest of mankind can in this matter supply the experience.

A quaint little French proverb is this, " L'espoir du pendu que la corde casse," when they wish to express the idea of a very faint ground indeed for hope. When all that a man who is already hanging can hope for is that the cord may perchance break, his chance of a reprieve is but small. He has most legitimate ground for hope who has already done what in him lay to deserve success, hence foresight and forethought are a valuable possession : the one to see in advance the possibilities, the other to think how best to turn them to account :

> "When all is done, lerne this my sonne
> Not friend, nor skill, nor wit at will,
> Nor ship, nor clod, but onelie God,
>   Doth all in all.
> Man taketh paine, God giueth gaine,
> Man doth his best, God doth the rest,
> Man knew well intendes, God foizon * sendes
>   Else want he shall."

The value of forethought in various directions is enforced in the following wisdom-chips: " A wise man will make more opportunities than he finds " ; " Hasty

* In Cotgrave's Dictionary defined as " store, plentie, abundance, great fulnesse, enough."

climbers have sudden falls "; * "Count not your chickens before they are hatched "; "He that would enjoy the fruit must not gather the flower "; "Short reflection may save long regret "; "From bad to worse is poor exchange "; "Haste makes waste "; "Leave not to hazard what forethought may provide for "; "Cast not away the dirty water till thou hast clean "; "Little chips will kindle a large fire "; "Look before you leap "; "Beware of—had I known this before "; "Better be sure first than sorry after "; "Be wisely worldly, not worldly wise "; "Take heed that the relish be not spoiled by the cost "; "Heaven is a cheap purchase, whatever it costs "; "Ask thy purse what thou shouldest buy "; "He that measureth not himself is measured "; "When a fool hath bethought himself, the market is over "; "If things could be done twice all would be wise "; "Small beginnings may have great endings "; "A forest is in an acorn "; "Every maybe hath a maybe not "; "While it is fine weather mend your sails "; "Measure thrice before cutting once "; "Haste trips up its own heels "; "Take more time, that you may have done the sooner "; "Wisdom not only gets but retains "; "Defer not till to-morrow to be wise "; "Safe bind, safe find "; "A little wariness may save much weariness "; "Haste is a poor apology "; "That which the fool has to do in the end the wise man does at first "; and even then the dilatory man may never compass the task, for our position in life on the morrow depends largely upon our attitude of to-day,

---

* "Babel's projectors, seeking a name, found confusion ; and Icarus, by flying too high, melted his waxen wings and fell into the sea." " *Grey cap for a green head.*" Gray express the idea very forcibly:

> " Ambition this shall tempt to rise,
> Then hurl the wretch from high,
> To bitter scorn a sacrifice,
> And grinning infamy ! "

and the remedy of to-morrow may come too late. "Our deeds determine us as much as we determine our deeds." It has been said that if we cannot go backward and change what has been we can go forward and change what is, but even this unfortunately is only partly true, and the shadow of the past may darken the future, do what we will.* Hence the adage, "To-morrow is untouched," cannot be accepted without reservation.

Other proverbs that may well be quoted in praise of forethought are these : "Little stumble may save big fall "; "He who begins and does not finish, loses his labour "; "Put out your arm no further than your sleeve will reach "; "To change and to better are not always the same thing "; "Quick choice, long repentance."

> "Take warning at once, that a worse may not hap,
> Foresight is the stopper of many a gap."

The French say truly enough that "Tout le monde est sage après coup," an equivalent saying to our, "After-wit is everybody's wit "; and the Portuguese declare that "An empty purse makes a man wise, but too late,"—a most unfortunate state of things. Another well-known adage is "Festina lente "—tarry a little that we make our end the sooner. "Presto et bene non conviene " — hastily and well rarely meet. A Ciceronian maxim was, "Certis rebus certa signa præ-currunt "—certain signs are the forerunners of certain events, or, as we say in English, "Coming events cast their shadows before."

> "Often do the spirits
> Of great events stride on before the events,
> And in to-day already walks to-morrow." †

---

* "Life is like wine, he that would drink it pure must not drain it to the dregs."—*Sir William Temple.*

† *Coleridge.*

"Chi va piano va lontano" — he who goes gently travels far. A quaint old proverb tells us that "It is good to have a hatch before your door" — in order, that is, that one may not rush out too impetuously, but that a momentary pause may give opportunity for a moment's consideration. One of the most startling proverbs on this need of forethought is the Arab "Live, thou ass, until the clover sprouts" — a better day is coming, despondency must give place to patience and to hope.

The manufacture of excuses has not escaped the notice of the proverb-makers and users. These excuses take two forms — the excuses that omission calls for, and those that commission needs — that black may look at least grey, if not absolutely white. A very good example of the former is this, "Am I my brother's keeper?" — originally the plea of a murderer, and ever after the excuse of those who would wrap themselves up in their selfishness, and shut their eyes, their hearts, their consciences, their pockets, to the needs of the suffering. It has been well said that "Apologies only account for that which they do not alter." In some few cases, such as "A bad workman finds fault with his tools," or "The creaking wheel blames the badness of the road," the utterance is quaint and not unwholesome, and very true to human nature; but in most of these proverbs dealing with excuses there is an actual incitement to evil, a justification of wrongdoing, an implication that people are only honest because it pays better or because the chance of knavery is for the time being debarred to them. We have so often heard the declaration that "Opportunity makes the thief," that it has lost its meaning; but if we really think it out a moment, how abominable in teaching it is! A similar saying is this, "A bad padlock invites a picklock," an insinuation that we would all be dishonest if we got the opportunity; while the Spaniards say, "Puerta abierta al santo tiento"—an open door tempts a saint. Shakespeare's utterance, "How oft the sight of means to do ill deeds makes ill deeds done," may express a sad truth, but after all we would fain believe that things are not quite so bad as not a few of our proverbs would imply : there is surely yet some little virtue and honesty left.

Fortune, good or ill, is not by any means overlooked. Thus we find the philosophic reflection, "Fortune can take nothing from us but what she gave"; and the warning, "Fortune is constant in nothing but inconstancy." We are warned yet again that "When fortune comes smiling she often designs the most mischief." All, however, is not blind chance; the hand of God is guiding; "There's a divinity that shapes our ends, rough hew them how we will." Nor is the hand of man without its influence, for "To him that is willing ways are not wanting," and "If you weave your web God will find the thread." The Italians say, "Vien la fortuna a chi la procura"—good fortune is to him who earns it; while the French declare, "Qui ne se lasse pas lasse l'adversité"—he who does not tire tires adversity, and steady perseverance will conquer ill-fortune. "La fortune aide aux audacieux," say the French again, while the Romans declared, "Fortes fortuna adjuvat"—fortune assists the brave, the classic reading of our more homely version, "Nothing venture, nothing have."

The victim of ill-fortune is reminded that "It is a long lane that has no turning"; or, as Gower puts it :

> "Sometime I drew into memoire
> Howe sorowe maie not euer last."

The French have a saying, "The wind in a man's

face makes him wise," equivalent to the English adage,
"Adversity makes a man wise, not rich," and so the
Psalmist sings, "It is good for me that I have been
afflicted, that I might learn thy statutes." Trouble
works, however, in a twofold way, and while some it
softens, others it hardens.

It is a matter of common observation that misfortunes often fall most unexpectedly, and that they
seldom come singly.

> "O soden hap, O thou fortune unstable,
> Like to the scorpion so deceivable,
> That flatrest with thy hed whan thou wilt sting." *

"Mischiefs," says an old proverb, "come by the pound
and go away by the ounce," and the Italians have a
practically identical saying. These calamities come
sometimes in such a flood that no resistance to their
attack seems of any avail, hence the quaint and homely
adage, "There is no fence against a flail." The Romans
had the saw, "Mustelam habes"—you have a weasel
in your house, which they applied to those with
whom everything seemed to turn out unfortunately :
to meet a weasel being considered by the Romans an
ill-omen.

It has been said that each man is the architect of
his own fortune.† The statement is not wholly true,
but it is sufficiently so to justify such proverbs as
"As you have made your bed, so you must lie";
"As you brew, so must you drink"; and we must be
prepared to take the consequences of our own fault.
Zeno, the philosopher, having detected his servant in
a theft, ordered him to be whipped ; the servant, in
excuse for what he had done, said it was decreed by

---

* CHAUCER, *The Marchaunt's Tale.*

† "Men at some time are masters of their fates."—SHAKESPEARE,
Julius Cæsar.

the fates that he should be a thief, alluding to the doctrine of fatalism which his master maintained. And so, too, it was decreed, said Zeno, that you should be whipped. It has been well said that "Presumption first blinds a man, and then sets him running." The Germans say, "Wer da fallt, über ihm laufen alle Welt"—he that falls down all the world runs over. All are ready to bear a hand in beating the man whom fortune buffets ; and, as an old proverb says, "When the tree is fallen every man goeth to it with his hatchet." This kicking a man when he is down would appear a mean and contemptible proceeding were it not dignified by being termed the survival of the fittest in the struggle for existence, and this somehow throws a halo of philosophy on the proceeding, and the kicker is seen to be working out a law of the universe, in which the kicked also has an essential place.

We are told, truly enough, that "Half a loaf is better than no bread," that "A man had better be half-blind than have both his eyes out." Burke declares that "He that wrestles with us strengthens our nerves and sharpens our skill ; our antagonist is our helper"; and the French say, "On apprend en faillant"—one learns by failing. Riches entail responsibility and anxiety, and a poet of the reign of Queen Elizabeth would have us believe that they are on the whole more trouble than gain :

> "Take upp thy fortune wythe good hape,
> Wyth rytches thou doste fyle thy lappe ;
> Yet lesse were better for thy store,
> Thy quyetnes sholde be the more."

One compensation of poverty is perhaps seen in the adage, "He that is down need fear no fall." We are told, too, that "A threadbare coat is armour against the highwayman"; and Chaucer, in "The Wif of Bathe's Tale," tells how

"The poure man whan he goth by the way,
Before the theves he may sing and play,"

since he has nothing to lose, and therefore nothing to fear.

The sad but just law of retribution finds its due recognition in our proverb lore. The following may be taken as a few examples of this : "He that toucheth pitch shall be defiled therewith"; "Over-reachers most ordinarily over-reach themselves"; "A guilty mind punishes itself"; "He that will not be saved needs no preacher"; "He who sows thorns must not go barefoot"; "He who sows the wind shall reap the whirlwind"; "Hoist with his own petard." Shakespeare tells us how

"Diseases, desperate grown,
By desperate appliance are relieved,
Or not at all";

and of one elsewhere who cries: "I have lost my reputation! I have lost the immortal part, sir, of myself, and what remains is bestial." Do we not see again the dread law of retribution in the passage:

"Suspicion always haunts the guilty mind :
The thief doth fear each bush an officer,"

and Gay tells us how at last all has to be faced, and the responsibility of one's actions has to be realised—

"Then comes a reckoning when the banquet's o'er,
The dreadful reckoning, and men smile no more."

As an alternative to a picture so sombre, we may quote the declaration, that "Chastisement is the knife that tells we still abide in the Vine."

Detraction, hypocrisy, ingratitude are all scourged by proverbs, but one feels over and over again how very much the proverbial wisdom of our ancestors seemed to dwell on the darker side of things. One may find a dozen adages that have ingratitude as their theme, but scarcely one that sings the praise of sweet thankfulness, and in like manner pretension, boasting, time-serving, self-interest have their attendant proverbs, while the praise of gentle modesty and sweet self-surrender finds little or no place. It may, perhaps, be said that this latter end is reached practically by the denouncing of the evil, but this is scarcely so—a scathing attack on falsehood is in its time needful, but there is still place and need for the recognition of the spotless beauty of truth. Denunciation may do much, but sweet persuasiveness yet more.

Shakespeare, in his " Cymbeline," writes of deadly slander—

> " Whose edge is sharper than the sword ; whose tongue
> Outvenoms all the worms of Nile ";

and again, in " Much Ado about Nothing," we find the line—" Done to death by slanderous tongues "; and yet again warns us that " No might nor greatness in mortality can censure 'scape," and that " Back-wounding calumny the whitest virtue strikes." Byron writes in his " Childe Harold's Pilgrimage " of those whose evil task is " Sapping a solemn creed with solemn sneer," and Thomson tells how " Still the world prevailed, and its dread laugh,"—a laugh "which scarce the firm philosopher can scorn."

The following adages may be quoted :— " Envy shoots at others and wounds itself "; " Envy never does a good turn but when it designs an evil one "; " Malice seldom wants a mark to aim at "; " ' They say ' is a poisoned arrow." The Welsh say—" Faults are thick where love is thin." Other sayings are— " One jeer going forth brings back another "; " Once in people's mouths, 'tis hard to get out of them again "; " Those who have most need of credit seldom get much "; "The evil which issues from thy mouth falls into thy bosom "; "The sting of a reproach is in the truth of it ";* "He that prepares a net for another should not shut his own eyes"; "Respect is better got by deserving than by exacting"; "Little minds, like weak liquors, are soon soured"; "Suspicion, like bats, fly by twilight"; "In a little mind everything is little"; "Despise none and despair of none"; "Faint praise is disparagement"; "A blow from a frying-pan blacks, though it may not hurt"; "Truth is truth, though spoken by an enemy"; "Harm set, harm get"; "Envy never enriched any man."

In a curious manuscript of the fifteenth century may be found "the answere which God gave to a certyn creture that desired to wit whate thinge was moost plesure to hym in this worlde." The answer is a very full one, fuller than we can quote, but it includes the following precepts :—"Suffre noysous wordis with a meke harte, for that pleseth me more than thow beate thy body with as many roddys as growen in an hundred wodys. Have compassion on the seeke and poore, for that pleaseth me more than thow fasteth fifty wynter brede and water. Saye no bakbyting wordis, but shon from them and love thy nayghber and turne alle that he saithe or dothe to good, me onely love and alle other for me, for that pleseth me more than if thowe every daye goo upon a whele stikking fulle of nayles that shulde prik thy bodye." Another manuscript of the same date that has come under our notice, in the Library of Jesus College, Cambridge, introduces a personification of the deadly sins,

---

* The friends of a Roman patrician condemned by Tiberias to death, dwelt strongly on the injustice of the sentence. "That," said he, "my friends, is my greatest consolation, you do not surely wish that I had been guilty ! "

and each is treated with much graphic power, thus, under the heading of " Invidia " we find—

> " I am full sory in my hert
> Of other mens welefare and whert :
> I ban and bakbyte wykkedly,
> And hynder all that I may sikerly."

The sneaking treachery of the envious man, grieved to the heart at the welfare of others, and doing them what evil he can safely compass, is very forcibly painted, and this of " Ira," in its picture of down-right brutality, is as graphic—

> " I chide and feght and manas fast ;
> All my fomen I wylle doun kast,
> Mercy on thaym I wylle none haue
> But vengeance take, so God me saue."

Revenge, however sweet it may appear, always costs more than it is worth, so that to be of this mind is to scourge oneself with one's own flail. Thus the adage says truly enough, " To be angry is to revenge the faults of others on ourselves." Another useful hint is that " Anger is danger, and even the anger of the righteous is not always righteous anger." How full, too, of wisdom the precept that " Anger should set with the sun but not rise with it," carrying on with vindictive perseverance into the present and the future the evil of the past. Other proverbs are :— " Anger begins with folly and ends with repentance "; " Anger makes a rich man hated, and a poor man scorned "; " Anger is more hurtful than the injury that caused it "; " A man in a passion rides a horse that runs away with him "; " Anger may glance into the breast of a good man, but rests only in the bosom of fools "; " An angry man opens his mouth and shuts his eyes "; and to these many others bearing on the subject might be added.

Other excellent wisdom chips are these :—"Religion is the best armour in the world, but the worst cloak"; "Imitate good but do not counterfeit it"; "Roguery with pretext is double roguery"; "Better the blame of the just than the praise of the wicked." Of all the virtues it has been said that gratitude has the shortest memory—"Eaten bread is soon forgotten." The Spaniards have, too, a very graphic proverb: "Cria el cuervo y sacarte ha los ojos"—breed up a crow and he will tear out your eyes; while the French say: "Otez un vilain, du gibet, il vous y mettra"—save a thief from the gallows and he will place you there.

Pretension is exposed in many proverbs. An excellent one is this: "The best horseman is always on his feet." This is sometimes varied into "The man on the wall is the best player." It is in either version an obvious satire on the looker-on, who always tells how he could have done the thing better. Other good saws are these: "In a calm all can steer"; "Vainglory blossoms but does not bear"; "All his geese are swans"; "We cannot all do everything"; "Not even the youngest is infallible"; "Conceit in weakest bodies strongest works"; "Presumption blinds a man and then sets him running"; "Vanity has no greater foe than itself"; "A small mind has usually still room for pride"; "Insolence is pride with her mask pulled off"; "Arrogance is a weed that grows on poor soil."

Sir Thomas More reminds us that "Pride, as the proverb is, must needs have a shame," while a yet older writer declares that "Loste and deignouse pride and ille avisement mishapnes oftentide," and centuries even before this we find the warning that "A haughty spirit goes before a fall." Shakespeare puts the matter very pithily — "Who knows himself a braggart (let him fear this : for it will come to pass), That every braggart shall be found an ass." "Brag is a good dog, but hold-fast is a better," we are told ; a less familiar version found in old collections of proverbs being, "Brag is a good dog, but dares not bite." A very quaint old saw against boasting and pretension is this, "We hounds killed the hare, quoth the lap-dog"; while another good doggy adage is the warning that "A snappish cur must be tied short." "Great boasters," we are told, "are little doers,"* even as "Great promisers are bad paymasters." It is equally true, the statement that "One sword keeps another in its sheath." A quaint proverb hath it that "My father's name was Loaf, and I die of hunger," a Spanish satire on those who, in poorest circumstances, yet boast of their kindred,† while a very true Italian saw is that "Many are brave when the enemy is running." On the other hand, "A brave retreat is a brave exploit." Throughout our pages we have made but slight reference to Biblical sayings since these are so readily accessible to all, and are, we may presume, so well known, but we cannot here quite forbear, for the counsel—"Let not him that girdeth on his harness boast himself as he that putteth it off"—seems so particularly happy a termination to our proverbs on pretension and boasting. Having thus broken through our procedure, we are tempted to add yet one more reference from the same source, the splendid irony on the man, "Wiser in his own conceit

---

* "But did this boaster threaten, did he pray,
  Or, by his own example, urge their stay?
  None, none of these, but ran himself away."
  —DRYDEN, *Ovid's Metamorphoses*, Book xiii.

† The Spanish revel in these proverbs of sarcastic nature. Another, for instance, is, "Praise me, friends, I love my daughters," applied to those who expect commendation for fulfilling the most obvious duties.

than seven men that can render a reason"—a race not yet extinct.

The following proverbs, dealing with various phases of self-interest, have more or less of worldly wisdom in them, and are worth quotation:—"Better go round than fall in the ditch"; "Better say here it is than here it was"; "Better cut the shoe than pinch the foot"; "If you wish a thing done—go; if not—send"; "Light not a blaze that you cannot extinguish"; "A hook's well lost to catch a salmon"; "Buyers want a hundred eyes; sellers, two"; "All is lost that is poured into a cracked dish"; "Those who put on livery must put on patience"; "Of two evils choose the less"; "Better one's house too little one day than too large all the year beside"; "Sometimes it is better to give your apple than to eat it yourself"; "Venture not all in one bottom"; "A man's gift makes room for him"; "An ass laden with gold overtakes everything"; "If you grease a cause well it will stretch"; "Praise the bridge by which you pass over"; "It is wit to pick a lock, but wisdom to let it alone"; "Those disposed for mischief will never want occasion"; "A petitioner that spares his purse angles without his bait."

In "The Ship of Fools," 1570, we find the line, "Aungels worke wonders in Westminster Hall," the angel being a coin of that period, and the Hall the great seat of Justice, or at all events, of Law. The Romans had a proverb—"Bos in lingua"—an ox on the tongue. As some of the ancient money was stamped with the device of an ox, the proverb was a delicate way of saying that a man had been bribed to be silent. We are told that Demosthenes, having received a present from some who wished to obtain a privilege that they were fearful he would oppose, appeared in the court with his throat muffled up,

R

pretending that he had so violent a cold as to be incapable of speaking ; but one of the members of the court suspected the matter, and quoted this proverb, intimating that it was not the cold but the bribe that had debarred him from speech. Another of these old Roman proverbs was, "Argenteis hastis pugna et omnia expugnabis" — if only one fights with silver spear they will be all-conquering. A similar cynical maxim appreciative of the power of bribery and corruption is that, "Where gold avails argument fails." Another old Roman adage was, "Oleum et operam perdere" — to lose both oil and labour. This was applied to those who had spent much time, given much labour, made considerable pecuniary sacrifice, to attain some object, and had, after all, failed in doing so. Those who contended in the public games freely anointed their limbs with oil to make them supple ere entering on the contest, and so if, after all, they were conquered they lost both oil and labour. In like manner, the student poring over his books and burning the midnight oil, if he failed in the acquisition of knowledge, lost oil and labour. The ancients tell how a man, having a suit at law, sent to the judge a present of a vessel of oil, but his antagonist sent a fatted pig, and this turned the scale in his favour, and he gained his cause. Justice may well be represented as blind when such proceedings are possible. The first man complained and reminded the judge of his gift, but the judge told him that a great pig had rushed in and overturned the oil, so that it and his labour in bringing it had been lost. Whether the proverb grew out of the story or the story out of the proverb it is now impossible to pronounce any opinion upon.

Other keen proverbs are :—" He that finds a thing steals it if he restores it not"; "What will not make

a pot may make a lid"; "The best patch is off the
same cloth"; "Break not eggs with a hatchet"; "Ease
and honour are seldom bedfellows"; "Stretch your
legs according to your coverlet"; "Pin not your faith
on another's sleeve"; "As a man is finded so the law
is ended"; "Live and let live"; "An ill agreement
is better than a good judgment"; "Misreckoning is no
payment"; "Name not a rope in his house that hanged
himself." A very marked example of this delicacy
of feeling is seen in the saying, "Father disappeared
about assizes - time, and we asked no questions!"
"Take away fuel and you take away fire"; "No
man is impatient with his creditors"; "Command
yourself and you may command much else."

Turning our attention awhile in other directions, we
find the Spaniard's warning, "Cada cuba bucele al
vino que tiene"—the cask smells of the liquid it
held; a man's surroundings stamp him, and he is
known by the company he keeps. Self - interest is
blatant in the Spanish saying that "People don't give
black puddings to those who kill no pigs"; and the
same cynical teaching is found in the French adage,
"To one who has a pie in the oven you may give
a piece of your cake."* The French version of "To
him that hath shall be given," is, "He who eats
chicken gets chicken."† The Spanish proverbs, as we
have seen, have a strong tinge of mocking sarcasm
in them; here are two more examples: "Give away
for the good of your soul what you cannot eat";
"Steal the pig but give away the feet in alms." There
is a delightful touch of human nature in the French
saying, "No one is so open-handed as he who has

* In Germany they say, "Siedet der Topf, so blühet die Freundschaft"
—while the pot boils the friendship blooms.

† In Welsh proverb lore, "Have a horse of your own and then you
can borrow another."

nothing to give," or its Scotch equivalent, "They are aye gudewilly o' their horse that hae nane." Another canny Scotch experience is that "He that lacks (disparages) my mare would buy my mare." Self-interest degenerates into self-abasement in the Arab counsel, "If the king at noon-day says it is night, behold the stars." The Persian warning, "It is ill sport between the cotton and the fire," is very graphic. The old Roman, "Aliam quercum excute," the advice to go and shake some other tree, since enough has been gathered here, is expressive. It is equivalent to telling one's importunate neighbour that he must really try fresh ground at last ; to advise one's friend to cease from the pursuit they have been following, since they have reaped from it all the advantage it is likely to yield to them. A dignified and noble saying is this, "Deridet sed non derideor"—he laugheth, but I am not laughed at ; the impertinence is suffered, is passed unregarded, and falls flat and dead.

Custom and habit exercise their influence on our proverb lore ; thus we are told, wisely enough, that "Custom is the plague of wise men, the idol of fools." Kelly tells a good story, in illustration of this bowing to custom, of a captain's wife whose husband the South Sea Islanders had eaten, being consoled by a friend : "Mais, madame, que voulez-vous ? Chaque peuple a ses usages." The power of habit is immense ; an old saying tells us that "Habit is overcome by habit," but ordinarily the habit in possession fights hard, and is not readily dispossessed. Hence it is of solemn warning to "Kill the cockatrice while yet in the egg." It is one of the most familiar of truisms that "Habit becomes second nature," and that "What is bred in the bone will never come out of the flesh." To check at the beginning may be difficult, but to overcome in the end may be impossible. "Can the Ethiopian," asks the prophet, "change his skin or the leopard his spots? Then may you also do good that are accustomed to do evil." As the bough of a tree bent from its usual direction returns to its old position so soon as the temporary force to which it yielded is removed, so do men return to their old habits so soon as the motives, whether of interest or fear, which had influenced them, are done away. "Nature," says Lord Bacon, "is often hidden, sometimes overcome, seldom extinguished. Let not a man trust his victory over his nature too far; for nature will be buried a great time and yet revive upon the occasion or temptation, like as it was with Æsop's damsel, turned from a cat to a woman, who sat very demurely at the board's end till a mouse ran before her." The same philosopher gives the following admirable caution: "A man's nature runs either to herbs or weeds: therefore let him seasonably water the one and destroy the other." The Spaniards say: "Mudar costumbre a par de muerte"—to change a habit is like death.

> "Ill habits gather by unseen degrees,
>   As brooks make rivers, rivers run to seas."

And Shakespeare, in the "Two Gentlemen of Verona," exclaims: "How use doth breed a habit in a man!" The ancient Romans declared: "Fabricando fit faber," which we find in French as "En forgeant ou devient forgeron"; in Spanish, as "El usar saca oficial"; in German, as "Uebung macht den meister"; and in English, as "Use makes the craftsman."

Boys catch the habit of stammering if thrown with those who stammer, and the Dutch declare: "Die bij kreupelen woont, leert hinken"—he that lives with cripples learns to limp. Fortunately, there are good habits as well as bad ones; hence the Romans taught: "Boni principii finis bonus," and the French say, "De bon commencement bonne fin "—we insensibly imitate what we habitually admire.

Experience teaches, and we propose to quote some few of the proverbial lessons that are of value in the conduct and wear and tear of life, and we commence with the homely bit of wisdom that, if realised, would save so much of worry and heartache: "What can't be cured must be endured."* Another good saying is: "Well begun is half done"—poetically rendered by the Italians in the counsel, "Begin your web, and God will find you thread." "Procrastination is the thief of time," is another well-worn and excellent adage. How valuable, again, are these: "Teaching of others teacheth the teacher"; "He teaches ill that teaches all"; "He that seeks trouble rarely misses it"; "He that is surety is not sure"; "Look before you leap"; "The horse that draws is most whipped"; "Blow first and sip after"; "At open doors dogs come in"; "He that is angry without cause must be pleased without amends"; "It is but lip-wisdom that lacks experience"; "Fetters, though of gold, are fetters still"; "Without danger, danger cannot be overcome"; "Experience is a dear school, but fools learn in no other"; "Some advice at fourpence is a groat too dear"; "The counsel that we favour we most scrutinise"; "He that sits to work in the market-place shall have many teachers"; "Valour that parleys is near surrender"; "As you salute you will be saluted"; "Responsibility must be shouldered, you cannot carry it under your arm"; "One eye-witness is better than ten hear-says"; "If you pity knaves you are no friend to honest men"; "Every man is a pilot in a calm sea"; "Plant the crab-tree where you will it will never bear

* "Things without all remedy
Should be without regard: what's done is done."
Macbeth.

pippins"; "Wide will wear, but narrow will tear." This
last, homely as it sounds, is excellent in its counsel in
praise of a wise liberality.

The ancient Roman, "Bis dat qui cito dat," that
is so often quoted in advocacy of prompt aid, re-
appears in modern Italy in the version, "A gift long
waited for is not given, but sold." "Say not to your
neighbour, Go, and come again, and to-morrow I will
give, when thou hast it by thee." "Hope deferred
maketh the heart sick,"* and ready help at the critical
moment might have averted a catastrophe. Another
very true classic adage is, "Beneficium accipere, liber-
tam est vendere"—accept a favour and you sell your
freedom. Excellent counsel is in the twin proverbs,
"Deliberating is not delaying," and "That is a wise
delay which maketh the road safe." An old writer †
very sagely puts it thus: "When we are in a strait
that we know not what to do, we must have a care
of doing we know not what," and thus save time by
giving time.

Advice for the conduct of life is freely bestowed
on us by our proverbial wisdom. We may well head
the examples we propose to give with the caution,
"In vain does he ask advice who will not follow it."

* "Is not a patron," says Dr Johnson to the Earl of Chesterfield,
"one who looks with unconcern on a man struggling for life in the
water, and when he has reached the land encumbers him with help?
The notice which you have been pleased to take of my labours had
been kind: but it has been delayed until I am indifferent, and cannot
enjoy it; till I am solitary, and cannot impart it; till I am known, and
do not want it."

† One Richard Nichols, of Warrington, writing in 1670 or thereabouts.
Many of his sayings are admirable; here are half-a-dozen of them:
"Self-denial makes a poor condition easy, and a rich one safe"; "A
good intention will not justify a bad action"; "Though time be not
lasting, yet what depends upon time is everlasting"; "The weak, when
watchful, are more safe than the strong when secure"; "He that has
all his religion in his prayers has no religion at all"; "The best way to
wipe off reproaches is to live so that none will believe them."

"Few things," says Dr Johnson, "are so liberally bestowed, or squandered with so little effect, as good advice." Another reading is that "He that will not be counselled cannot be helped." Some few specimens of counsel tendered are these: "At great bargains pause awhile"; "The best throw of the dice is to throw them away"; "Raise up no spirits that you cannot lay"; "Rather suffer a great evil than do a little one"; "Agree, for the law is costly"; "Avoid the pleasure that will bite to-morrow"; "Let the shipwrecks of others be your beacons"; "Let every man praise the bridge he goes over." Speak not ill of him who hath done you a courtesy, or whom you have made use of to your benefit. The Arabs in like spirit teach, "A well from which thou drinkest throw not a stone into it." An Italian saw sarcastically says, "Does thy neighbour annoy thee? lend him a zechin" —he will then keep out of the way. A Danish proverb wisely advises to "Take help of many, and counsel of few"; while a homely German proverb—"Henke nicht alles auf einen Nagel"—warns us not to hang all on one nail; or, as our equally homely English proverb has it, "Do not carry all your eggs in one basket"—have not all your ventures in one vessel.

The weather in this our changeable climate has supplied abundant store for popular lore; it would indeed suffice in itself to yield material for a goodly volume, and the result would be a collection of great literary and antiquarian interest.

One very familiar adage is the comforting statement that "It is an ill wind that blows no one any good." Shakespeare quotes it more than once; in one case it is rendered as "Ill blows the wind that profits nobody," and elsewhere, "Not the ill wind which blows no man good," while Tusser gives us the rhyming version—

"Except wind stands as never it stood,
It is an ill wind turns none to good."

Another old saw teaches that "Ill weather is seen soon enough when it comes," but this is indefensible, for while it is a wise counsel not to meet troubles half way, to exercise no forethought at all is mere lunacy. Such a proverb, again, as this, "Though the sun shine leave not your coat at home," is much too rigid in its insistence, and the advice, whether taken literally or metaphorically, would be at times absurd. If we try it, for instance, in this guise—Though surrounded by loving friends carry suspicion ever with you—we feel that the tension is needless. A much truer saying is this, "When the sun shines nobody minds him, but when he is eclipsed all consider him," and we realise at last on the withdrawal of the benefit of how great value it had been to us.

A wise and helpful Latin proverb is, "Sequitur Ver Hyemem"—spring succeeds winter, and sunshine follows rain. "After a storm, calm," or, as the French have it, "Apres la pluie vient le beau temps."

"What, man, plucke up your harte, bee of good cheere,
After cloudes blacke wee shall have wether clere."

"Heaviness may endure for a night, but joy cometh in the morning," is no discovery of yesterday.

"March winds and April showers bring forth the May flowers," and the French recognise the welcome assurance in their version, "Mars venteux, Avril pluvieux, font le Mai gai et gracieux," while across the Rhine the saying is again, "Märzen Wind and Aprilen Regen verheissen im Mai grossen segen." The value of dry weather at sowing time is indicated in the saying that "A bushel of March dust is worth a king's ransom"; while "February fill-dyke" is a testimony to the abundant rain that is ordinarily characteristic of that month; in France it is said that "Fevrier remplit les fosses: Mars les seche." This rain is of great value, and "All the months of the year curse a fair Februeer," and "If the grass look green in Janiveer 'twill look the worser all the year." The exigencies of rhyme are responsible for the miscalling of these month-names. A great many of these rustic weather proverbs are thrown into more or less, and ordinarily more, uncouth rhyme, no doubt as an aid to memory; thus we are told that "No weather's ill if the wind be still," that it is well should "September blow soft till the fruit's in the loft," and that "If the first of July be rainy weather, 'twill rain more or less four weeks together." We are taught again that "In February if thou hearest thunder thou wilt see a summer's wonder." Undoubtedly a thunderstorm in February might well be regarded as one of the least likely things to happen in July, while the hearing of its sonorous peals would certainly be a remarkable feat of vision. As the literal acceptance is so impossible we must perforce look a little below the surface, and when we recall that our ancestors were great at prognostics we see that we are expected to regard this ill-timed storm as an omen of coming events of startling nature. Thus Willford, in his "Nature's Secrets," teaches that "Thunder and lightning in winter is held ominous, portending factions, tumults, and bloody wars, and a thing seldome seen, according to ye old adigy, Winter's thunder is ye Sommer's wonder."*

---

* "Sondayes thundre should bryng ye death of learned men, judges, and others: Mondayes thundre ye death of women: Tuesdayes thundre plentie of graine: Wednesdayes thundre ye death of ye wicked: Thursdayes thundre plentie of sheepe and corne: Fridaies thundre ye slaughter of a great man and other horrible murders: Saturdayes thundre a generall plague and grate deathe."—LEONARD DIGGES, *A Prognostication Everlasting of Ryght Good Effecte*, 1556.

The countryman has abundant opportunity of study-
ing the varying aspects of Nature, hence he has discovered that "An evening red and morning grey will
set the traveller on his way";* though he seems to
have also observed that "If the sun in red should set,
the next day surely will be wet." The two statements
appear to directly contradict each other. On the other
hand we are told that when the reverse happens,
"The evening grey and morning red make the shepherd hang his head"; and that "If the sun should
set in grey the next will be a rainy day"; the sun
setting in a bank of clouds—the west in this country
being the direction in which we ordinarily look for
wet weather—the result on the morrow will probably
be rain. Hence, "A rainbow in the morning is the
shepherd's warning, a rainbow at night is the shepherd's delight"; or in Germany, "Regenborgen am
Morgen macht dem Schäfer sorgen : Regenborgen am
Abend ist dem Schäfer labend."

The statement that "The moon is made of green
cheese" may be mentioned in passing. Shacklock, in
the "Hatchet of Heresies," written in 1565, says, "They
may make theyr blinde brotherhode, and the ignorant
sort beleeve that the mone is made of grene chese,"
and many old writers introduce this venerable belief
in their plays and other works. We now-a-days
associate the idea with age, the green suggesting
mouldiness, but the word here means the very opposite, and refers really to a chesse not matured ; the
moon being new every month, the material of which
it was composed never got beyond the green or un-
ripe stage.

It is popularly held that "When the wind is in the

* Sometimes rendered as, "Evening red and morning grey, tokens
of a bonny day"; or, "An evening red and a morning grey are the
two sure signs of a fine day."

east 'tis good for neither man nor beast," and a quaint Spanish proverb advises, " Ask no favour during the Solano." This Solano is a wind that blows over from Africa, and is exceedingly hot and dry. It is also known as the sirocco. The moral clearly is that when people are in a state of irritation it is not advisable to lay one's needs before them, the time being inopportune.

Many of our weather proverbs are very naturally associated with various saints' days. Thus we get " St Martin's Summer " and " All Saints' Summer " in reference to the bright clear weather that we occasionally get in the late autumn, All Saints' Day being on the first, and St Martin's Day on the eleventh of November. Allusions to both will be found in Shakespeare ; thus, in " I. Henry VI."—" Expect St Martin's Summer, halcyon days." The eighteenth of October was in like manner called " St Luke's little Summer." Another old adage was, " If the day of St Paul be clear, then shall betide a happy year "; this day, the festival of the conversion of the saint, was in the calendar ascribed to January the 25th.

Another well-known belief is summed up in the old rhyme : " St Swithin's day if it do rain, for forty days it will remain." This date is July 15th, and it may not be generally known that, taking the year round, July is often a very rainy month. The Saint was Bishop of Winchester, and when he died, in the year 862, he desired to rest where the sweet rain of heaven might fall. His desire was respected, but later on the monks thought it beneath his and their dignity that he should be laid to rest in the graveyard, and so they proposed to re-inter the body in the choir, but when the day came the rain was so terrific that they had to postpone matters till the next day. This, however, was no better, nor was the next, or next, till at length, after forty such postponements, it dawned upon them that their late bishop felt a strong objection to the removal of his remains, and they at last had the sense to decide to let him rest in peace as he had desired, whereupon the sun burst forth, and it is to be hoped that they all lived happy ever after.

The subject of our book has a scope so all-embracing, a wisdom so piquant, an utterance so quaint, a wit so trenchant, a body of material so vast, an antiquity so remarkable that not a volume but a library would be needed to do it justice.

He who would desire to discourse wisely, comprehensively, on the proverbs of all times and of all countries has before him a task too great for fulfilment, if not too vast for ambition, and what to select from the sheer necessity of its inclusion, what to discard since the impossibility of completeness might be our plea in forgiveness of its absence, has been a problem constantly before us. Where there are many men there are many minds, and we shall be, doubtless, blamed alike by some for what they find, and, no less, for what they fail to find. Could our readers see, as we now see before us on reaching this our last page, the great bulk of material that we have accumulated, and that remains unused, they would realise the better the vastness of the field—the ever-recurring problem and responsibility of selection.

The subject has been, from the first page to the last, one of abounding interest to us, and we would fain hope that we have succeeded in imbuing our readers with something of the pleasure that we have ourselves derived from a study in itself so full of charm.

Elliot Stock, 62 Paternoster Row, London, E.C.